Pasta & Italian

Practical Cookery

Pasta & Italian

p

NOTE

Cup measurements in this book are for American cups. Tablespoons are assumed to
be 15 ml. Unless otherwise stated, milk is assumed to be full fat, eggs are medium
and pepper is freshly ground black pepper.

Recipes using uncooked eggs should be
avoided by infants, the elderly, pregnant women and anyone
suffering from an illness

Contents

Fish & Seafood (continued)

Meat

Chicken & Poultry

Pasta

Pizzas & Bread

Introduction

Italian food, including the many pasta dishes, pizzas and risottos, as well as the decadent desserts, are enjoyed all around the world. This inspirational cookbook aims to bring a little bit of Italy into your kitchen!

Glorious sunlight, spectacular beaches, luscious countryside, rugged mountains, world-famous museums and art galleries, elegant designer shops, picturesque villages and magnificent cities – if this were not enough, Italy also boasts one of the longest and finest culinary traditions in the whole of Europe.

The ancient Romans loved good food and plenty of it, vying with each other to produce increasingly lavish and outlandish banquets. One of the earliest cookbooks written by Apicius, a gourmet in the first century, includes an appalling recipe for dormouse stuffed with walnuts! Overseas trade as the Roman Empire expanded brought new ingredients, and agriculture began to flourish at home. However, even then, wine production was just as prodigious as it is today.

With the collapse of the Roman Empire, the diet returned to plainer fare, relying on the wealth of cereals, fruit and vegetables that could be cultivated on the fertile plains. However, with the Renaissance, an interest in and enthusiasm for fine food revived and, once again, there were wealthy families who presided over extravagant banquets.

Italian pastry cooks were valued throughout the courts of Europe and were generally acknowledged as the best in the world. When Catherine de' Medici went to Paris to marry the future King Henri II, she took an army of Italian cooks with her and changed French culinary traditions irrevocably. A new middle class developed who also took an interest in eating well, creating a bourgeois cuisine characterized by fresh flavours and simple, unsauced dishes. The poor, of course, continued with a peasant subsistence.

The very finest produce and freshest ingredients still characterize Italian cuisine as a whole. Although modern transportation makes it possible for more exotic ingredients to travel across the world, Italian

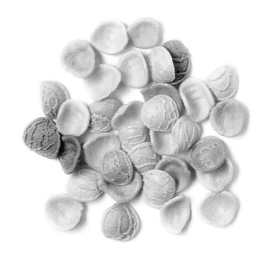

cooking still centres on home-grown produce. Over 60 per cent of the land is devoted to crops and pasture. With a climate that ranges from very cold in the Alps and Apennines to semi-tropical along the coast of the Ligurian Sea, the range of produce is extensive: olives, oranges, lemons, figs, grapes pomegranates, almonds, wheat, potatoes, tomatoes, sugar beet, maize and rice.

Livestock includes cattle and buffalo, sheep, goats, pigs and chickens. In a single year, Italy produces nearly 6.5 million tonnes of wine, nearly 2.5 million tonnes of olives, about 500,000 tonnes of olive oil, over 4.5 million tonnes of tomatoes and 120 million chickens. An impressive amount, you'll agree!

The introduction to this book continues to explore Italy, region by region, to discover the different types of food that is identified with a specific area of the country. Seasonal ingredients are also examined to provide the reader with as much insight into the type of produce used by the very discerning people of Italy.

Ragu Sauce

3 tbsp olive oil

45 g/1½ oz butter

2 large onions, chopped

4 celery stalks, sliced thinly

175 g/6 oz streaky bacon, chopped

2 garlic cloves, chopped

500 g/1 lb 2 oz minced (ground) lean beef

2 tbsp tomato purée (paste)

1 tbsp flour

400 g/14 oz can chopped tomatoes

150 ml/¼ pint /⅔ cup beef stock

150 ml/¼ pint /¼ cup red wine

2 tsp dried oregano

½ tsp freshly grated nutmeg

salt and pepper

1 Heat the oil and butter in a pan over a medium heat. Add the onions, celery and bacon and fry for 5 minutes, stirring.

2 Stir in the garlic and minced (ground) beef and cook, stirring until the meat has lost its redness. Lower the heat and cook for 10 minutes, stirring.

3 Increase the heat to medium, stir in the tomato purée (paste) and the flour and cook for 1-2 minutes. Stir in the tomatoes, stock and wine and bring to the boil, stirring. Season and stir in the oregano and nutmeg. Cover and simmer for 45 minutes, stirring. The sauce is now ready to use.

Regional Cooking

To talk about Italian cuisine is somewhat misleading, as it is not a single entity. The country has been united only since 17 March, 1861 and Italians still have a powerful sense of their regional identity.

Regional cuisine is a source of pride and considerable competition. Sicilians are dismissed as *mangimaccaroni* (pasta eaters), while they express their contempt for Neapolitan cooking with the term *mangiafoglie* (vegetable eaters). Each region bases its cuisine on local ingredients, so the best ham comes from the area where pigs are raised, fish and seafood feature in coastal regions, butter is used in dishes from the north of Italy where there is dairy farming, while olive oil is characteristic of southern recipes.

Abruzzi & Molise

This was once a single region and although it has now been divided into two separate provinces, they remain closely associated. Located in northern Italy to the east of Rome, the area is well-known for its high-quality cured meats and cheese. The cuisine is traditional and also features lamb and fish and seafood in the coastal areas. Peperoncino a tiny, fiery hot, dried red chilli is from Abruzzi.

Basilicata

If the Italian peninsula looks like a boot, Basilicata is located on the arch of the foot. The landscape is rugged and inhospitable, with much of the region being over 2,000 metres/6,500 feet above sea level.

It is hardly surprising, therefore, that the cuisine is warming and filling, featuring substantial soups in particular. Cured meats, pork, lamb and game are typical ingredients and freshwater fish are abundant in the more mountainous areas.

Calabria

In the south, on Italy's toe, Calabria is a region of dramatic contrasts – superb beaches and towering mountains. Excellent fish and seafood typify the local cuisine, which is well known for its swordfish and tuna dishes. Fruit and vegetables are abundant, particularly oranges, lemons, aubergines (eggplants) and olives. Like other southern regions, desserts are a speciality, often based on local figs, honey or almonds.

Campania

Naples on the west coast is the home of pizza, now known across the world from Sydney to New York and the region bases many of its other dishes on the wonderful sun-ripened tomatoes grown locally. Fish and seafood feature strongly in the Neapolitan diet and robust herb-flavoured stews, redolent with garlic, are popular. Pastries and fruit desserts are also characteristic.

Emilia-Romagna

A central Italian province, Emilia-Romagna's capital is the beautiful medieval city of Bologna, nicknamed *la grassa*, the fat city, and home to some of the best restaurants in the country. A gourmet paradise, the region is famous for Parmesan cheese and Parma ham from Parma, balsamic vinegar from the area around Modena, cotechino, mortadella and other cured meats

and, of course, *spaghetti alla bolognese*. Butter, cream and other dairy products feature in the fine food of the region and a wide range of pasta dishes is popular.

Lazio

Capital of the region and the country, Rome is a cosmopolitan and sophisticated city with some of the best restaurants – and ice cream parlours – in Europe. Fruit and vegetables are abundant and lamb and veal dishes are characteristic of the region, which is famous for *saltimbocca*, which literally means "jump in the mouth". Here, they have perfected the art of preparing high-quality ingredients in simple, but delicious ways that retain the individual flavours. A Roman speciality is *supplì al telefono* – "telephone wires" – mozzarella cheese wrapped in balls of cooked rice and deep-fried. The mozzarella is stringy, hence the name of the dish.

Liguria

A northern province with a long coastline, Liguria is well known for its superb fish and seafood. It is also said to produce the best basil in the whole of Italy and it is where pesto sauce was first invented.

The ancient port of Genoa was one of the first places in Europe to import Asian spices and highly seasoned dishes are still particularly characteristic of this area.

Lombardy

An important rice-growing region in north-west Italy, this is the home of risotto and there are probably as many variations of this dish as there

Regional Cooking

are cooks. Dairy produce features in the cuisine and Lombardy is credited with the invention of butter, as well as mascarpone cheese. Vegetable soups, stews and pot roasts are characteristic of this region. Bresaola, cured raw beef, is a local speciality that is often served wrapped around soft goat's cheese.

Marches

With its long coastline and high mountains, this region is blessed with both abundant seafood and game. Pasta, pork and olives also feature and methods of preparation are even more elaborate than those of neighbouring Umbria.

Piedmont

On the borders of France and Switzerland, Piedmont in the north-west is strongly influenced by its neighbours. A fertile, arable region, it is well known for rice, polenta and gnocchi and is said to grow the finest onions in Italy. Gorgonzola, one of the world's greatest cheeses, comes from this region although, sadly, the little village that gave it its name has now been subsumed by the urban sprawl of Milan. Piedmontese garlic is said to be the best in Italy and the local white truffles are a gourmet's dream.

Puglia

On the heel of Italy, this region produces excellent olives, herbs, vegetables and fruit, particularly melons and figs. Fish and seafood are abundant and the region is known for its oyster and mussel dishes. Calzone, a sort of inside out pizza, was invented here.

Sardinia

This Mediterranean island is famous for its luxurious desserts and extravagant pastries, many of them featuring honey, nuts and home-grown fruit. Hardly surprisingly, fish and seafood – tuna, eel, mullet, sea bass, lobster and mussels – are central to Sardinian cuisine and spit-roasted suckling pig is the national dish served on feast days. *Sardo* is a mild-tasting pecorino cheese produced in Sardinia.

Sicily

Like their southern neighbours, Sicilians have a sweet tooth, which they indulge with superb cakes, desserts and ice cream, often incorporating locally grown almonds, pistachios and citrus fruits. Pasta dishes are an important part of the diet and fish and seafood, including tuna, swordfish and mussels, feature prominently.

Trentino Alto-Adage

A mountainous region in the north-east, Trentino has been strongly influenced by its Austrian neighbour. Smoked sausage and dumplings are characteristic of the cuisine, which is also well known for its filled pasta.

Tuscany

The fertile plains of Tuscany are ideal for farming and the region produces superb fruit and vegetables. Cattle are raised here and both steak and veal dishes feature on the Tuscan menu, together with a wide range of game. Tripe is a local speciality and *Panforte di Siena*, a traditional Christmas cake made with honey and nuts, comes from the city of Siena. A grain known as *farro* is grown almost exclusively in Tuscany, where it is used to make a nourishing soup.

Umbria

Pork, lamb, game and freshwater fish, prepared and served simply but deliciously, characterize the excellent cuisine of the region. Fragrant black truffles are a feature and Umbrian cooking makes good use of its high-quality olive oil. Umbria is also famous for *imbrecciata*, a hearty soup made with lentils, chick-peas (garbanzo beans) and haricot (navy) beans.

Veneto and Friuli

An intensively farmed area in the north-east of Italy, this region produces cereals and almost 20 per cent of the country's wine. Polenta and risotto feature in the cuisine, as well as an extensive range of fish and seafood. *Risi e bisi*, rice and peas, is a traditional dish which was served every year at the Doge's banquet in Venice to honour the city's patron saint, Mark.

Basic Recipes

These recipes form the basis of several of the dishes contained throughout this book. Many of these basic recipes can be made in advance and stored in the refrigerator until required.

Basic Tomato Sauce

2 tbsp olive oil

1 small onion, chopped

1 garlic clove, chopped

400 g/14 oz can chopped tomatoes

2 tbsp chopped parsley

1 tsp dried oregano

2 bay leaves

2 tbsp tomato purée (paste)

1 tsp sugar

salt and pepper

1 Heat the oil in a pan over a medium heat and fry the onion for 2-3 minutes or until translucent. Add the garlic and fry for 1 minute.

2 Stir in the chopped tomatoes, parsley, oregano, bay leaves, tomato purée (paste), sugar, and salt and pepper to taste.

3 Bring the sauce to the boil, then simmer, uncovered, for 15–20 minutes or until the sauce has reduced by half. Taste the sauce and adjust the seasoning if necessary. Discard the bay leaves just before serving.

Béchamel Sauce

300 ml/½ pint/1¼ cups milk

2 bay leaves

3 cloves

1 small onion

60 g/2 oz/¼ cup butter, plus extra for greasing

45 g/1½ oz/6 tbsp flour

300 ml/½ pint/1¼ cups single (light) cream

large pinch of freshly grated nutmeg

salt and pepper

1 Pour the milk into a small pan and add the bay leaves. Press the cloves into the onion, add to the pan and bring the milk to the boil. Remove the pan from the heat and set aside to cool.

2 Strain the milk into a jug and rinse the pan. Melt the butter in the pan and stir in the flour. Stir for 1 minute, then gradually pour on the milk, stirring constantly. Cook the sauce for 3 minutes, then pour on the cream and bring it to the boil. Remove from the heat and season with nutmeg, salt and pepper to taste.

Lamb Sauce

2 tbsp olive oil

1 large onion, sliced

2 celery stalks, thinly sliced

500 g/1 lb 2 oz lean lamb, minced (ground)

3 tbsp tomato purée (paste)

150 g/5½ oz bottled sun-dried tomatoes, drained and chopped

1 tsp dried oregano

1 tbsp red wine vinegar

150 ml/¼ pint/⅔ cup chicken stock

salt and pepper

1 Heat the oil in a frying pan (skillet) over a medium heat and fry the onion and celery until the onion is translucent, about 3 minutes. Add the lamb and fry, stirring frequently, until it browns.

2 Stir in the tomato purée (paste), sun-dried tomatoes, oregano, vinegar and stock. Season with salt and pepper to taste.

3 Bring to the boil and cook, uncovered, for 20 minutes or until the meat has absorbed the stock. Taste and adjust the seasoning if necessary.

Cheese Sauce

25 g/1 oz/2 tbsp butter

1 tbsp flour

250 ml/9 fl oz/1 cup milk

2 tbsp single (light) cream

pinch of freshly grated nutmeg

45 g/1½ oz mature (sharp) Cheddar, grated

1 tbsp freshly grated Parmesan

salt and pepper

1 Melt the butter in a pan, stir in the flour and cook for 1 minute. Gradually pour on the milk, stirring all the time. Stir in the cream and season the sauce with nutmeg, salt and pepper to taste.

2 Simmer the sauce for 5 minutes to reduce, then remove it from the heat and stir in the cheeses. Stir until the cheeses have melted and blended into the sauce.

Espagnole Sauce

2 tbsp butter

25 g/1 oz/¼ cup plain (all-purpose) flour

1 tsp tomato purée (paste)

250 ml/9 fl oz/1⅛ cups hot veal stock

1 tbsp Madeira

1½ tsp white wine vinegar

2 tbsp olive oil

25 g/1 oz bacon, diced

25 g/1 oz carrot, diced

25 g/1 oz onion, diced

15 g/½ oz celery, diced

15 g/½ oz leek, diced

15 g/½ oz fennel, diced

1 fresh thyme sprig

1 bay leaf

1 Melt the butter in a pan, add the flour and cook, stirring, until lightly coloured. Add the tomato purée (paste), then stir in the hot veal stock, Madeira and white wine vinegar and cook for 2 minutes.

2 Heat the oil in a separate pan, add the bacon, carrot, onion, celery, leek, fennel, thyme sprig and bay leaf and fry until the vegetables have softened. Remove the vegetables from the pan with a slotted spoon and drain thoroughly. Add the vegetables to the sauce and leave to simmer for 4 hours, stirring occasionally. Strain the sauce before using.

Italian Red Wine Sauce

150 ml/¼ pint /⅝ cup Brown Stock (see page 30)

150 ml/¼ pint /⅔ cup Espagnole Sauce (see left)

125 ml/4 fl oz/½ cup red wine

2 tbsp red wine vinegar

4 tbsp shallots, chopped

1 bay leaf

1 thyme sprig

pepper

1 First make a demi-glace sauce. Put the Brown Stock and Espagnole Sauce in a pan and heat for 10 minutes, stirring occasionally.

2 Meanwhile, put the red wine, red wine vinegar, shallots, bay leaf and thyme in a pan, bring to the boil and reduce by three-quarters.

3 Strain the demi-glace sauce and add to the pan containing the Red Wine Sauce and leave to simmer for 20 minutes, stirring occasionally. Season with pepper to taste and strain the sauce before using.

Basic Recipes

Italian Cheese Sauce

2 tbsp butter

25 g/1 oz/¼ cup plain (all-purpose) flour

300 ml/½ pint/1¼ cups hot milk

pinch of nutmeg

pinch of dried thyme

2 tbsp white wine vinegar

3 tbsp double (heavy) cream

60 g/2 oz/½ cup grated Mozzarella cheese

60 g/2 oz/½ cup Parmesan cheese

1 tsp English mustard

2 tbsp soured cream

salt and pepper

1 Melt the butter in a pan and stir in the flour. Cook, stirring, over a low heat until the roux is light in colour and crumbly in texture. Stir in the hot milk and cook, stirring, for 15 minutes until thick and smooth.

2 Add the nutmeg, thyme, white wine vinegar and season to taste. Stir in the cream and mix well.

3 Stir in the cheeses, mustard and cream and mix until the cheeses have melted and blended into the sauce.

Fish Stock

900 g/2 lb non-oily fish pieces, such as heads, tails, trimmings and bones

150 ml/¼ pint/⅔ cup white wine

1 onion, chopped

1 carrot, sliced

1 celery stick (stalk), sliced

4 black peppercorns

1 bouquet garni

1.75 litres/3 pints/7½ cups water

1 Put the fish pieces, wine, onion, carrot, celery, black peppercorns, bouquet garni and water in a large pan and leave to simmer for 30 minutes, stirring occasionally. Strain and blot the fat from the surface with kitchen paper (towels) before using.

Garlic Mayonnaise

2 garlic cloves, crushed

8 tbsp mayonnaise

chopped parsley

salt and pepper

1 Put the mayonnaise in a bowl. Add the garlic, parsley and salt and pepper to taste and mix together well.

Brown Stock

900 g/ 2 lb veal bones and shin of beef

1 leek, sliced

1 onion, chopped

1 celery stick (stalk), sliced

1 carrot, sliced

1 bouquet garni

150 ml/¼ pint/⅔ cup white wine vinegar

1 thyme sprig

1.75 litres/3 pints/7½ cups cold water

1 Roast the veal bones and shin of beef in their own juices in the oven for 40 minutes.

2 Transfer the bones to a large pan and add the leeks, onion, celery, carrots, bouquet garni, white wine vinegar and thyme and cover with the cold water. Leave to simmer over a very low heat for about 3 hours. Strain and blot the fat from the surface with kitchen paper (towels) before using.

How to Use This Book

Each recipe contains a wealth of useful information, including a breakdown of nutritional quantities, preparation and cooking times, and level of difficulty. All of this information is explained in detail below.

This amount of time represents the actual cooking time.

The nutritional information provided for each recipe is per serving or per portion. Optional ingredients, variations or serving suggestions have not been included in the calculations.

The number of chef's hats represents the difficulty of each recipe, ranging from easy (1 chef's hat) to difficult (5 chef's hats).

This amount of time represents the preparation of ingredients, including cooling, chilling and soaking times.

The ingredients for each recipe are listed in the order that they are used.

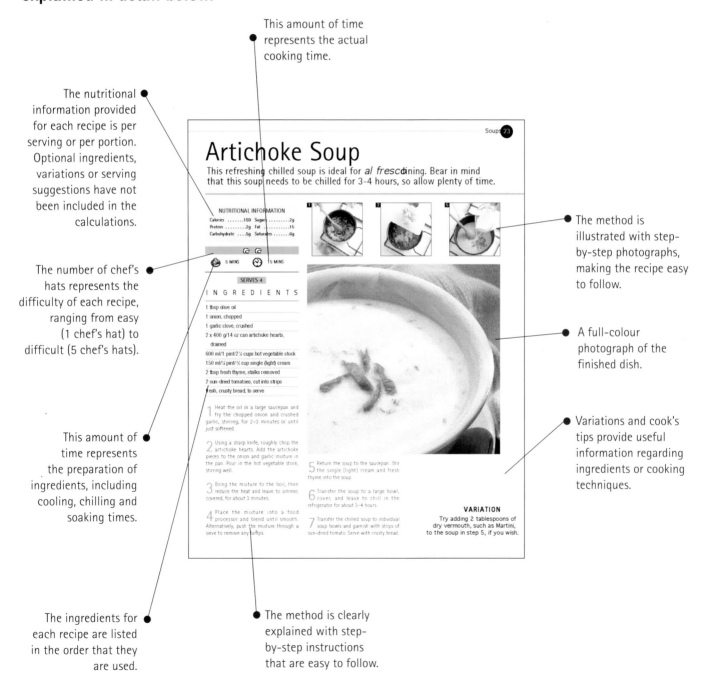

The method is illustrated with step-by-step photographs, making the recipe easy to follow.

A full-colour photograph of the finished dish.

Variations and cook's tips provide useful information regarding ingredients or cooking techniques.

The method is clearly explained with step-by-step instructions that are easy to follow.

Soups 23

Artichoke Soup

This refreshing chilled soup is ideal for *al fresco* dining. Bear in mind that this soup needs to be chilled for 3-4 hours, so allow plenty of time.

NUTRITIONAL INFORMATION

Calories 159   Sugar 2g
Protein . . . . .2g   Fat 15
Carbohydrate . . . .5g   Saturates 6g

5 MINS   15 MINS

SERVES 4

INGREDIENTS

1 tbsp olive oil

1 onion, chopped

1 garlic clove, crushed

2 x 400 g/14 oz can artichoke hearts, drained

600 ml/1 pint/2 ½ cups hot vegetable stock

150 ml/¼ pint/⅔ cup single (light) cream

2 tbsp fresh thyme, stalks removed

2 sun-dried tomatoes, cut into strips

fresh, crusty bread, to serve

1 Heat the oil in a large saucepan and fry the chopped onion and crushed garlic, stirring, for 2-3 minutes or until just softened.

2 Using a sharp knife, roughly chop the artichoke hearts. Add the artichoke pieces to the onion and garlic mixture in the pan. Pour in the hot vegetable stock, stirring well.

3 Bring the mixture to the boil, then reduce the heat and leave to simmer, covered, for about 3 minutes.

4 Place the mixture into a food processor and blend until smooth. Alternatively, push the mixture through a sieve to remove any lumps.

5 Return the soup to the saucepan. Stir the single (light) cream and fresh thyme into the soup.

6 Transfer the soup to a large bowl, cover, and leave to chill in the refrigerator for about 3-4 hours.

7 Transfer the chilled soup to individual soup bowls and garnish with strips of sun-dried tomato. Serve with crusty bread.

VARIATION
Try adding 2 tablespoons of dry vermouth, such as Martini, to the soup in step 5, if you wish.

Soups

Soups are an important part of the Italian cuisine. They vary in consistency from light and delicate to hearty main meal soups. Texture is always apparent – Italians rarely serve smooth soups. Some may be partially puréed but the identity of the ingredients is never entirely obliterated. There are regional characteristics, too. In the north, soups

are often based on rice, while in Tuscany, thick bean- or bread-based soups are popular. Tomato, garlic and pasta soups are typical of the south. Minestrone is known world-wide but the best-known version probably comes from Milan. However, all varieties are full of vegetables and are delicious and satisfying. Fish soups also abound in one guise or another, and most of these are village specialities, so the variety is unlimited and always tasty.

Tuscan Onion Soup

This soup is best made with white onions, which have a mild flavour. If you cannot get hold of them, try using large Spanish onions instead.

NUTRITIONAL INFORMATION

Calories . . . . . . .390 Sugars 0g
Protein . . . . .9g Fat 33g
Carbohydrate . . .15g Saturates 14g

 5–10 MINS 40–45 MINS

SERVES 4

INGREDIENTS

50 g/1¾ oz pancetta ham, diced

1 tbsp olive oil

4 large white onions, sliced thinly into rings

3 garlic cloves, chopped

850 ml/1½ pints/3½ cups hot chicken or
  ham stock

4 slices ciabatta or other Italian bread

50 g/1¾ oz/3 tbsp butter

75 g/2¾ oz Gruyère or Cheddar

salt and pepper

1 Dry fry the pancetta in a large saucepan for 3–4 minutes until it begins to brown. Remove the pancetta from the pan and set aside until required.

2 Add the oil to the pan and cook the onions and garlic over a high heat for

4 minutes. Reduce the heat, cover and cook for 15 minutes or until the onions are lightly caramelized.

3 Add the stock to the saucepan and bring to the boil. Reduce the heat and leave the mixture to simmer, covered, for about 10 minutes.

4 Toast the slices of ciabatta on both sides, under a preheated grill (broiler),

for 2–3 minutes or until golden. Spread the ciabatta with butter and top with the Gruyère or Cheddar cheese. Cut the bread into bite-size pieces.

5 Add the reserved pancetta to the soup and season with salt and pepper to taste.

6 Pour into 4 soup bowls and top with the toasted bread.

COOK'S TIP

Pancetta is similar to bacon, but it is air- and salt-cured for about 6 months. Pancetta is available from most delicatessens and some large supermarkets. If you cannot obtain pancetta use unsmoked bacon instead.

Tuscan Bean Soup

A thick and creamy soup that is based on a traditional Tuscan recipe. If you use dried beans, the preparation and cooking times will be longer.

NUTRITIONAL INFORMATION

Calories 250   Sugars 4g
Protein ....13g   Fat 10g
Carbohydrate ...29g   Saturates 2g

2 MINS   10 MINS

SERVES 4

INGREDIENTS

225 g/8 oz dried butter beans, soaked overnight, or 2 x 400 g/14 oz can butter beans

1 tbsp olive oil

2 garlic cloves, crushed

1 vegetable or chicken stock cube, crumbled

150 ml/¼ pint/⅔ cup milk

2 tbsp chopped fresh oregano

salt and pepper

1 If you are using dried beans that have been soaked overnight, drain them thoroughly. Bring a large pan of water to the boil, add the beans and boil for 10 minutes. Cover the pan and simmer for a further 30 minutes or until tender. Drain the beans, reserving the cooking liquid. If you are using canned beans, drain them thoroughly and reserve the liquid.

2 Heat the oil in a large frying pan (skillet) and fry the garlic for 2–3 minutes or until just beginning to brown.

3 Add the beans and 400 ml/14 fl oz/1⅔ cup of the reserved liquid to the pan (skillet), stirring. You may need to add a little water if there is insufficient liquid. Stir in the crumbled stock cube. Bring the mixture to the boil and then remove the pan from the heat.

4 Place the bean mixture in a food processor and blend to form a smooth purée. Alternatively, mash the bean mixture to a smooth consistency. Season to taste with salt and pepper and stir in the milk.

5 Pour the soup back into the pan and gently heat to just below boiling point. Stir in the chopped oregano just before serving.

Pumpkin Soup

This thick, creamy soup has a wonderful, warming golden colour.
It is flavoured with orange and thyme.

NUTRITIONAL INFORMATION

Calories . . . . .111 Sugars 4g
Protein . . . . .2g Fat 6g
Carbohydrate . . . .5g Saturates 2g

 10 MINS   35–40 MINS

SERVES 4

INGREDIENTS

2 tbsp olive oil

2 medium onions, chopped

2 cloves garlic, chopped

900 g/2 lb pumpkin, peeled and cut into
    2.5 cm/1 inch chunks

1.5 litres /2 ¾ pints/6 ¼ cups boiling
    vegetable or chicken stock

finely grated rind and juice of 1 orange

3 tbsp fresh thyme, stalks removed

150 ml/¼ pint/⅔ cup milk

salt and pepper

crusty bread, to serve

1 Heat the olive oil in a large saucepan.
Add the onions to the pan and cook
for 3–4 minutes or until softened. Add the
garlic and pumpkin and cook for a further
2 minutes, stirring well.

2 Add the boiling vegetable or chicken
stock, orange rind and juice and 2
tablespoons of the thyme to the pan.
Leave to simmer, covered, for 20 minutes
or until the pumpkin is tender.

3 Place the mixture in a food processor
and blend until smooth. Alternatively,
mash the mixture with a potato masher
until smooth. Season to taste.

4 Return the soup to the saucepan and
add the milk. Reheat the soup for 3–4
minutes or until it is piping hot but not
boiling.

5 Sprinkle with the remaining fresh
thyme just before serving.

6 Divide the soup among 4 warm soup
bowls and serve with lots of fresh
crusty bread.

COOK'S TIP

Pumpkins are usually
large vegetables. To make things
a little easier, ask the greengrocer
to cut a chunk off for you.
Alternatively, make double the
quantity and freeze the soup
for up to 3 months.

Artichoke Soup

This refreshing chilled soup is ideal for *al fresco* dining. Bear in mind that this soup needs to be chilled for 3-4 hours, so allow plenty of time.

NUTRITIONAL INFORMATION

Calories 159   Sugars 2g
Protein . . . . .2g   Fat 15
Carbohydrate . . . .5g   Saturates 6g

 5 MINS   15 MINS

SERVES 4

I N G R E D I E N T S

1 tbsp olive oil

1 onion, chopped

1 garlic clove, crushed

2 x 400 g/14 oz can artichoke hearts,
   drained

600 ml/1 pint/2 ½ cups hot vegetable stock

150 ml/¼ pint/⅔ cup single (light) cream

2 tbsp fresh thyme, stalks removed

2 sun-dried tomatoes, cut into strips

fresh, crusty bread, to serve

1 Heat the oil in a large saucepan and fry the chopped onion and crushed garlic, stirring, for 2–3 minutes or until just softened.

2 Using a sharp knife, roughly chop the artichoke hearts. Add the artichoke pieces to the onion and garlic mixture in the pan. Pour in the hot vegetable stock, stirring well.

3 Bring the mixture to the boil, then reduce the heat and leave to simmer, covered, for about 3 minutes.

4 Place the mixture into a food processor and blend until smooth. Alternatively, push the mixture through a sieve to remove any lumps.

5 Return the soup to the saucepan. Stir the single (light) cream and fresh thyme into the soup.

6 Transfer the soup to a large bowl, cover, and leave to chill in the refrigerator for about 3–4 hours.

7 Transfer the chilled soup to individual soup bowls and garnish with strips of sun-dried tomato. Serve with crusty bread.

VARIATION

Try adding 2 tablespoons of dry vermouth, such as Martini, to the soup in step 5, if you wish.

Cream of Artichoke Soup

A creamy soup with the unique, subtle flavouring of Jerusalem artichokes and a garnish of grated carrots for extra crunch.

NUTRITIONAL INFORMATION

Calories 19   Sugars 0g
Protein . . . . .0.4g   Fat 2g
Carbohydrate . . .0.7g   Saturates 0.7g

 10–15 MINS 55–60 MINS

SERVES 6

I N G R E D I E N T S

750 g/1 lb 10 oz Jerusalem artichokes

1 lemon, sliced thickly

60 g/2 oz/¼ cup butter or margarine

2 onions, chopped

1 garlic clove, crushed

1.25 litres/2¼ pints/5½ cups chicken or
   vegetable stock

2 bay leaves

¼ tsp ground mace or ground nutmeg

1 tbsp lemon juice

150 ml/¼ pint/⅔ cup single (light) cream or
   natural fromage frais

salt and pepper

TO GARNISH

coarsely grated carrot

chopped fresh parsley or coriander
   (cilantro)

1 Peel and slice the artichokes. Put into a bowl of water with the lemon slices.

2 Melt the butter or margarine in a large saucepan. Add the onions and garlic and fry gently for 3–4 minutes until soft but not coloured.

3 Drain the artichokes (discarding the lemon) and add to the pan. Mix well and cook gently for 2–3 minutes without allowing to colour.

4 Add the stock, seasoning, bay leaves, mace or nutmeg and lemon juice. Bring slowly to the boil, then cover and simmer gently for about 30 minutes until the vegetables are very tender.

5 Discard the bay leaves. Cool the soup slightly then press through a sieve (strainer) or blend in a food processor until smooth. If liked, a little of the soup may be only partially puréed and added to the rest of the puréed soup, to give extra texture.

6 Pour into a clean pan and bring to the boil. Adjust the seasoning and stir in the cream or fromage frais. Reheat gently without boiling. Garnish with grated carrot and chopped parsley or coriander (cilantro).

Spinach & Mascarpone Soup

Spinach is the basis for this delicious soup, but use sorrel or watercress instead for a pleasant change.

NUTRITIONAL INFORMATION

Calories	537	Sugars	.........2g
Protein	.........6g	Fat	..........53g
Carbohydrate	....9g	Saturates	......29g

5 MINS   35 MINS

SERVES 4

INGREDIENTS

60 g/2 oz/¼ cup butter

1 bunch spring onions (scallions), trimmed and chopped

2 celery sticks, chopped

350 g/12 oz/3 cups spinach or sorrel, or 3 bunches watercress

850 ml /1 ½ pints/3 ½ cups vegetable stock

225 g/8 oz/1 cup Mascarpone cheese

1 tbsp olive oil

2 slices thick-cut bread, cut into cubes

½ tsp caraway seeds

salt and pepper

sesame bread sticks, to serve

1 Melt half the butter in a very large saucepan. Add the spring onions (scallions) and celery and cook gently for about 5 minutes, or until softened.

2 Pack the spinach, sorrel or watercress into the saucepan. Add the vegetable stock and bring to the boil; then reduce the heat and simmer, covered, for 15–20 minutes.

3 Transfer the soup to a blender or food processor and blend until smooth, or pass through a sieve. Return to the saucepan.

4 Add the Mascarpone cheese to the soup and heat gently, stirring, until smooth and blended. Taste and season with salt and pepper.

5 Heat the remaining butter with the oil in a frying pan (skillet). Add the bread cubes and fry in the hot oil until golden brown, adding the caraway seeds towards the end of cooking, so that they do not burn.

6 Ladle the soup into 4 warmed bowls. Sprinkle with the croûtons and serve at once, accompanied by the sesame bread sticks.

VARIATIONS

Any leafy vegetable can be used to make this soup to give variations to the flavour. For anyone who grows their own vegetables, it is the perfect recipe for experimenting with a glut of produce. Try young beetroot (beet) leaves or surplus lettuces for a change.

Calabrian Mushroom Soup

The Calabrian mountains in southern Italy provide large amounts of wild mushrooms that are rich in flavour and colour.

NUTRITIONAL INFORMATION

Calories 452   Sugars 5g
Protein . . . . .15g   Fat 26g
Carbohydrate . . .42g   Saturates 12g

 5 MINS   25–30 MINS

SERVES 4

I N G R E D I E N T S

2 tbsp olive oil

1 onion, chopped

450g/1 lb mixed mushrooms, such as ceps, oyster and button

300 ml/ ½ pint/1 ¼ cup milk

850 ml/1 ½ pints/3 ¾ cups hot vegetable stock

8 slices of rustic bread or French stick

2 garlic cloves, crushed

50 g/1 ¾ oz/3 tbsp butter, melted

75 g/2 ¾ oz Gruyère cheese, finely grated

salt and pepper

1 Heat the oil in a large frying pan (skillet) and cook the onion for 3–4 minutes or until soft and golden.

2 Wipe each mushroom with a damp cloth and cut any large mushrooms into smaller, bite-size pieces.

3 Add the mushrooms to the pan, stirring quickly to coat them in the oil.

4 Add the milk to the pan, bring to the boil, cover and leave to simmer for about 5 minutes. Gradually stir in the hot vegetable stock and season with salt and pepper to taste.

5 Under a preheated grill (broiler), toast the bread on both sides until golden.

6 Mix together the garlic and butter and spoon generously over the toast.

7 Place the toast in the bottom of a large tureen or divide it among 4 individual serving bowls and pour over the hot soup. Top with the grated Gruyère cheese and serve at once.

COOK'S TIP

Mushrooms absorb liquid, which can lessen the flavour and affect cooking properties. Therefore, carefully wipe them with a damp cloth rather than rinsing them in water.

Green Soup

This fresh-tasting soup with green (dwarf) beans, cucumber and watercress can be served warm, or chilled on a hot summer day.

NUTRITIONAL INFORMATION

Calories 121   Sugars 2g
Protein . . . . .2g   Fat 8g
Carbohydrate . . .10g   Saturates 1g

 5 MINS   25–30 MINS

SERVES 4

INGREDIENTS

1 tbsp olive oil

1 onion, chopped

1 garlic clove, chopped

200 g/7 oz potato, peeled and cut into
    2.5 cm/1 inch cubes

700 ml/1 ¼ pints/scant 3 cups vegetable or
    chicken stock

1 small cucumber or ½ large cucumber, cut
    into chunks

80 g/3 oz bunch watercress

125 g/4 ½ oz green (dwarf) beans, trimmed
    and halved lengthwise

salt and pepper

VARIATION

Try using 125 g/4½ oz
mange tout (snow peas)
instead of the beans, if
you prefer.

1 Heat the oil in a large pan and fry the onion and garlic for 3–4 minutes or until softened.

2 Add the cubed potato and fry for a further 2–3 minutes.

3 Stir in the stock, bring to the boil and leave to simmer for 5 minutes.

4 Add the cucumber to the pan and cook for a further 3 minutes or until the potatoes are tender. Test by inserting the tip of a knife into the potato cubes – it should pass through easily.

5 Add the watercress and allow to wilt. Then place the soup in a food processor and blend until smooth. Alternatively, before adding the watercress, mash the soup with a potato masher and push through a sieve, then chop the watercress finely and stir into the soup.

6 Bring a small pan of water to the boil and steam the beans for 3–4 minutes or until tender.

7 Add the beans to the soup, season and warm through.

Red Bean Soup

Beans feature widely in Italian soups, making them hearty and tasty. The beans need to be soaked overnight, so prepare well in advance.

NUTRITIONAL INFORMATION

Calories 184   Sugars 5g
Protein . . . . .4g   Fat 11g
Carbohydrate . . .19g   Saturates 2g

5–10 MINS   3¾ HOURS

SERVES 6

I N G R E D I E N T S

175 g/6 oz/scant 1 cup dried red kidney
   beans, soaked overnight

1.7 litres/3 pints/7½ cups water

1 large ham bone or bacon knuckle

2 carrots, chopped

1 large onion, chopped

2 celery stalks, sliced thinly

1 leek, trimmed, washed and sliced

1–2 bay leaves

2 tbsp olive oil

2–3 tomatoes, peeled and chopped

1 garlic clove, crushed

1 tbsp tomato purée (paste)

60 g/2 oz/4½ tbsp arborio or Italian rice

125–175 g/4–6 oz green cabbage,
   shredded finely

salt and pepper

1 Drain the beans and place them in a saucepan with enough water to cover. Bring to the boil, then boil for 15 minutes to remove any harmful toxins. Reduce the heat and simmer for 45 minutes.

2 Drain the beans and put into a clean saucepan with the water, ham bone or knuckle, carrots, onion, celery, leek, bay leaves and olive oil. Bring to the boil, then cover and simmer for 1 hour or until the beans are very tender.

3 Discard the bay leaves and bone, reserving any ham pieces from the bone. Remove a small cupful of the beans and reserve. Purée or liquidize the soup in a food processor or blender, or push through a coarse sieve (strainer), and return to a clean pan.

4 Add the tomatoes, garlic, tomato purée (paste), rice and season. Bring back to the boil and simmer for about 15 minutes or until the rice is tender.

5 Add the cabbage and reserved beans and ham, and continue to simmer for 5 minutes. Adjust the seasoning and serve very hot. If liked, a piece of toasted crusty bread may be put in the base of each soup bowl before ladling in the soup. If the soup is too thick, add a little boiling water or stock.

Vegetable & Bean Soup

This wonderful combination of cannellini beans, vegetables and vermicelli is made even richer by the addition of pesto and dried mushrooms.

NUTRITIONAL INFORMATION

Calories	294	Sugars	.........2g
Protein	........11g	Fat	..........16g
Carbohydrate	...30g	Saturates	.......2g

30 MINS   30 MINS

SERVES 4

I N G R E D I E N T S

1 small aubergine (eggplant)

2 large tomatoes

1 potato, peeled

1 carrot, peeled

1 leek

425 g/15 oz can cannellini beans

850 ml/1½ pints/3¾ cups hot vegetable or
   chicken stock

2 tsp dried basil

15 g/½ oz dried porcini mushrooms,
   soaked for 10 minutes in enough warm
   water to cover

50 g/1¾ oz/¼ cup vermicelli

3 tbsp pesto (see page 31 or use shop
   bought)

freshly grated Parmesan cheese, to serve
   (optional)

1 Slice the aubergine (eggplant) into rings about 1 cm/½ inch thick, then cut each ring into 4.

2 Cut the tomatoes and potato into small dice. Cut the carrot into sticks, about 2.5 cm/1 inch long and cut the leek into rings.

3 Place the cannellini beans and their liquid in a large saucepan. Add the aubergine (eggplant), tomatoes, potatoes, carrot and leek, stirring to mix.

4 Add the stock to the pan and bring to the boil. Reduce the heat and leave to simmer for 15 minutes.

5 Add the basil, dried mushrooms and their soaking liquid and the vermicelli and simmer for 5 minutes or until all of the vegetables are tender.

6 Remove the pan from the heat and stir in the pesto.

7 Serve with freshly grated Parmesan cheese, if using.

Chickpea (Garbanzo Bean) Soup

A thick vegetable soup which is a delicious meal in itself. Serve with Parmesan cheese and warm sun-dried tomato-flavoured ciabatta bread.

NUTRITIONAL INFORMATION

Calories	297	Sugars	.........0g
Protein	........11g	Fat	..........18g
Carbohydrate	...24g	Saturates	.......2g

5 MINS   15 MINS

SERVES 4

INGREDIENTS

2 tbsp olive oil

2 leeks, sliced

2 courgettes (zucchini), diced

2 garlic cloves, crushed

2 x 400 g/14 oz cans chopped tomatoes

1 tbsp tomato purée (paste)

1 fresh bay leaf

850 ml/1 ½ pints/3 ¾ cups chicken stock

400 g/14 oz can chickpeas (garbanzo beans), drained and rinsed

225 g/8 oz spinach

salt and pepper

TO SERVE

Parmesan cheese

sun-dried tomato bread

COOK'S TIP

Chickpeas (garbanzo beans) are used extensively in North African cuisine and are also found in Italian, Spanish, Middle Eastern and Indian cooking. They have a deliciously nutty flavour with a firm texture and are an excellent canned product.

1 Heat the oil in a large saucepan, add the leeks and courgettes (zucchini) and cook briskly for 5 minutes, stirring constantly.

2 Add the garlic, tomatoes, tomato purée (paste), bay leaf, stock and chickpeas (garbanzo beans). Bring to the boil and simmer for 5 minutes.

3 Shred the spinach finely, add to the soup and cook for 2 minutes. Season.

4 Remove the bay leaf from the soup and discard.

5 Serve the soup with freshly grated Parmesan cheese and sun-dried tomato bread.

Potato & Pesto Soup

Fresh pesto is a treat to the taste buds and very different in flavour from that available from supermarkets. Store fresh pesto in the refrigerator.

NUTRITIONAL INFORMATION

Calories 548   Sugars 0g
Protein ....11g   Fat 52g
Carbohydrate ...10g   Saturates 18g

5–10 MINS   50 MINS

SERVES 4

INGREDIENTS

3 slices rindless, smoked, fatty bacon

450 g/1 lb floury potatoes

450 g/ 1 lb onions

2 tbsp olive oil

25 g/1 oz/2 tbsp butter

600 ml/1 pint/2 ½ cups chicken stock

600 ml/1 pint/2 ½ cups milk

100 g/3 ½ oz/¾ cup dried conchigliette

150 ml/ ¼ pint/⅝ cup double (heavy) cream

chopped fresh parsley

salt and pepper

freshly grated Parmesan cheese and garlic
  bread, to serve

PESTO SAUCE

60 g/2 oz/1 cup finely chopped fresh
  parsley

2 garlic cloves, crushed

60 g/2 oz/⅔ cup pine nuts (kernels),
  crushed

2 tbsp chopped fresh basil leaves

60 g/2 oz/⅔ cup freshly grated Parmesan
  cheese

white pepper

150 ml/ ¼ pint/⅝ cup olive oil

1 To make the pesto sauce, put all of the ingredients in a blender or food processor and process for 2 minutes, or blend by hand using a pestle and mortar.

2 Finely chop the bacon, potatoes and onions. Fry the bacon in a large pan over a medium heat for 4 minutes. Add the butter, potatoes and onions and cook for 12 minutes, stirring constantly.

3 Add the stock and milk to the pan, bring to the boil and simmer for 10 minutes. Add the conchigliette and simmer for a further 10-12 minutes.

4 Blend in the cream and simmer for 5 minutes. Add the parsley, salt and pepper and 2 tbsp pesto sauce. Transfer the soup to serving bowls and serve with Parmesan cheese and fresh garlic bread.

Creamy Tomato Soup

This quick and easy creamy soup has a lovely fresh tomato flavour. Basil leaves complement tomatoes perfectly.

NUTRITIONAL INFORMATION

Calories 218   Sugars 10g
Protein . . . . .3g   Fat 19g
Carbohydrate . . .10g   Saturates 11g

  5 MINS   25–30 MINS

SERVES 4

I N G R E D I E N T S

50 g/1 ¾ oz/3 tbsp butter

700 g/1 lb 9 oz ripe tomatoes, preferably
  plum, roughly chopped

850 ml/1 ½ pints/3 ¾ hot vegetable stock

50 g/1 ¾ oz/¼ cup ground almonds

150 ml/¼ pint/⅔ cup milk or single (light)
  cream

1 tsp sugar

2 tbsp shredded basil leaves

salt and pepper

1 Melt the butter in a large saucepan. Add the tomatoes and cook for 5 minutes until the skins start to wrinkle. Season to taste with salt and pepper.

2 Add the stock to the pan, bring to the boil, cover and simmer for 10 minutes.

3 Meanwhile, under a preheated grill (broiler), lightly toast the ground almonds until they are golden-brown. This will take only 1-2 minutes, so watch them closely.

4 Remove the soup from the heat and place in a food processor and blend the mixture to form a smooth consistency. Alternatively, mash the soup with a potato masher until smooth.

5 Pass the soup through a sieve to remove any tomato skin or pips.

6 Place the soup in the pan and return to the heat. Stir in the milk or cream, toasted ground almonds and sugar. Warm the soup through and add the shredded basil leaves just before serving.

7 Transfer the creamy tomato soup to warm soup bowls and serve hot.

COOK'S TIP

Very fine breadcrumbs can be used instead of the ground almonds, if you prefer. Toast them in the same way as the almonds and add with the milk or cream in step 6.

Minestrone Soup

Minestrone translates as 'big soup' in Italian. It is made all over Italy, but this version comes from Livorno, a port on the western coast.

NUTRITIONAL INFORMATION

Calories	311	Sugars	. . . . .8g
Protein	. . . . .12g	Fat	. . . . .19g
Carbohydrate	. . .26g	Saturates	. . . . . . .5g

10 MINS   30 MINS

SERVES 4

I N G R E D I E N T S

1 tbsp olive oil

100 g/3 ½ oz pancetta ham, diced

2 medium onions, chopped

2 cloves garlic, crushed

1 potato, peeled and cut into 1 cm/
    ½ inch cubes

1 carrot, peeled and cut into chunks

1 leek, sliced into rings

¼ green cabbage, shredded

1 stick celery, chopped

450 g/1 lb can chopped tomatoes

200 g/7 oz can flageolet (small navy)
    beans, drained and rinsed

600 ml/1 pint/2 ½ cups hot ham or chicken
    stock, diluted with 600 ml/1 pint/2 ½ cups
    boiling water

bouquet garni (2 bay leaves, 2 sprigs
    rosemary and 2 sprigs thyme, tied
    together)

salt and pepper

freshly grated Parmesan cheese, to serve

1 Heat the olive oil in a large saucepan. Add the diced pancetta, chopped onions and garlic and fry for about 5 minutes, stirring, or until the onions are soft and golden.

2 Add the prepared potato, carrot, leek, cabbage and celery to the saucepan. Cook for a further 2 minutes, stirring frequently, to coat all of the vegetables in the oil.

3 Add the tomatoes, flageolet (small navy) beans, hot ham or chicken stock and bouquet garni to the pan, stirring to mix. Leave the soup to simmer, covered, for 15–20 minutes or until all of the vegetables are just tender.

4 Remove the bouquet garni, season with salt and pepper to taste and serve with plenty of freshly grated Parmesan cheese.

Tomato & Pasta Soup

Plum tomatoes are ideal for making soups and sauces
as they have denser, less watery flesh than rounder varieties.

NUTRITIONAL INFORMATION

Calories . . . . . . .503 Sugars 16g
Protein . . . . .9g Fat 28g
Carbohydrate . . .59g Saturates 17g

  5 MINS   50–55 MINS

SERVES 4

INGREDIENTS

60 g/2 oz/4 tbsp unsalted butter

1 large onion, chopped

600 ml/1 pint/2 ½ cups vegetable stock

900 g/2 lb Italian plum tomatoes, skinned
    and roughly chopped

pinch of bicarbonate of soda (baking soda)

225 g/8 oz/2 cups dried fusilli

1 tbsp caster (superfine) sugar

150 ml/¼ pint/⅔ cup double (heavy) cream

salt and pepper

fresh basil leaves, to garnish

 1 Melt the butter in a large pan, add the
onion and fry for 3 minutes, stirring.
Add 300 ml/½ pint/1¼ cups of vegetable
stock to the pan, with the chopped
tomatoes and bicarbonate of soda (baking

soda). Bring the soup to the boil and
simmer for 20 minutes.

2 Remove the pan from the heat and
set aside to cool. Purée the soup in
a blender or food processor and pour
through a fine strainer back into
the saucepan.

3 Add the remaining vegetable stock
and the fusilli to the pan, and season
to taste with salt and pepper.

VARIATION

To make orange and tomato
soup, simply use half the
quantity of vegetable stock,
topped up with the same amount
of fresh orange juice and garnish
the soup with orange rind.

Brown Lentil & Pasta Soup

In Italy, this soup is called *Minestrade Lentiche*. A *minestra* is a soup cooked with pasta; here, farfalline, a small bow-shaped variety, is used.

NUTRITIONAL INFORMATION

Calories	225	Sugars	.........1g
Protein	........13g	Fat	...........8g
Carbohydrate	...27g	Saturates	.......3g

5 MINS   25 MINS

SERVES 4

I N G R E D I E N T S

4 rashers streaky bacon, cut into small
  squares

1 onion, chopped

2 garlic cloves, crushed

2 sticks celery, chopped

50 g/1 ¾ oz/ ¼ cup farfalline or spaghetti,
  broken into small pieces

1 x 400 g/14 oz can brown lentils, drained

1.2 litres/2 pints/5 cups hot ham or
  vegetable stock

2 tbsp chopped, fresh mint

1 Place the bacon in a large frying pan
  (skillet) together with the onions,
garlic and celery. Dry fry for 4–5 minutes,
stirring, until the onion is tender and the
bacon is just beginning to brown.

2 Add the pasta to the pan (skillet) and
  cook, stirring, for about 1 minute to
coat the pasta in the oil.

3 Add the lentils and the stock and
  bring to the boil. Reduce the heat and
leave to simmer for 12–15 minutes or
until the pasta is tender.

4 Remove the pan (skillet) from the heat
  and stir in the chopped fresh mint.

5 Transfer the soup to warm soup bowls
  and serve immeditely.

COOK'S TIP

If you prefer to use dried
lentils, add the stock before
the pasta and cook for 1–1¼
hours until the lentils are tender.
Add the pasta and cook for a further
12–15 minutes.

Minestrone & Pasta Soup

Italian cooks have created some very heart-warming soups and this is the most famous of all.

NUTRITIONAL INFORMATION

Calories . . . . .231 Sugars 3g
Protein . . . . .8g Fat 16g
Carbohydrate . . .14g Saturates 7g

10 MINS   1¾ HOURS

SERVES 10

INGREDIENTS

3 garlic cloves

3 large onions

2 celery sticks (sticks)

2 large carrots

2 large potatoes

100 g/3 ½ oz French (green) beans

100 g/3 ½ oz courgettes (zucchini)

60 g/2 oz/4 tbsp butter

50 ml/2 fl oz/ ¼ cup olive oil

60 g/2 oz rindless fatty bacon, finely diced

1.5 litres/2 ¾ pints/6 ⅞ cups vegetable or
   chicken stock

1 bunch fresh basil, finely chopped

100 g/3 ½ oz chopped tomatoes

2 tbsp tomato purée (paste)

100 g/3 ½ oz Parmesan cheese rind

90 g/3 oz dried spaghetti, broken up

salt and pepper

freshly grated Parmesan cheese, to serve

1 Finely chop the garlic, onions, celery, carrots, potatoes, beans and courgettes (zucchini).

2 Heat the butter and oil together in a large saucepan, add the bacon and cook for 2 minutes.

3 Add the garlic and onion and fry for 2 minutes, then stir in the celery, carrots and potatoes and fry for a further 2 minutes.

4 Add the beans to the pan and fry for 2 minutes. Stir in the courgettes (zucchini) and fry for a further 2 minutes. Cover the pan and cook all the vegetables, stirring frequently, for 15 minutes.

5 Add the stock, basil, tomatoes, tomato purée (paste) and cheese rind and season to taste. Bring to the boil, lower the heat and simmer for 1 hour. Remove and discard the cheese rind.

6 Add the spaghetti to the pan and cook for 20 minutes. Serve in large, warm soup bowls; sprinkle with freshly grated Parmesan cheese.

Bean & Pasta Soup

A dish with proud Mediterranean origins, this soup is a winter warmer.
Serve with warm, crusty bread and, if you like, a slice of cheese.

NUTRITIONAL INFORMATION

Calories 463   Sugars 5g
Protein . . . . .13g   Fat 33g
Carbohydrate . . .30g   Saturates 7g

5–10 MINS   1¼ HOURS

SERVES 4

I N G R E D I E N T S

225 g/8 oz/generous 1 cup dried haricot
   (navy) beans, soaked, drained and rinsed

4 tbsp olive oil

2 large onions, sliced

3 garlic cloves, chopped

400 g/14 oz can chopped tomatoes

1 tsp dried oregano

1 tsp tomato purée (paste)

850 ml/1 ½ pints/3 ½ cups water

90 g/3 oz small pasta shapes, such as fusilli
   or conchigliette

125 g/4 ½ oz sun-dried tomatoes, drained
   and sliced thinly

1 tbsp chopped coriander (cilantro),
   or flat-leaf parsley

2 tbsp freshly grated Parmesan

salt and pepper

1 Put the soaked beans into a large pan,
cover with cold water and bring them
to the boil. Boil rapidly for 15 minutes to
remove any harmful toxins. Drain the
beans in a colander.

2 Heat the oil in a pan over a medium
heat and fry the onions until they are
just beginning to change colour. Stir in the
garlic and cook for 1 further minute. Stir

in the chopped tomatoes, oregano and the
tomato purée (paste) and pour on the
water. Add the beans, bring to the boil and
cover the pan. Simmer for 45 minutes or
until the beans are almost tender.

3 Add the pasta, season the soup with
salt and pepper to taste and stir in the
sun-dried tomatoes. Return the soup to

the boil, partly cover the pan and continue
cooking for 10 minutes, or until the pasta
is nearly tender.

4 Stir in the chopped coriander
(cilantro) or parsley. Taste the soup
and adjust the seasoning if necessary.
Transfer to a warmed soup tureen to serve.
Sprinkle with the cheese and serve hot.

Ravioli alla Parmigiana

This soup is traditionally served at Easter and Christmas in the province of Parma.

NUTRITIONAL INFORMATION

Calories ...... .554	Sugars 3g	
Protein .... .26g	Fat .... .24g	
Carbohydrate ...64g	Saturates 9g	

 4½–5 HOURS ⏲ 25 MINS

SERVES 4

INGREDIENTS

285 g/10 oz basic pasta dough

1.2 litres/2 pints/5 cups veal stock

freshly grated Parmesan cheese, to serve

FILLING

125 ml/4 fl oz/ ½ cup Espagnole Sauce

100 g/3 ½ oz/1 cup freshly grated

Parmesan cheese

100 g/3 ½ oz/1 ⅔ cup fine white

breadcrumbs

2 eggs

1 small onion, finely chopped

1 tsp freshly grated nutmeg

1 Make the basic pasta dough and the Espagnole Sauce (see page 15).

2 Carefully roll out 2 sheets of the pasta dough and cover with a damp tea towel (dish cloth) while you make the filling for the ravioli.

3 To make the filling, place the freshly grated Parmesan cheese, fine white breadcrumbs, eggs, Espagnole Sauce, finely chopped onion and the freshly grated nutmeg in a large mixing bowl, and mix together well.

4 Place spoonfuls of the filling at regular intervals on 1 sheet of pasta dough. Cover with the second sheet of pasta dough, then cut into squares and seal the edges.

5 Bring the veal stock to the boil in a large saucepan.

6 Add the ravioli to the pan and cook for about 15 minutes.

7 Transfer the soup and ravioli to warm serving bowls and serve, generously sprinkled with Parmesan cheese.

COOK'S TIP

It is advisable to prepare the basic pasta dough and the Espagnole Sauce (see page 15) well in advance, or buy ready-made equivalents if you are short of time.

Lemon & Chicken Soup

This delicately flavoured summer soup is surprisingly easy to make, and tastes delicious.

NUTRITIONAL INFORMATION

Calories 506	Sugars 4g	
Protein 19g	Fat 31g	
Carbohydrate . . .41g	Saturates 19g	

5–10 MINS   1¼ HOURS

SERVES 4

INGREDIENTS

60 g/2 oz/4 tbsp butter

8 shallots, thinly sliced

2 carrots, thinly sliced

2 celery sticks (stalks), thinly sliced

225 g/8 oz boned chicken breasts, finely chopped

3 lemons

1.2 litres/2 pints/5 cups chicken stock

225 g/8 oz dried spaghetti, broken into small pieces

150 ml/¼ pint/⅝ cup double (heavy) cream

salt and white pepper

TO GARNISH

fresh parsley sprig

3 lemon slices, halved

COOK'S TIP

You can prepare this soup up to the end of step 3 in advance, so that all you need do before serving is heat it through before adding the pasta and the finishing touches.

1 Melt the butter in a large saucepan. Add the shallots, carrots, celery and chicken and cook over a low heat, stirring occasionally, for 8 minutes.

2 Thinly pare the lemons and blanch the lemon rind in boiling water for 3 minutes. Squeeze the juice from the lemons.

3 Add the lemon rind and juice to the pan, together with the chicken stock. Bring slowly to the boil over a low heat and simmer for 40 minutes, stirring occasionally.

4 Add the spaghetti to the pan and cook for 15 minutes. Season to taste with salt and white pepper and add the cream. Heat through, but do not allow the soup to boil or it will curdle.

5 Pour the soup into a tureen or individual bowls, garnish with the parsley and half slices of lemon and serve immediately.

Chicken & Pasta Broth

This satisfying soup makes a good lunch or supper dish and you can use any vegetables you like. Children will love the tiny pasta shapes.

NUTRITIONAL INFORMATION

Calories	185	Sugars	.........5g
Protein	........17g	Fat	...........5g
Carbohydrate	...20g	Saturates	.......1g

5 MINS   15-20 MINS

SERVES 6

INGREDIENTS

350 g/12 oz boneless chicken breasts

2 tbsp sunflower oil

1 medium onion, diced

250 g/9 oz/1 ½ cups carrots, diced

250 g/9 oz cauliflower florets

850 ml/1 ½ pints/3 ¾ cups chicken stock

2 tsp dried mixed herbs

125 g/4 ½ oz small pasta shapes

salt and pepper

Parmesan cheese (optional) and crusty
   bread, to serve

1 Using a sharp knife, finely dice the chicken, discarding any skin.

2 Heat the oil in a large saucepan and quickly sauté the chicken, onion, carrots and cauliflower until they are lightly coloured.

3 Stir in the chicken stock and dried mixed herbs and bring to the boil.

4 Add the pasta shapes to the pan and return to the boil. Cover the pan and leave the broth to simmer for 10 minutes, stirring occasionally to prevent the pasta shapes from sticking together.

5 Season the broth with salt and pepper to taste and sprinkle with Parmesan cheese, if using. Serve the broth with fresh crusty bread.

COOK'S TIP

You can use any small pasta shapes for this soup – try conchigliette or ditalini or even spaghetti broken up into small pieces. To make a fun soup for children you could add animal-shaped or alphabet pasta.

Chicken & Bean Soup

This hearty and nourishing soup, combining chickpeas (garbanzo beans) and chicken, is an ideal starter for a family supper.

NUTRITIONAL INFORMATION

Calories 347   Sugars 2g
Protein ....28g   Fat 11g
Carbohydrate ...37g   Saturates 4g

5 MINS   1¾ HOURS

SERVES 4

INGREDIENTS

25 g/1 oz/2 tbsp butter

3 spring onions (scallions), chopped

2 garlic cloves, crushed

1 fresh marjoram sprig, finely chopped

350 g/12 oz boned chicken breasts, diced

1.2 litres/2 pints/5 cups chicken stock

350 g/12 oz can chickpeas (garbanzo
beans), drained

1 bouquet garni

1 red (bell) pepper, diced

1 green (bell) pepper, diced

115 g/4 oz/1 cup small dried pasta shapes,
    such as elbow macaroni

salt and white pepper

croûtons, to serve

COOK'S TIP

If you prefer, you can use dried chickpeas (garbanzo beans). Cover with cold water and set aside to soak for 5–8 hours. Drain and add the beans to the soup, according to the recipe, and allow an additional 30 minutes– 1 hour cooking time.

1 Melt the butter in a large saucepan. Add the spring onions (scallions), garlic, sprig of fresh marjoram and the diced chicken and cook, stirring frequently, over a medium heat for 5 minutes.

2 Add the chicken stock, chickpeas (garbanzo beans) and bouquet garni and season with salt and white pepper.

3 Bring the soup to the boil, lower the heat and simmer for about 2 hours.

4 Add the diced (bell) peppers and pasta to the pan, then simmer for a further 20 minutes.

5 Transfer the soup to a warm tureen. To serve, ladle the soup into individual serving bowls and serve immediately, garnished with the croûtons.

Tuscan Veal Broth

Veal plays an important role in Italian cuisine and there are dozens of recipes for all cuts of this meat.

NUTRITIONAL INFORMATION

Calories ....420 Sugars 5g
Protein ....54g Fat 7g
Carbohydrate ...37g Saturates 2g

2¼ HOURS   4¾ HOURS

SERVES 4

INGREDIENTS

60 g/2 oz/⅓ cup dried peas, soaked for
   2 hours and drained

900 g/2 lb boned neck of veal, diced

1.2 litres/2 pints/5 cups beef or brown
   stock (see Cook's Tip)

600 ml/1 pint/2½ cups water

60 g/2 oz/⅓ cup barley, washed

1 large carrot, diced

1 small turnip (about 175 g/6 oz), diced

1 large leek, thinly sliced

1 red onion, finely chopped

100 g/3½ oz chopped tomatoes

1 fresh basil sprig

100 g/3½ oz/¾ cup dried vermicelli

salt and white pepper

1 Put the peas, veal, stock and water into a large pan and bring to the boil over a low heat. Using a slotted spoon, skim off any scum that rises to the surface.

2 When all of the scum has been removed, add the barley and a pinch of salt to the mixture. Simmer gently over a low heat for 25 minutes.

3 Add the carrot, turnip, leek, onion, tomatoes and basil to the pan, and season with salt and pepper to taste. Leave to simmer for about 2 hours, skimming the surface from time to time to remove any scum. Remove the pan from the heat and set aside for 2 hours.

4 Set the pan over a medium heat and bring to the boil. Add the vermicelli and cook for 12 minutes. Season with salt and pepper to taste; remove and discard the basil. Ladle into soup bowls and serve immediately.

COOK'S TIP

The best brown stock is made with veal bones and shin of beef roasted with dripping (drippings) in the oven for 40 minutes. Transfer the bones to a pan and add sliced leeks, onion, celery and carrots, a bouquet garni, white wine vinegar and a thyme sprig and cover with cold water. Simmer over a very low heat for 3 hours; strain before use.

Veal & Wild Mushroom Soup

Wild mushrooms are available commercially and an increasing range of cultivated varieties is now to be found in many supermarkets.

NUTRITIONAL INFORMATION

Calories 413	Sugars 3g
Protein 28g	Fat 22g
Carbohydrate . . .28g	Saturates 12g

🍲 5 MINS   🕐 3¼ HOURS

SERVES 4

I N G R E D I E N T S

450 g/1 lb veal, thinly sliced

450 g/1 lb veal bones

1.2 litres/2 pints/5 cups water

1 small onion

6 peppercorns

1 tsp cloves

pinch of mace

140 g/5 oz oyster and shiitake mushrooms, roughly chopped

150 ml/¼ pint/⅔ cup double (heavy) cream

100 g/3½ oz/¾ cup dried vermicelli

1 tbsp cornflour (cornstarch)

3 tbsp milk

salt and pepper

COOK'S TIP

You can make this soup with the more inexpensive cuts of veal, such as breast or neck slices. These are lean and the long cooking time ensures that the meat is really tender.

1 Put the veal, bones and water into a large saucepan. Bring to the boil and lower the heat. Add the onion, peppercorns, cloves and mace and simmer for about 3 hours, until the veal stock is reduced by one-third.

2 Strain the stock, skim off any fat on the surface with a slotted spoon, and pour the stock into a clean saucepan. Add the veal meat to the pan.

3 Add the mushrooms and cream, bring to the boil over a low heat and then leave to simmer for 12 minutes, stirring occasionally.

4 Meanwhile, cook the vermicelli in lightly salted boiling water for 10 minutes or until tender, but still firm to the bite. Drain and keep warm.

5 Mix the cornflour (cornstarch) and milk to form a smooth paste. Stir into the soup to thicken. Season to taste with salt and pepper and just before serving, add the vermicelli. Transfer the soup to a warm tureen and serve immediately.

Veal & Ham Soup

Veal and ham is a classic combination, complemented here with the addition of sherry to create a richly-flavoured Italian soup.

NUTRITIONAL INFORMATION

Calories . . . . .501 Sugars 10g
Protein . . . . .38g Fat 18g
Carbohydrate . . .28g Saturates 10g

5 MINS   3¼ HOURS

SERVES 4

INGREDIENTS

60 g/2 oz/4 tbsp butter

1 onion, diced

1 carrot, diced

1 celery stick (stalk), diced

450 g/1 lb veal, very thinly sliced

450 g/1 lb ham, thinly sliced

60 g/2 oz/ ½ cup plain (all-purpose) flour

1 litre/1 ¾ pints/4 ⅜ cups beef stock

1 bay leaf

8 black peppercorns

pinch of salt

3 tbsp redcurrant jelly

150 ml/ ¼ pint/ ⅝ cup cream sherry

100 g/3 ½ oz/ ¾ cup dried vermicelli

garlic croûtons (see Cook's Tip), to serve

1 Melt the butter in a large pan. Add the onions, carrot, celery, veal and ham and cook over a low heat for 6 minutes.

2 Sprinkle over the flour and cook, stirring constantly, for a further 2 minutes. Gradually stir in the stock, then add the bay leaf, peppercorns and salt. Bring to the boil and simmer for 1 hour.

3 Remove the pan from the heat and add the redcurrant jelly and cream

sherry, stirring to combine. Set aside for about 4 hours.

4 Remove the bay leaf from the pan and discard. Reheat the soup over a very low heat until warmed through.

5 Meanwhile, cook the vermicelli in a saucepan of lightly salted boiling water for 10-12 minutes. Stir the vermicelli into the soup and transfer to soup bowls. Serve with garlic croûtons.

COOK'S TIP

To make garlic croûtons, remove the crusts from 3 slices of day-old white bread. Cut the bread into 5 mm/¼ inch cubes. Heat 3 tbsp oil over a low heat and stir-fry 1–2 chopped garlic cloves for 1–2 minutes. Remove the garlic and add the bread. Cook, stirring frequently, until golden. Remove with a slotted spoon and drain.

Fish Soup

There are many varieties of fish soup in Italy, some including shellfish. This one, from Tuscany, is more like a chowder.

NUTRITIONAL INFORMATION

Calories ....305 Sugars 3g
Protein ....47g Fat 7g
Carbohydrate ....11g Saturates 1g

🍲 5–10 MINS   ⏱ 1 HOUR

SERVES 6

I N G R E D I E N T S

1 kg/2 lb 4 oz assorted prepared fish
    (including mixed fish fillets, squid, etc.)

2 onions, sliced thinly

2 celery stalks, sliced thinly

a few sprigs of parsley

2 bay leaves

150 ml/ ¼ pint/ ⅔ cup white wine

1 litre/1 ¾ pints/4 cups water

2 tbsp olive oil

1 garlic clove, crushed

1 carrot, chopped finely

400 g/14 oz can peeled tomatoes, puréed

2 potatoes, chopped

1 tbsp tomato purée (paste)

1 tsp chopped fresh oregano or ½ tsp
    dried oregano

350 g/12 oz fresh mussels

175 g/6 oz peeled prawns (shrimp)

2 tbsp chopped fresh parsley

salt and pepper

crusty bread, to serve

1 Cut the fish into slices and put into a pan with half the onion and celery, the parsley, bay leaves, wine and water. Bring to the boil, cover and simmer for 25 minutes.

2 Strain the fish stock and discard the vegetables. Skin the fish, remove any bones and reserve.

3 Heat the oil in a pan. Fry the remaining onion and celery with the garlic and carrot until soft but not coloured, stirring occasionally. Add the puréed canned tomatoes, potatoes, tomato purée (paste), oregano, reserved stock and seasoning. Bring to the boil and simmer for about 15 minutes or until the potato is almost tender.

4 Meanwhile, thoroughly scrub the mussels. Add the mussels to the pan with the prawns (shrimp) and leave to simmer for about 5 minutes or until the mussels have opened (discard any that remain closed).

5 Return the fish to the soup with the chopped parsley, bring back to the boil and simmer for 5 minutes. Adjust the seasoning.

6 Serve the soup in warmed bowls with chunks of fresh crusty bread, or put a toasted slice of crusty bread in the bottom of each bowl before adding the soup. If possible, remove a few half shells from the mussels before serving.

Mussel & Potato Soup

This quick and easy soup would make a delicious summer lunch, served with fresh crusty bread.

NUTRITIONAL INFORMATION

Calories 804   Sugars 3g
Protein . . . . .17g   Fat 68g
Carbohydrate . . .32g   Saturates 38g

🧊 10 MINS   🕐 35 MINS

SERVES 4

I N G R E D I E N T S

750 g/1 lb 10 oz mussels

2 tbsp olive oil

100 g/3½ oz/7 tbsp unsalted butter

2 slices rindless fatty bacon, chopped

1 onion, chopped

2 garlic cloves, crushed

60 g/2 oz/½ cup plain (all-purpose) flour

450 g/1 lb potatoes, thinly sliced

100 g/3½ oz/¾ cup dried conchigliette

300 ml/½ pint/1¼ cups double (heavy)
   cream

1 tbsp lemon juice

2 egg yolks

salt and pepper

T O   G A R N I S H

2 tbsp finely chopped fresh parsley

lemon wedges

1 Debeard the mussels and scrub them under cold water for 5 minutes. Discard any mussels that do not close immediately when sharply tapped.

2 Bring a large pan of water to the boil, add the mussels, oil and a little pepper. Cook until the mussels open. (discard any mussels that remain closed.)

3 Drain the mussels, reserving the cooking liquid. Remove the mussels from their shells.

4 Melt the butter in a large saucepan, add the bacon, onion and garlic and cook for 4 minutes. Carefully stir in the flour. Measure 1.2 litres/2 pints/5 cups of the reserved cooking liquid and stir it into the pan.

5 Add the potatoes to the pan and simmer for 5 minutes. Add the conchigliette and simmer for a further 10 minutes.

6 Add the cream and lemon juice, season to taste with salt and pepper, then add the mussels to the pan.

7 Blend the egg yolks with 1–2 tbsp of the remaining cooking liquid, stir into the pan and cook for 4 minutes.

8 Ladle the soup into 4 warm individual soup bowls, garnish with the chopped fresh parsley and lemon wedges and serve immediately.

Italian Fish Stew

This robust stew is full of Mediterranean flavours. If you do not want to prepare the fish yourself, ask your local fishmonger to do it for you.

NUTRITIONAL INFORMATION

Calories ....236 Sugars 4g
Protein ....20g Fat 7g
Carbohydrate ...25g Saturates 1g

5-10 MINS   25 MINS

SERVES 4

INGREDIENTS

2 tbsp olive oil

2 red onions, finely chopped

1 garlic clove, crushed

2 courgettes (zucchini), sliced

400 g/14 oz can chopped tomatoes

850 ml/1 ½ pints/3 ½ cups fish or vegetable
   stock

90 g/3 oz dried pasta shapes

350 g/12 oz firm white fish, such as cod,
   haddock or hake

1 tbsp chopped fresh basil or oregano or
   1 tsp dried oregano

1 tsp grated lemon rind

1 tbsp cornflour (cornstarch)

1 tbsp water

salt and pepper

sprigs of fresh basil or oregano, to garnish

  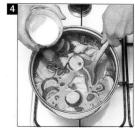

1 Heat the oil in a large saucepan and fry the onions and garlic for 5 minutes. Add the courgettes (zucchini) and cook for 2–3 minutes, stirring often.

2 Add the tomatoes and stock to the saucepan and bring to the boil. Add the pasta, cover and reduce the heat. Simmer for 5 minutes.

3 Skin and bone the fish, then cut it into chunks. Add to the saucepan with the basil or oregano and lemon rind and cook gently for 5 minutes until the fish is opaque and flakes easily (take care not to overcook it).

4 Blend the cornflour (cornstarch) with the water and stir into the stew. Cook gently for 2 minutes, stirring, until thickened. Season with salt and pepper to taste and ladle into 4 warmed soup bowls. Garnish with basil or oregano and serve.

Starters & Snacks

Starters are known as antipasto in Italy which is translated as meaning 'before the main course'. Antipasti usually come in three categories: meat, fish and vegetables. There are many varieties of cold meats, including ham, invariably sliced paper-thin. All varieties of fish are popular in Italy,

including inkfish, octopus and cuttlefish. Seafood is also highly prized, especially huge prawns (shrimp), mussels and fresh sardines. Numerous vegetables feature in Italian cuisine and are an important part of the daily diet. They are served as a starter, as an accompaniment to main dishes, or as a course on their own. In Italy, vegetables are cooked only until 'al dente' and still slightly crisp. This ensures that they retain more nutrients and the colours remain bright and appealing.

Spinach & Ricotta Patties

Nudo or naked is the word used to describe this mixture, which can also be made into thin pancakes or used as a filling for tortelloni.

NUTRITIONAL INFORMATION

Calories 374	Sugars 4g	
Protein 16g	Fat 31g	
Carbohydrate 9g	Saturates 19g	

5 MINS   30 MINS

SERVES 4

INGREDIENTS

450 g/1 lb fresh spinach

250 g/9 oz ricotta cheese

1 egg, beaten

2 tsp fennel seeds, lightly crushed

50 g/1¾ oz pecorino or Parmesan cheese, finely grated, plus extra to garnish

25 g/1 oz plain (all-purpose) flour, mixed with 1 tsp dried thyme

75 g/2¾ oz/5 tbsp butter

2 garlic cloves, crushed

salt and pepper

tomato wedges, to serve

1 Wash the spinach and trim off any long stalks. Place in a pan, cover and cook for 4–5 minutes until wilted. This will probably have to be done in batches as the volume of spinach is quite large. Place in a colander and leave to drain and cool.

2 Mash the ricotta and beat in the egg and the fennel seeds. Season with plenty of salt and pepper, then stir in the pecorino or Parmesan cheese.

3 Squeeze as much excess water as possible from the spinach and finely chop the leaves. Stir the spinach into the cheese mixture.

4 Taking about 1 tablespoon of the spinach and cheese mixture, shape it into a ball and flatten it slightly to form a patty. Gently roll in the seasoned flour. Continue this process until all of the mixture has been used up.

5 Half-fill a large frying pan (skillet) with water and bring to the boil.

Carefully add the patties and cook for 3–4 minutes or until they rise to the surface. Remove with a perforated spoon.

6 Melt the butter in a pan. Add the garlic and cook for 2–3 minutes. Pour the garlic butter over the patties, season with freshly ground black pepper and serve at once.

(Bell) Pepper Salad

Colourful marinated Mediterranean vegetables make a tasty starter.
Serve with fresh bread or Tomato Toasts (see below).

NUTRITIONAL INFORMATION

Calories . . . . . . .234 Sugars 4g
Protein . . . . .6g Fat 17g
Carbohydrate . . .15g Saturates 2g

   5–10 MINS   35 MINS

SERVES 4

INGREDIENTS

1 onion

2 red (bell) peppers

2 yellow (bell) peppers

3 tbsp olive oil

2 large courgettes (zucchini), sliced

2 garlic cloves, sliced

1 tbsp balsamic vinegar

50 g/1¾ oz anchovy fillets, chopped

25 g/1 oz/¼ cup black olives,
   halved and pitted

1 tbsp chopped fresh basil

salt and pepper

TOMATO TOASTS

small stick of French bread

1 garlic clove, crushed

1 tomato, peeled and chopped

2 tbsp olive oil

1 Cut the onion into wedges. Core and deseed the (bell) peppers and cut into thick slices.

2 Heat the oil in a large heavy-based frying pan (skillet). Add the onion, (bell) peppers, courgettes (zucchini) and garlic and fry gently for 20 minutes, stirring occasionally.

3 Add the vinegar, anchovies, olives and seasoning to taste, mix thoroughly and leave to cool.

4 Spoon on to individual plates and sprinkle with the basil.

5 To make the tomato toasts, cut the French bread diagonally into 1 cm/½ inch slices.

6 Mix the garlic, tomato, oil and seasoning together, and spread thinly over each slice of bread.

7 Place the bread on a baking tray (cookie sheet), drizzle with the olive oil and bake in a preheated oven, 220°C/425°F/Gas Mark 7, for 5–10 minutes until crisp. Serve the Tomato Toasts with the (Bell) Pepper Salad.

Aubergine (Eggplant) Rolls

Thin slices of aubergine (eggplant) are fried in olive oil and garlic, and then topped with pesto sauce and finely sliced Mozzarella.

NUTRITIONAL INFORMATION

Calories . . . . .278 Sugars 2g
Protein . . . . .4g Fat 28g
Carbohydrate . . . .2g Saturates 7g

15-20 MINS   20 MINS

SERVES 4

I N G R E D I E N T S

2 aubergines (eggplant), sliced thinly
  lengthways

5 tbsp olive oil

1 garlic clove, crushed

4 tbsp pesto

175 g/6 oz/1½ cups Mozzarella, grated

basil leaves, torn into pieces

salt and pepper

fresh basil leaves, to garnish

1 Sprinkle the aubergine (eggplant) slices liberally with salt and leave for 10–15 minutes to extract the bitter juices. Turn the slices over and repeat. Rinse well with cold water and drain on paper towels.

2 Heat the olive oil in a large frying pan (skillet) and add the garlic. Fry the aubergine (eggplant) slices lightly on both sides, a few at a time. Drain them on paper towels.

3 Spread the pesto on to one side of the aubergine (eggplant) slices. Top with the grated Mozzarella and sprinkle with the torn basil leaves. Season with a little salt and pepper. Roll up the slices and secure with wooden cocktail sticks (toothpicks).

4 Arrange the aubergine (eggplant) rolls in a greased ovenproof baking dish. Place in a preheated oven, 180°C/350°F/Gas Mark 4, and bake for 8–10 minutes.

5 Transfer the aubergine (eggplant) rolls to a warmed serving plate. Scatter with fresh basil leaves and serve at once.

Stewed Artichokes

This is a traditional Roman dish. The artichokes are stewed in olive oil with fresh herbs.

NUTRITIONAL INFORMATION

Calories 129   Sugars 0g
Protein ....4g   Fat 8g
Carbohydrate ...10g   Saturates 1g

 5 MINS   50 MINS

SERVES 4

INGREDIENTS

4 small globe artichokes

olive oil

4 garlic cloves, peeled

2 bay leaves

finely grated rind and juice of 1 lemon

2 tbsp fresh marjoram

lemon wedges, to serve

1 Using a sharp knife, carefully peel away the tough outer leaves surrounding the artichokes. Trim the stems to about 2.5 cm/1 inch.

2 Using a knife, cut each artichoke in half and scoop out the choke (heart).

3 Place the artichokes in a large heavy-based pan. Pour over enough olive oil to half cover the artichokes in the pan.

4 Add the garlic cloves, bay leaves and half of the grated lemon rind.

5 Start to heat the artichokes gently, cover the pan and continue to cook over a low heat for about 40 minutes. It is important that the artichokes should be stewed in the oil, not fried.

6 Once the artichokes are tender, remove them with a perforated spoon and drain thoroughly. Remove the bay leaves and discard.

7 Transfer the artichokes to warm serving plates. Garnish the artichokes with the remaining grated lemon rind, fresh marjoram and a little lemon juice. Serve with lemon wedges.

COOK'S TIP

To prevent the artichokes from oxidizing and turning brown before cooking, brush them with a little lemon juice. In addition, use the oil used for cooking the artichokes for salad dressings – it will impart a lovely lemon and herb flavour.

Baked Fennel Gratinati

Fennel is a common ingredient in Italian cooking. In this dish its distinctive flavour is offset by the smooth Béchamel Sauce.

NUTRITIONAL INFORMATION

Calories 426   Sugars 9g
Protein . . . . .13g   Fat 35g
Carbohydrate . . .16g   Saturates 19g

 5-10 MINS   45 MINS

SERVES 4

INGREDIENTS

4 heads fennel

25 g/1 oz/ 2 tbsp butter

150 ml/¼ pint/½ cup dry white wine

Béchamel Sauce (see page 14),
    enriched with 2 egg yolks

25 g/1 oz/½ cup fresh white breadcrumbs

3 tbsp freshly grated Parmesan

salt and pepper

fennel fronds, to garnish

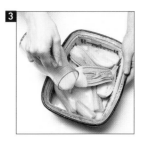

1 Remove any bruised or tough outer stalks of fennel and cut each head in half. Put into a saucepan of boiling salted water and simmer for 20 minutes until tender, then drain.

2 Butter an ovenproof dish liberally and arrange the drained fennel in it.

3 Mix the wine into the Béchamel Sauce and season with salt and pepper to taste. Pour over the fennel.

4 Sprinkle evenly with the breadcrumbs and then the Parmesan.

5 Place in a preheated oven, 200°C/400°F/Gas Mark 6, and bake for 20 minutes until the top is golden. Serve garnished with fennel fronds.

Pancakes with Smoked Fish

These are delicious as a starter or light supper dish
and you can vary the filling with whichever fish you prefer.

NUTRITIONAL INFORMATION

Calories 399   Sugars 6g
Protein . . . . .36g   Fat 18g
Carbohydrate . . .25g   Saturates 10g

15 MINS   1 HR 20 MINS

Makes 12 pancakes

INGREDIENTS

PANCAKES

100 g/3 ½ oz flour

½ tsp salt

1 egg, beaten

300 ml/ ½ pint/1 ¼ cups milk

1 tbsp oil, for frying

SAUCE

450 g/1 lb smoked haddock, skinned

300 ml/ ½ pint/1 ¼ cups milk

40 g/1 ½ oz/3 tbsp butter or margarine

40 g/1 ½ oz flour

300 ml/ ½ pint/1 ¼ cups fish stock

75 g/2 ¾ oz Parmesan cheese, grated

100 g/3 ½ oz frozen peas, defrosted

100 g/3 ½ oz prawns (shrimp), cooked
and peeled

50 g/1 ¾ oz Gruyère cheese, grated

salt and pepper

1 To make the pancake batter, sift the flour and salt into a large bowl and make a well in the centre. Add the egg and, using a wooden spoon, begin to draw in the flour. Slowly add the milk and beat together to form a smooth batter. Set aside until required.

2 Place the fish in a large frying pan (skillet), add the milk and bring to the boil. Simmer for 10 minutes or until the fish begins to flake. Drain thoroughly, reserving the milk.

3 Melt the butter in a saucepan. Add the flour, mix to a paste and cook for 2–3 minutes. Remove the pan from the heat and add the reserved milk a little at a time, stirring to make a smooth sauce. Repeat with the fish stock. Return to the heat and bring to the boil, stirring. Stir in the Parmesan and season with salt and pepper to taste.

4 Grease a frying pan (skillet) with oil. Add 2 tablespoons of the pancake batter, swirling it around the pan and cook for 2–3 minutes. Loosen the sides with a palette knife (spatula) and flip over the pancake. Cook for 2–3 minutes until golden; repeat. Stack the pancakes with sheets of baking parchment between them and keep warm in the oven.

5 Stir the flaked fish, peas and prawns (shrimp) into half of the sauce and use to fill each pancake. Pour over the remaining sauce, top with the Gruyère and bake for 20 minutes until golden.

Mozzarella Snack

These deep-fried Mozzarella sandwiches are a tasty snack at any time of the day, or serve smaller triangles as an antipasto with drinks.

NUTRITIONAL INFORMATION

Calories	379	Sugars	.........4g
Protein	........20g	Fat	..........22g
Carbohydrate	...28g	Saturates	.......5g

 20 MINS 5–10 MINS

SERVES 4

I N G R E D I E N T S

8 slices bread, preferably slightly stale, crusts removed

100 g/3 ½ oz Mozzarella cheese, sliced thickly

50 g/1 ¾ oz black olives, chopped

8 canned anchovy fillets, drained and chopped

16 fresh basil leaves

4 eggs, beaten

150 ml/5 floz/ ⅔ cup milk

oil, for deep-frying

salt and pepper

1 Cut each slice of bread into 2 triangles. Top 8 of the bread triangles with the Mozzarella slices, olives and chopped anchovies.

2 Place the basil leaves on top and season with salt and pepper to taste.

3 Lay the other 8 triangles of bread over the top and press down round the edges to seal.

4 Mix the eggs and milk and pour into an ovenproof dish. Add the sandwiches and leave to soak for about 5 minutes.

5 Heat the oil in a large saucepan to 180°–190°C/350°–375°F or until a cube of bread browns in 30 seconds.

6 Before cooking the sandwiches, squeeze the edges together again.

7 Carefully place the sandwiches in the oil and deep-fry for 2 minutes or until golden, turning once. Remove the sandwiches with a perforated spoon and drain on absorbent kitchen paper. Serve immediately while still hot.

Garlic & Pine Nut Tarts

A crisp lining of bread is filled with garlic butter and pine nuts to make a delightful light meal.

NUTRITIONAL INFORMATION

Calories 435   Sugars 1g
Protein . . . . .6g   Fat 39g
Carbohydrate . . .17g   Saturates 20g

  20 MINS   15 MINS

SERVES 4

I N G R E D I E N T S

4 slices wholemeal or granary bread

50 g/1¾ oz pine nuts

150 g/5½ oz/10 tbsp butter

5 garlic cloves, peeled and halved

2 tbsp fresh oregano, chopped, plus extra
  for garnish

4 black olives, halved

oregano leaves, to garnish

1 Using a rolling pin, flatten the bread slightly. Using a pastry cutter, cut out 4 circles of bread to fit your individual tart tins (pans) – they should measure about 10 cm/4 inches across. Reserve the offcuts of bread and leave them in the refrigerator for 10 minutes or until required.

VARIATION

Puff pastry can be used for the tarts. Use 200 g/7oz puff pastry to line 4 tart tins (pans). Leave the pastry to chill for 20 minutes. Line the tins (pans) with the pastry and foil and bake blind for 10 minutes. Remove the foil and bake for 3–4 minutes or until the pastry is set. Cool, then continue from step 2, adding 2 tbsp breadcrumbs to the mixture.

2 Meanwhile, place the pine nuts on a baking tray (cookie sheet). Toast the pine nuts under a preheated grill (broiler) for 2–3 minutes or until golden.

3 Put the bread offcuts, pine nuts, butter, garlic and oregano into a food processor and blend for about 20 seconds. Alternatively, pound the ingredients by hand in a mortar and pestle. The mixture should have a rough texture.

4 Spoon the pine nut butter mixture into the lined tin (pan) and top with the olives. Bake in a preheated oven at 200°C/400°F/Gas Mark 6 for 10–15 minutes or until golden.

5 Transfer the tarts to serving plates and serve warm, garnished with the fresh oregano leaves.

Onion & Mozzarella Tarts

These individual tarts are delicious hot or cold and are great for lunchboxes or picnics.

NUTRITIONAL INFORMATION

Calories 327   Sugars 3g
Protein . . . . .5g   Fat 23g
Carbohydrate . . .25g   Saturates 9g

45 MINS   45 MINS

SERVES 4

I N G R E D I E N T S

250g/9 oz packet puff pastry, defrosted
  if frozen

2 medium red onions

1 red (bell) pepper

8 cherry tomatoes, halved

100g/3½ oz Mozzarella cheese,
  cut into chunks

8 sprigs thyme

1 Roll out the pastry to make 4 x 7.5 cm/ 3 inch squares. Using a sharp knife, trim the edges of the pastry, reserving the trimmings. Leave the pastry to chill in the refrigerator for 30 minutes.

2 Place the pastry squares on a baking tray (cookie sheet). Brush a little water along each edge of the pastry squares and use the reserved pastry trimmings to make a rim around each tart.

3 Cut the red onions into thin wedges and halve and deseed the (bell) peppers.

4 Place the onions and (bell) pepper in a roasting tin (pan). Cook under a preheated grill (broiler) for 15 minutes or until charred.

5 Place the roasted (bell) pepper halves in a polythene bag and leave to sweat for 10 minutes. Peel off the skin from the (bell) peppers and cut the flesh into strips.

6 Line the pastry squares with squares of foil. Bake in a preheated oven at 200°C/400°F/Gas Mark 6 for 10 minutes. Remove the foil squares and bake for a further 5 minutes.

7 Place the onions, (bell) pepper strips, tomatoes and cheese in each tart and sprinkle with the fresh thyme.

8 Return to the oven for 15 minutes or until the pastry is golden. Serve hot.

Bruschetta with Tomatoes

Using ripe tomatoes and the best olive oil will make this Tuscan dish absolutely delicious.

NUTRITIONAL INFORMATION

Calories	330	Sugars	.........4g
Protein	.........8g	Fat	..........14g
Carbohydrate	...45g	Saturates	.......2g

 15 MINS   5 MINS

SERVES 4

I N G R E D I E N T S

300 g/10½ oz cherry tomatoes

4 sun-dried tomatoes

4 tbsp extra virgin olive oil

16 fresh basil leaves, shredded

2 garlic cloves, peeled

8 slices ciabatta

salt and pepper

1 Using a sharp knife, cut the cherry tomatoes in half.

2 Using a sharp knife, slice the sun-dried tomatoes into strips.

3 Place the cherry tomatoes and sun-dried tomatoes in a bowl. Add the olive oil and the shredded basil leaves and toss to mix well. Season to taste with a little salt and pepper.

4 Using a sharp knife, cut the garlic cloves in half. Lightly toast the ciabatta bread.

5 Rub the garlic, cut-side down, over both sides of the lightly toasted ciabatta bread.

6 Top the ciabatta bread with the tomato mixture and serve immediately.

Baked Fennel

Fennel is used extensively in northern Italy. It is a very versatile vegetable, which is good cooked or used raw in salads.

NUTRITIONAL INFORMATION

Calories 111   Sugars 6g
Protein . . . . .7g   Fat 7g
Carbohydrate . . . .7g   Saturates 3g

10 MINS   35 MINS

SERVES 4

INGREDIENTS

2 fennel bulbs

2 celery sticks, cut into 7.5 cm/3 inch sticks

6 sun-dried tomatoes, halved

200 g/7 oz passata (tomato paste)

2 tsp dried oregano

50 g/1¾ oz Parmesan cheese, grated

1 Using a sharp knife, trim the fennel, discarding any tough outer leaves, and cut the bulb into quarters.

2 Bring a large pan of water to the boil, add the fennel and celery and cook for 8–10 minutes or until just tender. Remove with a perforated spoon and drain.

3 Place the fennel pieces, celery and sun-dried tomatoes in a large ovenproof dish.

4 Mix the passata (tomato paste) and oregano and pour the mixture over the fennel.

5 Sprinkle with the Parmesan cheese and bake in a preheated oven at 190°C/375°F/Gas Mark 5 for 20 minutes or until hot. Serve as a starter with bread or as a vegetable side dish.

Bean & Tomato Casserole

This quick and easy casserole can be eaten as a healthy supper dish or as a side dish to accompany sausages or grilled fish.

NUTRITIONAL INFORMATION

Calories 273   Sugars 8g
Protein . . . . .15g   Fat 7g
Carbohydrate . . .40g   Saturates 1g

 10 MINS   15 MINS

SERVES 4

I N G R E D I E N T S

400g/14 oz can cannellini beans

400g/14 oz can borlotti beans

2 tbsp olive oil

1 stick celery

2 garlic cloves, chopped

175 g/6 oz baby onions, halved

450 g/1 lb tomatoes

75 g/2¾ oz rocket (arugula)

1 Drain both cans of beans and reserve 6 tbsp of the liquid.

2 Heat the oil in a large pan. Add the celery, garlic and onions and sauté for 5 minutes or until the onions are golden.

3 Cut a cross in the base of each tomato and plunge them into a bowl of boiling water for 30 seconds until the skins split. Remove the tomatoes with a perforated spoon and leave until cool enough to handle. Peel off the skin and chop the flesh.

4 Add the tomato flesh and the reserved bean liquid to the pan and cook for 5 minutes.

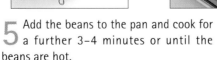

5 Add the beans to the pan and cook for a further 3–4 minutes or until the beans are hot.

6 Stir in the rocket (arugula) and allow to wilt slightly before serving. Serve hot.

VARIATION
For a spicier tasting dish, add 1–2 teaspoons of hot pepper sauce with the cannellini and borlotti beans in step 5.

Cured Meats, Olives & Tomatoes

This is a typical *antipasto* dish with the cold cured meats, stuffed olives and fresh tomatoes, basil and balsamic vinegar.

NUTRITIONAL INFORMATION

Calories	.312	Sugars	.1g
Protein	12g	Fat	28g
Carbohydrate	.2g	Saturates	.1g

 10 MINS   5 MINS

SERVES 4

INGREDIENTS

4 plum tomatoes

1 tbsp balsamic vinegar

6 canned anchovy fillets, drained and rinsed

2 tbsp capers, drained and rinsed

125 g/4 ½ oz green olives, pitted

175 g/6 oz mixed, cured meats, sliced

8 fresh basil leaves

1 tbsp extra virgin olive oil

salt and pepper

crusty bread, to serve

1 Using a sharp knife, cut the tomatoes into evenly-sized slices. Sprinkle the tomato slices with the balsamic vinegar and a little salt and pepper to taste, and set aside.

2 Chop the anchovy fillets into pieces measuring about the same length as the olives.

3 Push a piece of anchovy and a caper into each olive.

4 Arrange the sliced meat on 4 individual serving plates together with the tomatoes, filled olives and basil leaves.

5 Lightly drizzle the olive oil over the sliced meat, tomatoes and olives.

6 Serve the cured meats, olives and tomatoes with plenty of fresh crusty bread.

COOK'S TIP

The cured meats for this recipe are up to your individual taste. They can include a selection of Parma ham (prosciutto), pancetta, bresaola (dried salt beef) and salame di Milano (pork and beef sausage).

Figs & Parma Ham (Prosciutto)

This colourful fresh salad is delicious at any time of the year. Prosciutto di Parma is thought to be the best ham in the world.

NUTRITIONAL INFORMATION

Calories	121	Sugars	6g
Protein	1g	Fat	11g
Carbohydrate	6g	Saturates	2g

 15 MINS   🕐 5 MINS

SERVES 4

I N G R E D I E N T S

40 g/1½ oz rocket (arugula)

4 fresh figs

4 slices Parma ham (prosciutto)

4 tbsp olive oil

1 tbsp fresh orange juice

1 tbsp clear honey

1 small red chilli

1 Tear the rocket (arugula) into more manageable pieces and arrange on 4 serving plates.

2 Using a sharp knife, cut each of the figs into quarters and place them on top of the rocket (arugula) leaves.

3 Using a sharp knife, cut the Parma ham (prosciutto) into strips and scatter over the rocket (arugula) and figs.

4 Place the oil, orange juice and honey in a screw-top jar. Shake the jar until the mixture emulsifies and forms a thick dressing. Transfer to a bowl.

5 Using a sharp knife, dice the chilli, remembering not to touch your face before you have washed your hands (see Cook's Tip, below). Add the chopped chilli to the dressing and mix well.

6 Drizzle the dressing over the Parma ham (prosciutto), rocket (arugula) and figs, tossing to mix well. Serve at once.

COOK'S TIP

Chillies can burn the skin for several hours after chopping, so it is advisable to wear gloves when you are handling the very hot varieties.

Crostini alla Fiorentina

Serve as a starter, or simply spread on small pieces of crusty fried bread (crostini) as an appetizer with drinks.

NUTRITIONAL INFORMATION

Calories 393   Sugars 2g
Protein . . . . .17g   Fat 25g
Carbohydrate . . .19g   Saturates 9g

   10 MINS   40–45 MINS

SERVES 4

I N G R E D I E N T S

3 tbsp olive oil

1 onion, chopped

1 celery stalk, chopped

1 carrot, chopped

1–2 garlic cloves, crushed

125 g/4½ oz chicken livers

125 g/4½ oz calf's, lamb's or pig's liver

150 ml/¼ pint/⅔ cup red wine

1 tbsp tomato purée (paste)

2 tbsp chopped fresh parsley

3–4 canned anchovy fillets, chopped finely

2 tbsp stock or water

25–40 g/1–1½ oz/2–3 tbsp butter

1 tbsp capers

salt and pepper

small pieces of fried crusty bread, to serve

chopped parsley, to garnish

1 Heat the oil in a pan, add the onion, celery, carrot and garlic, and cook gently for 4–5 minutes or until the onion is soft, but not coloured.

2 Meanwhile, rinse and dry the chicken livers. Dry the calf's or other liver, and slice into strips. Add the liver to the pan and fry gently for a few minutes until the strips are well sealed on all sides.

3 Add half of the wine and cook until it has mostly evaporated. Then add the rest of the wine, tomato purée (paste), half of the parsley, the anchovy fillets, stock or water, a little salt and plenty of black pepper.

4 Cover the pan and leave to simmer, stirring occasionally, for 15–20 minutes or until tender and most of the liquid has been absorbed.

5 Leave the mixture to cool a little, then either coarsely mince or put into a food processor and process to a chunky purée.

6 Return to the pan and add the butter, capers and remaining parsley. Heat through gently until the butter melts. Adjust the seasoning and turn out into a bowl. Serve warm or cold spread on the slices of crusty bread and sprinkled with chopped parsley.

Mussels in White Wine

This soup of mussels, cooked in white wine with onions and cream, can be served as an appetizer or a main dish with plenty of crusty bread.

NUTRITIONAL INFORMATION

Calories 396   Sugars 2g
Protein . . . . .23g   Fat 24g
Carbohydrate . . . .8g   Saturates 15g

5–10 MINS   25 MINS

SERVES 4

I N G R E D I E N T S

about 3 litres/5¼ pints/12 cups fresh
 mussels

60 g/2 oz/¼ cup butter

1 large onion, chopped very finely

2–3 garlic cloves, crushed

350 ml/12 fl oz/1½ cups dry white wine

150 ml/¼ pint/⅔ cup water

2 tbsp lemon juice

good pinch of finely grated lemon rind

1 bouquet garni sachet

1 tbsp plain (all-purpose) flour

4 tbsp single (light) or double (thick) cream

2–3 tbsp chopped fresh parsley

salt and pepper

warm crusty bread, to serve

1 Scrub the mussels in several changes of cold water to remove all mud, sand, barnacles, etc. Pull off all the 'beards'. All of the mussels must be tightly closed; if they don't close when given a sharp tap, they must be discarded.

2 Melt half the butter in a large saucepan. Add the onion and garlic, and fry gently until soft but not coloured.

3 Add the wine, water, lemon juice and rind, bouquet garni and plenty of seasoning. Bring to the boil then cover and simmer for 4–5 minutes.

4 Add the mussels to the pan, cover tightly and simmer for 5 minutes, shaking the pan frequently, until all the mussels have opened. Discard any mussels which have not opened. Remove the bouquet garni.

5 Remove the empty half shell from each mussel. Blend the remaining butter with the flour and whisk into the soup, a little at a time. Simmer gently for 2–3 minutes until slightly thickened.

6 Add the cream and half the parsley to the soup and reheat gently. Adjust the seasoning. Ladle the mussels and soup into warmed large soup bowls, sprinkle with the remaining parsley and serve with plenty of warm crusty bread.

Deep-Fried Seafood

Deep-fried seafood is popular all around the Mediterranean, where fish of all kinds is fresh and abundant.

NUTRITIONAL INFORMATION

Calories 393   Sugars 0.2g
Protein . . . . .27g   Fat 26g
Carbohydrate . . .12g   Saturates 3g

🖐 5 MINS   🕐 15 MINS

SERVES 4

INGREDIENTS

200 g/7 oz prepared squid

200 g/7 oz blue (raw) tiger prawns
   (shrimp), peeled

150 g/5 ½ oz whitebait

oil, for deep-frying

50 g/1 ½ oz plain (all-purpose) flour

1 tsp dried basil

salt and pepper

TO SERVE

garlic mayonnaise (see page 16)

lemon wedges

1 Carefully rinse the squid, prawns (shrimp) and whitebait under cold running water, completely removing any dirt or grit.

2 Using a sharp knife, slice the squid into rings, leaving the tentacles whole.

3 Heat the oil in a large saucepan to 180°–190°C/350°–375°F or until a cube of bread browns in 30 seconds.

4 Place the flour in a bowl, add the basil and season with salt and pepper to taste. Mix together well.

5 Roll the squid, prawns (shrimp) and whitebait in the seasoned flour until coated all over. Carefully shake off any excess flour.

6 Cook the seafood in the heated oil, in batches, for 2–3 minutes or until crispy and golden all over. Remove all of the seafood with a perforated spoon and leave to drain thoroughly on kitchen paper.

7 Transfer the deep-fried seafood to serving plates and serve with garlic mayonnaise (see page 16) and a few lemon wedges.

Pasta with Bacon & Tomatoes

As this dish cooks, the mouth-watering aroma of bacon, sweet tomatoes and oregano is a feast in itself.

NUTRITIONAL INFORMATION

Calories . . . . .431 Sugars 8g
Protein . . . . .10g Fat 29g
Carbohydrate . . .34g Saturates 14g

 10 MINS   35 MINS

SERVES 4

I N G R E D I E N T S

900 g/2 lb small, sweet tomatoes

6 slices rindless smoked bacon

60 g/2 oz/4 tbsp butter

1 onion, chopped

1 garlic clove, crushed

4 fresh oregano sprigs, finely chopped

450 g/1 lb/4 cups dried orecchiette

1 tbsp olive oil

salt and pepper

freshly grated Pecorino cheese, to serve

1 Blanch the tomatoes in boiling water. Drain, skin and seed the tomatoes, then roughly chop the flesh.

2 Using a sharp knife, chop the bacon into small dice.

3 Melt the butter in a saucepan. Add the bacon and fry until it is golden.

4 Add the onion and garlic and fry over a medium heat for 5-7 minutes, until just softened.

5 Add the tomatoes and oregano to the pan and then season to taste with salt and pepper. Lower the heat and simmer for 10-12 minutes.

6 Bring a large pan of lightly salted water to the boil. Add the orecchiette and oil and cook for 12 minutes, until just tender, but still firm to the bite. Drain the pasta and transfer to a warm serving dish or bowl.

7 Spoon the bacon and tomato sauce over the pasta, toss to coat and serve with the cheese.

COOK'S TIP

For an authentic Italian flavour use pancetta, rather than ordinary bacon. This kind of bacon is streaked with fat and adds flavour to traditional dishes. It is available smoked and unsmoked from supermarkets and delicatessens.

Chorizo & Mushroom Pasta

Simple and quick to make, this spicy dish is sure to set the taste buds tingling.

NUTRITIONAL INFORMATION

Calories	.495	Sugars	1g
Protein	15g	Fat	35g
Carbohydrate	33g	Saturates	5g

🧊 5 MINS 🕐 20 MINS

SERVES 6

INGREDIENTS

680 g/1½ lb dried vermicelli

125 ml/4 fl oz/½ cup olive oil

2 garlic cloves

125 g/4½ oz chorizo, sliced

225 g/8 oz wild mushrooms

3 fresh red chillies, chopped

2 tbsp freshly grated Parmesan cheese

salt and pepper

10 anchovy fillets, to garnish

1 Bring a large saucepan of lightly salted water to the boil. Add the vermicelli and 1 tablespoon of the oil and cook for 8–10 minutes or until just tender, but still firm to the bite.

2 Drain the pasta thoroughly, place on a large, warm serving plate and keep warm.

3 Meanwhile, heat the remaining oil in a large frying pan (skillet). Add the garlic and fry for 1 minute.

4 Add the chorizo and wild mushrooms and cook for 4 minutes,

5 Add the chopped chillies and cook for 1 further minute.

6 Pour the chorizo and wild mushroom mixture over the vermicelli and season with a little salt and pepper.

7 Sprinkle with freshly grated Parmesan cheese, garnish with a lattice of anchovy fillets and serve immediately.

COOK'S TIP

Many varieties of mushrooms are cultivated and indistinguishable from the wild varieties. Mixed colour oyster mushrooms are used here, but you could also use chanterelles. Chanterelles shrink during cooking, so you may need more.

Smoked Ham Linguini

Served with freshly-made Italian bread or tossed with pesto, this makes a mouth-watering light lunch.

NUTRITIONAL INFORMATION

Calories	537	Sugars	.........4g
Protein	........22g	Fat	..........29g
Carbohydrate	....71g	Saturates	.......8g

 25 MINS   15 MINS

SERVES 4

INGREDIENTS

450 g/1 lb dried linguini

450 g/1 lb green broccoli florets

225 g/8 oz Italian smoked ham

150 ml/¼ pint/⅝ cup Italian Cheese Sauce
(see page 16)

salt and pepper

Italian bread, such as ciabatta or focaccia,
to serve

1 Bring a large saucepan pan of lightly salted water to the boil. Add the linguini and broccoli florets and cook for about 10 minutes, or until the linguini is tender, but still firm to the bite.

2 Drain the linguini and broccoli thoroughly, set aside and keep warm until required.

3 Cut the Italian smoked ham into thin strips.

4 Toss the linguini, broccoli and ham into the Italian Cheese Sauce and gently warm through over a very low heat.

5 Transfer the pasta mixture to a warm serving dish. Sprinkle with pepper and serve with Italian bread.

COOK'S TIP

There are many types of Italian bread which would be suitable to serve with this dish. Ciabatta is made with olive oil and is available plain and with different ingredients, such as olives or sun-dried tomatoes.

Pancetta & Pecorino Cakes

This makes an excellent light meal when served with a topping of pesto or anchovy sauce.

NUTRITIONAL INFORMATION

Calories	.619	Sugars	.4g
Protein	.22g	Fat	.29g
Carbohydrate	.71g	Saturates	.8g

 20 MINS   25 MINS

SERVES 4

INGREDIENTS

25 g/1 oz/2 tbsp butter, plus extra for
 greasing

100 g/3½ oz pancetta, rind removed

225 g/8 oz/2 cups self-raising
 (self-rising) flour

75 g/2¾ oz/⅞ cup grated pecorino cheese

150 ml/¼ pint/⅝ cup milk, plus extra
 for glazing

1 tbsp tomato ketchup

1 tsp Worcestershire sauce

400 g/14 oz/3½ cups dried farfalle

1 tbsp olive oil

salt and pepper

3 tbsp Pesto or anchovy sauce (optional)

green salad, to serve

1 Grease a baking tray (cookie sheet) with butter. Grill (broil) the pancetta until it is cooked. Allow the pancetta to cool, then chop finely.

2 Sift together the flour and a pinch of salt into a mixing bowl. Add the butter and rub in with your fingertips. When the butter and flour have been thoroughly incorporated, add the pancetta and one-third of the grated cheese.

3 Mix together the milk, tomato ketchup and Worcestershire sauce and add to the dry ingredients, mixing to make a soft dough.

4 Roll out the dough on a lightly floured board to make an 18 cm/7 inch round. Brush with a little milk to glaze and cut into 8 wedges.

5 Arrange the dough wedges on the prepared baking tray (cookie sheet)

and sprinkle over the remaining cheese. Bake in a preheated oven at 200°C/ 400°F/Gas Mark 6 for 20 minutes.

6 Meanwhile, bring a saucepan of lightly salted water to the boil. Add the farfalle and the oil and cook for 8–10 minutes until just tender, but still firm to the bite. Drain and transfer to a large serving dish. Top with the pancetta and pecorino cakes. Serve with the sauce of your choice and a green salad.

Aubergine (Eggplant) & Pasta

Prepare the marinated aubergines well in advance so that all you have to do is cook the pasta.

NUTRITIONAL INFORMATION

Calories 378   Sugars 3g
Protein ....12g   Fat 30g
Carbohydrate ...16g   Saturates 3g

12¼ HOURS   15 MINS

SERVES 4

I N G R E D I E N T S

150 ml/¼ pint/⅝ cup vegetable stock
150 ml/¼ pint/⅝ cup white wine vinegar
2 tsp balsamic vinegar
3 tbsp olive oil
fresh oregano sprig
450 g/1 lb aubergine (eggplant), peeled and
   thinly sliced
400 g/14 oz dried linguine

M A R I N A D E

2 tbsp extra virgin oil
2 garlic cloves, crushed
2 tbsp chopped fresh oregano
2 tbsp finely chopped roasted almonds
2 tbsp diced red (bell) pepper
2 tbsp lime juice
grated rind and juice of 1 orange
salt and pepper

1 Put the vegetable stock, wine vinegar and balsamic vinegar into a saucepan and bring to the boil over a low heat. Add 2 tsp of the olive oil and the sprig of oregano and simmer gently for about 1 minute.

2 Add the aubergine (eggplant) slices to the pan, remove from the heat and set aside for 10 minutes.

3 Meanwhile make the marinade. Combine the oil, garlic, fresh oregano, almonds, (bell) pepper, lime juice, orange rind and juice together in a large bowl and season to taste.

4 Carefully remove the aubergine (eggplant) from the saucepan with a slotted spoon, and drain well. Add the aubergine (eggplant) slices to the marinade, mixing well, and set aside in the refrigerator for about 12 hours.

5 Bring a large pan of lightly salted water to the boil. Add half of the remaining oil and the linguine and cook for 8–10 minutes until just tender. Drain the pasta thoroughly and toss with the remaining oil while still warm. Arrange the pasta on a serving plate with the aubergine (eggplant) slices and the marinade and serve.

Spinach & Ricotta Shells

This is a classic combination in which the smooth, creamy cheese balances the sharper taste of the spinach.

NUTRITIONAL INFORMATION

Calories	672	Sugars	........10g
Protein	........23g	Fat	..........26g
Carbohydrate	...93g	Saturates	.......8g

  5 MINS   🕐 40 MINS

SERVES 4

INGREDIENTS

400 g/14 oz dried lumache rigate grande

5 tbsp olive oil

60 g/2 oz/1 cup fresh white breadcrumbs

125 ml/4 fl oz/½ cup milk

300 g/10½ oz frozen spinach, thawed
 and drained

225 g/8 oz/1 cup ricotta cheese

pinch of freshly grated nutmeg

400 g/14 oz can chopped tomatoes, drained

1 garlic clove, crushed

salt and pepper

1 Bring a large saucepan of lightly salted water to the boil. Add the lumache and 1 tbsp of the olive oil and cook for 8–10 minutes until just tender, but still firm to the bite. Drain the pasta, refresh under cold water and set aside until required.

2 Put the breadcrumbs, milk and 3 tbsp of the remaining olive oil in a food processor and work to combine.

3 Add the spinach and ricotta cheese to the food processor and work to a smooth mixture. Transfer to a bowl, stir in the nutmeg, and season with salt and pepper to taste.

4 Mix together the tomatoes, garlic and remaining oil and spoon the mixture into the base of a large ovenproof dish.

5 Using a teaspoon, fill the lumache with the spinach and ricotta mixture and arrange on top of the tomato mixture in the dish. Cover and bake in a preheated oven at 180°C/350°F/Gas 4 for 20 minutes. Serve hot.

COOK'S TIP

Ricotta is a creamy Italian cheese traditionally made from ewes' milk whey. It is soft and white, with a smooth texture and a slightly sweet flavour. It should be used within 2–3 days of purchase.

Spinach & Anchovy Pasta

This colourful light meal can be made with a variety of different pasta, including spaghetti and linguine.

NUTRITIONAL INFORMATION

Calories 619	Sugars 5g	
Protein 21g	Fat 31g	
Carbohydrate . . .67g	Saturates 3g	

🥔 10 MINS   🕐 25 MINS

SERVES 4

I N G R E D I E N T S

900 g/2 lb fresh, young spinach leaves

400 g/14 oz dried fettuccine

6 tbsp olive oil

3 tbsp pine nuts (kernels)

3 garlic cloves, crushed

8 canned anchovy fillets, drained and
   chopped

salt

1 Trim off any tough spinach stalks. Rinse the spinach leaves and place them in a large saucepan with only the water that is clinging to them after washing. Cover and cook over a high heat, shaking the pan from time, until the spinach has wilted, but retains its colour. Drain well, set aside and keep warm.

COOK'S TIP

If you are in a hurry, you can use frozen spinach. Thaw and drain it thoroughly, pressing out as much moisture as possible. Cut the leaves into strips and add to the dish with the anchovies in step 4.

2 Bring a large saucepan of lightly salted water to the boil. Add the fettuccine and 1 tablespoon of the oil and cook for 8–10 minutes until it is just tender, but still firm to the bite.

3 Heat 4 tablespoons of the remaining oil in a saucepan. Add the pine kernels (nuts) and fry until golden. Remove the pine kernels (nuts) from the pan and set aside until required.

4 Add the garlic to the pan and fry until golden. Add the anchovies and stir in the spinach. Cook, stirring, for 2-3 minutes, until heated through. Return the pine nuts (kernels) to the pan.

5 Drain the fettuccine, toss in the remaining olive oil and transfer to a warm serving dish. Spoon the anchovy and spinach sauce over the fettucine, toss lightly and serve immediately.

Tagliarini with Gorgonzola

This simple, creamy pasta sauce is a classic Italian recipe. You could use Danish blue cheese instead of the Gorgonzola, if you prefer.

NUTRITIONAL INFORMATION

Calories	904	Sugars 4g
Protein	........27g	Fat 53g
Carbohydrate	...83g	Saturates 36g

5 MINS   20 MINS

SERVES 4

INGREDIENTS

25 g/1 oz/2 tbsp butter

225 g/8 oz Gorgonzola cheese, roughly crumbled

150 ml/¼ pint/⅝ cup double (heavy) cream

30 ml/2 tbsp dry white wine

1 tsp cornflour (cornstarch)

4 fresh sage sprigs, finely chopped

400 g/14 oz dried tagliarini

2 tbsp olive oil

salt and white pepper

1 Melt the butter in a heavy-based pan. Stir in 175 g/6 oz of the cheese and melt, over a low heat, for about 2 minutes.

2 Add the cream, wine and cornflour (cornstarch) and beat with a whisk until fully incorporated.

COOK'S TIP

Gorgonzola is one of the world's oldest veined cheeses and, arguably, its finest. When buying, always check that it is creamy yellow with delicate green veining. Avoid hard or discoloured cheese. It should have a rich, piquant aroma, not a bitter smell.

3 Stir in the sage and season to taste with salt and white pepper. Bring to the boil over a low heat, whisking constantly, until the sauce thickens. Remove from the heat and set aside while you cook the pasta.

4 Bring a large saucepan of lightly salted water to the boil. Add the tagliarini and 1 tbsp of the olive oil. Cook the pasta for 8–10 minutes or until just

tender, drain thoroughly and toss in the remaining olive oil. Transfer the pasta to a serving dish and keep warm.

5 Reheat the sauce over a low heat, whisking constantly. Spoon the Gorgonzola sauce over the tagliarini, generously sprinkle over the remaining cheese and serve immediately.

Spaghetti with Ricotta

This light pasta dish has a delicate flavour ideally suited for a summer lunch.

NUTRITIONAL INFORMATION

Calories	701	Sugars	........12g
Protein	........17g	Fat	..........40g
Carbohydrate	...73g	Saturates	......15g

5 MINS   25 MINS

SERVES 4

I N G R E D I E N T S

350 g/12 oz dried spaghetti

3 tbsp olive oil

40 g/1 ½ oz/3 tbsp butter

2 tbsp chopped fresh flat leaf parsley

125 g/4 ½ oz/1 cup freshly ground almonds

125 g/4 ½ oz/ ½ cup ricotta cheese

pinch of grated nutmeg

pinch of ground cinnamon

150 ml/ ¼ pint/ ⅝ cup crème fraîche
   (unsweetened yogurt)

125 ml/4 fl oz hot chicken stock

1 tbsp pine nuts (kernels)

salt and pepper

fresh flat leaf parsley sprigs, to garnish

1 Bring a pan of lightly salted water to the boil. Add the spaghetti and 1 tbsp of the oil and cook for 8–10 minutes until tender, but still firm to the bite.

2 Drain the pasta, return to the pan and toss with the butter and chopped parsley. Set aside and keep warm.

3 To make the sauce, mix together the ground almonds, ricotta cheese, nutmeg, cinnamon and crème fraîche (unsweetened yogurt) over a low heat to form a thick paste. Gradually stir in the remaining oil. When the oil has been fully incorporated, gradually stir in the hot chicken stock, until smooth. Season to taste with black pepper.

4 Transfer the spaghetti to a warm serving dish, pour over the sauce and toss together well (see Cook's Tip, right). Sprinkle over the pine nuts (kernels), garnish with the sprigs of flat leaf parsley and serve warm.

COOK'S TIP

Use two large forks to toss spaghetti or other long pasta, so that it is thoroughly coated with the sauce. Special spaghetti forks are available from some cookware departments and kitchen shops.

Three-Cheese Bake

Serve this dish while the cheese is still hot and melted, as cooked cheese turns very rubbery if it is allowed to cool down.

NUTRITIONAL INFORMATION

Calories	710	Sugars	. . . . .6g
Protein	. . . . .34g	Fat	. . . . .30g
Carbohydrate	. . .80g	Saturates	. . . . . .16g

 5 MINS   1 HOUR

SERVES 4

INGREDIENTS

butter, for greasing

400 g/14 oz dried penne

1 tbsp olive oil

2 eggs, beaten

350 g/12 oz/1½ cups ricotta cheese

4 fresh basil sprigs

100 g/3½ oz/1 cup grated Mozzarella or
    halloumi cheese

4 tbsp freshly grated Parmesan cheese

salt and pepper

fresh basil leaves (optional), to garnish

1 Lightly grease a large ovenproof dish with butter.

2 Bring a large pan of lightly salted water to the boil. Add the penne and olive oil and cook for 8–10 minutes until just tender, but still firm to the bite. Drain the pasta, set aside and keep warm.

3 Beat the eggs into the ricotta cheese and season to taste.

4 Spoon half of the penne into the base of the dish and cover with half of the basil leaves.

5 Spoon over half of the ricotta cheese mixture. Sprinkle over the Mozzarella or halloumi cheese and top with the remaining basil leaves. Cover with the remaining penne and then spoon over the remaining ricotta cheese mixture. Lightly sprinkle over the freshly grated Parmesan cheese.

6 Bake in a preheated oven at 190°C/375°F/Gas Mark 5 for 30–40 minutes, until golden brown and the cheese topping is hot and bubbling. Garnish with fresh basil leaves, if liked, and serve hot.

VARIATION

Try substituting smoked Bavarian cheese for the Mozzarella or halloumi and grated Cheddar cheese for the Parmesan, for a slightly different but just as delicious flavour.

Penne with Fried Mussels

This is quick and simple, but one of the nicest of Italian fried fish dishes, served with penne.

NUTRITIONAL INFORMATION

Calories 537   Sugars 2g
Protein . . . . .22g   Fat 24g
Carbohydrate . . .62g   Saturates 3g

10 MINS   25 MINS

SERVES 6

I N G R E D I E N T S

400 g/14 oz/3 ½ cups dried penne

125 ml/4 fl oz/ ½ cup olive oil

450 g/1 lb mussels, cooked and shelled

1 tsp sea salt

90 g/3 oz/ ⅔ cup flour

100 g/3 ½ oz sun-dried tomatoes, sliced

2 tbsp chopped fresh basil leaves

salt and pepper

1 lemon, thinly sliced, to garnish

1 Bring a large saucepan of lightly salted water to the boil. Add the penne and 1 tbsp of the olive oil and cook for 8–10 minutes or until the pasta is just tender, but still firm to the bite.

2 Drain the pasta thoroughly and place in a large, warm serving dish. Set aside and keep warm while you cook the mussels.

3 Lightly sprinkle the mussels with the sea salt. Season the flour with salt and pepper to taste, sprinkle into a bowl and toss the mussels in the flour until well coated.

4 Heat the remaining oil in a large frying pan (skillet). Add the mussels and fry, stirring frequently, until a golden brown colour.

5 Toss the mussels with the penne and sprinkle with the sun-dried tomatoes and basil leaves. Garnish with slices of lemon and serve immediately.

COOK'S TIP

Sun-dried tomatoes have become popular only quite recently. They are dried and preserved in oil. They have a concentrated, roasted flavour and a dense texture. They should be drained and chopped or sliced before using.

Baked Tuna & Ricotta Rigatoni

Ribbed tubes of pasta are filled with tuna and ricotta cheese and then baked in a creamy sauce.

NUTRITIONAL INFORMATION

Calories . . . . .949 Sugars 5g
Protein . . . . .51g Fat 48g
Carbohydrate . . .85g Saturates 26g

 10 MINS   45 MINS

SERVES 4

I N G R E D I E N T S

butter, for greasing

450 g/1 lb dried rigatoni

1 tbsp olive oil

200 g /7 oz can flaked tuna, drained

225 g/ 8 oz ricotta cheese

125 ml/4 fl oz/ ½ cup double (heavy) cream

225 g/8 oz/2 ⅔ cups grated
  Parmesan cheese

125 g/4 oz sun-dried tomatoes, drained
  and sliced

salt and pepper

1 Lightly grease a large ovenproof dish with butter.

2 Bring a large saucepan of lightly salted water to the boil. Add the rigatoni and olive oil and cook for 8–10 minutes until just tender, but still firm to the bite. Drain the pasta and set aside until cool enough to handle.

3 Meanwhile, in a bowl, mix together the tuna and ricotta cheese to form a soft paste. Spoon the mixture into a piping bag and use to fill the rigatoni. Arrange the filled pasta tubes side by side in the prepared ovenproof dish.

4 To make the sauce, mix the cream and Parmesan cheese and season with salt and pepper to taste. Spoon the sauce over the rigatoni and top with the sun-dried tomatoes, arranged in a criss-cross pattern. Bake in a preheated oven at 200°C/400°F/Gas Mark 6 for 20 minutes. Serve hot straight from the dish.

VARIATION

For a vegetarian alternative of this recipe, simply substitute a mixture of stoned (pitted) and chopped black olives and chopped walnuts for the tuna. Follow exactly the same cooking method.

Rotelle with Spicy Sauce

Prepare the sauce well in advance – it is a good idea to freeze batches of the sauce so that you always have some to hand.

NUTRITIONAL INFORMATION

Calories 530	Sugars 4g	
Protein 13g	Fat 18g	
Carbohydrate ...78g	Saturates 3g	

🧊 8¼ HOURS   🕐 40 MINS

SERVES 4

INGREDIENTS

200 ml/7 fl oz/⅞ cup Italian Red Wine Sauce (see page 15)

5 tbsp olive oil

3 garlic cloves, crushed

2 fresh red chillies, chopped

1 green chilli, chopped

400 g/14 oz/3½ cups dried rotelle

salt and pepper

warm Italian bread, to serve

1 Make the Italian Red Wine Sauce (see page 15).

2 Heat 4 tbsp of the oil in a saucepan. Add the garlic and chillies and fry for 3 minutes.

3 Stir in the Italian Red Wine Sauce, season with salt and pepper to taste, and simmer gently over a low heat for 20 minutes.

4 Bring a large saucepan of lightly salted water to the boil. Add the rotelle and the remaining oil and cook for 8 minutes, until just tender, but still firm to the bite. Drain the pasta.

5 Pour the Italian Red Wine Sauce over the rotelle and toss to mix.

6 Transfer to a warm serving dish and serve with warm Italian bread.

COOK'S TIP

Remove chilli seeds before chopping the chillies, as they are the hottest part, and shouldn't be allowed to slip into the food.

Tuna Stuffed Tomatoes

Deliciously sweet roasted tomatoes are filled with home-made lemon mayonnaise and tuna.

NUTRITIONAL INFORMATION

Calories 196   Sugars 2g
Protein ....9g   Fat 17g
Carbohydrate ....2g   Saturates 3g

5-10 MINS   25 MINS

SERVES 4

I N G R E D I E N T S

4 plum tomatoes

2 tbsp sun-dried tomato paste

2 egg yolks

2 tsp lemon juice

finely grated rind of 1 lemon

4 tbsp olive oil

115g/4 oz can tuna, drained

2 tbsp capers, rinsed

salt and pepper

TO GARNISH

2 sun-dried tomatoes, cut into strips

fresh basil leaves

1 Halve the tomatoes and scoop out the seeds. Divide the sun-dried tomato paste among the tomato halves and spread around the inside of the skin.

2 Place on a baking tray (cookie sheet) and roast in a preheated oven at 200°C/400°F/Gas Mark 6 for 12–15 minutes. Leave to cool slightly.

3 Meanwhile, make the mayonnaise. In a food processor, blend the egg yolks and lemon juice with the lemon rind until smooth. Once mixed and with the motor still running slowly, add the olive oil. Stop the processor as soon as the mayonnaise

has thickened. Alternatively, use a hand whisk, beating the mixture continuously until it thickens.

4 Add the tuna and capers to the mayonnaise and season.

5 Spoon the tuna mayonnaise mixture into the tomato shells and garnish with sun-dried tomato strips and basil leaves. Return to the oven for a few minutes or serve chilled.

COOK'S TIP

For a picnic, do not roast the tomatoes, just scoop out the seeds, drain, cut-side down on absorbent kitchen paper for 1 hour, and fill with the mayonnaise mixture. They are firmer and easier to handle this way. If you prefer, shop-bought mayonnaise may be used instead – just stir in the lemon rind.

Ciabatta Rolls

Sandwiches are always a welcome snack, but can be mundane. These crisp rolls filled with roast (bell) peppers and cheese are irresistible.

NUTRITIONAL INFORMATION

Calories 328	Sugars 6g
Protein 8g	Fat 19g
Carbohydrate ...34g	Saturates 9g

15 MINS   10 MINS

SERVES 4

INGREDIENTS

4 ciabatta rolls

2 tbsp olive oil

1 garlic clove, crushed

FILLING

1 red (bell) pepper

1 green (bell) pepper

1 yellow (bell) pepper

4 radishes, sliced

1 bunch watercress

100 g/3½ oz/8 tbsp cream cheese

1 Slice the ciabatta rolls in half. Heat the olive oil and crushed garlic in a saucepan. Pour the garlic and oil mixture over the cut surfaces of the rolls and leave to stand.

2 Halve the (bell) peppers and place, skin side uppermost, on a grill (broiler) rack. Cook under a hot grill (broiler) for 8–10 minutes, until just beginning to char. Remove the (bell) peppers from the grill (broiler), peel and slice thinly.

3 Arrange the radish slices on one half of each roll with a few watercress leaves. Spoon the cream cheese on top. Pile the (bell) peppers on top of the cream cheese and top with the other half of the roll. Serve immediately.

Fish & Seafood

Italians eat everything that comes out of the sea, from the smallest whitebait to the massive tuna fish. Fish markets in Italy are fascinating, with a huge variety of fish on

display, but as most of the fish comes from the Mediterranean it is not always easy to find an equivalent elsewhere. However, fresh or frozen imported fish of all kinds is increasingly appearing in fishmongers and supermarkets. After pasta, fish is probably the most important source of food in Italy, and in many recipes fish or seafood are served with one type of pasta or another – a winning combination!

Orange Mackerel

Mackerel can be quite rich, but when it is stuffed with oranges and toasted ground almonds it is tangy and light.

NUTRITIONAL INFORMATION

Calories 623   Sugars 7g
Protein ....42g   Fat 47g
Carbohydrate ....8g   Saturates 8g

🔥 15 MINS   🕐 35 MINS

SERVES 4

I N G R E D I E N T S

2 tbsp oil

4 spring onions (scallions), chopped

2 oranges

50 g/1¾ oz ground almonds

1 tbsp oats

50 g/1¾oz mixed green and black olives,
    pitted and chopped

8 mackerel fillets

salt and pepper

crisp salad, to serve

1 Heat the oil in a frying pan (skillet). Add the spring onions (scallions) and cook for 2 minutes.

2 Finely grate the rind of the oranges, then, using a sharp knife, cut away the remaining skin and white pith.

3 Using a sharp knife, segment the oranges by cutting down either side of the lines of pith to loosen each segment. Do this over a plate so that you can reserve any juices. Cut each orange segment in half.

4 Lightly toast the almonds, under a preheated grill (broiler), for 2–3 minutes or until golden; watch them carefully as they brown very quickly.

5 Mix the spring onions (scallions), oranges, ground almonds, oats and olives together in a bowl and season to taste with salt and pepper.

6 Spoon the orange mixture along the centre of each fillet. Roll up each fillet, securing it in place with a cocktail stick (toothpick) or skewer.

7 Bake in a preheated oven at 190°C/375°F/Gas Mark 5 for 25 minutes until the fish is tender.

8 Transfer to serving plates and serve warm with a salad.

Sea Bass with Olive Sauce

A favourite fish for chefs, the delicious sea bass is now becoming increasingly common in supermarkets and fish stores for family meals.

NUTRITIONAL INFORMATION

Calories 877   Sugars 3g
Protein ....50g   Fat 47g
Carbohydrate ...67g   Saturates 26g

 10 MINS   30 MINS

SERVES 4

INGREDIENTS

450 g/1 lb dried macaroni

1 tbsp olive oil

8 x 115 g/4 oz sea bass medallions

SAUCE

25 g/1 oz/2 tbsp butter

4 shallots, chopped

2 tbsp capers

175 g/6 oz/1 ½ cups stoned (pitted) green
   olives, chopped

4 tbsp balsamic vinegar

300 ml/½ pint/1 ¼ cups fish stock

300 ml/½ pint/1 ¼ cups double
   (heavy) cream

juice of 1 lemon

salt and pepper

TO GARNISH

lemon slices

shredded leek

shredded carrot

1 To make the sauce, melt the butter in a frying pan (skillet). Add the shallots and cook over a low heat for 4 minutes. Add the capers and olives and cook for a further 3 minutes.

2 Stir in the balsamic vinegar and fish stock, bring to the boil and reduce by half. Add the cream, stirring, and reduce again by half. Season to taste with salt and pepper and stir in the lemon juice. Remove the pan from the heat, set aside and keep warm.

3 Bring a large pan of lightly salted water to the boil. Add the pasta and olive oil and cook for about 12 minutes, until tender but still firm to the bite.

4 Meanwhile, lightly grill (broil) the sea bass medallions for 3–4 minutes on each side, until cooked through, but still moist and delicate.

5 Drain the pasta thoroughly and transfer to large individual serving dishes. Top the pasta with the fish medallions and pour over the olive sauce. Garnish with lemon slices, shredded leek and shredded carrot and serve immediately.

Baked Sea Bass

Sea bass is a delicious white-fleshed fish. If cooking two small fish, they can be grilled (broiled); if cooking one large fish, bake it in the oven.

NUTRITIONAL INFORMATION

Calories 378	Sugars 0g
Protein 62g	Fat 14g
Carbohydrate 0g	Saturates 2g

15–20 MINS   20–55 MINS

SERVES 4

I N G R E D I E N T S

1.4 kg/3 lb fresh sea bass or

   2 x 750 g/1 lb 10 oz sea bass, gutted

2–4 sprigs fresh rosemary

½ lemon, sliced thinly

2 tbsp olive oil

bay leaves and lemon wedges, to garnish

GARLIC SAUCE

2 tsp coarse sea salt

2 tsp capers

2 garlic cloves, crushed

4 tbsp water

2 fresh bay leaves

1 tsp lemon juice or wine vinegar

2 tbsp olive oil

pepper

1 Scrape off the scales from the fish and cut off the sharp fins. Make diagonal cuts along both sides. Wash and dry thoroughly. Place a sprig of rosemary in the cavity of each of the smaller fish with half the lemon slices; or two sprigs and all the lemon in the large fish.

2 To grill (broil), place in a foil-lined pan, brush with 1–2 tbsp oil and grill (broil) under a moderate heat for 5 minutes each side or until cooked through.

3 To bake: place the fish in a foil-lined dish or roasting tin (pan) brushed with oil, and brush the fish with the rest of the oil. Cook in a preheated oven, 190°C/375°F/Gas Mark 5, for 30 minutes for the small fish or 45–50 minutes for the large fish, until the thickest part of the fish is opaque.

4 For the sauce: crush the salt and capers with the garlic in a pestle and mortar and then work in the water. Or, work in a food processor or blender until smooth.

5 Bruise the bay leaves and remaining sprigs of rosemary and put in a bowl. Add the garlic mixture, lemon juice or vinegar and oil and pound together until the flavours are released. Season with pepper to taste.

6 Place the fish on a serving dish and, if liked, remove the skin. Spoon some of the sauce over the fish and serve the rest separately. Garnish with fresh bay leaves and lemon wedges.

Celery & Salt Cod Casserole

Salt cod is dried and salted in order to preserve it. It has an unusual flavour, which goes particularly well with celery in this dish.

NUTRITIONAL INFORMATION

Calories . . . . . . .173 Sugars 3g
Protein . . . . .14g Fat 12g
Carbohydrate . . . .3g Saturates 1g

25 MINS   25 MINS

SERVES 4

INGREDIENTS

250 g/9 oz salt cod, soaked overnight

1 tbsp oil

4 shallots, finely chopped

2 garlic cloves, chopped

3 celery sticks, chopped

1 x 400g/14 oz can tomatoes, chopped

150 ml/¼ pint/⅔ cup fish stock

50 g/1¾ oz pine nuts

2 tbsp roughly chopped tarragon

2 tbsp capers

crusty bread or mashed potato, to serve

1 Drain the salt cod, rinse it under plenty of running water and drain again thoroughly. Remove and discard any skin and bones. Pat the fish dry with paper towels and cut it into chunks.

2 Heat the oil in a large frying pan (skillet). Add the shallots and garlic and cook for 2–3 minutes. Add the celery and cook for a further 2 minutes, then add the tomatoes and stock.

3 Bring the mixture to the boil, reduce the heat and leave to simmer for about 5 minutes.

4 Add the fish and cook for 10 minutes or until tender.

5 Meanwhile, place the pine nuts on a baking tray (cookie sheet). Place under a preheated grill (broiler) and toast for 2–3 minutes or until golden.

6 Stir the tarragon, capers and pine nuts into the fish casserole and heat gently to warm through.

7 Transfer to serving plates and serve with lots of fresh crusty bread or mashed potato.

COOK'S TIP

Salt cod is a useful ingredient to keep in the storecupboard and, once soaked, can be used in the same way as any other fish. It does, however, have a stronger, salty flavour than normal. It can be found in fishmongers, larger supermarkets and delicatessens.

Spaghetti alla Bucaniera

Brill was once known as poor man's turbot, an unfair description as it is a delicately flavoured and delicious fish in its own right.

NUTRITIONAL INFORMATION

Calories 588   Sugars 5g
Protein . . . . .36g   Fat 18g
Carbohydrate . . .68g   Saturates 9g

 25 MINS   50 MINS

SERVES 4

I N G R E D I E N T S

90 g/3 oz/¾ cup plain (all-purpose) flour

450 g/1 lb brill or sole fillets,
  skinned and chopped

450 g/1 lb hake fillets,
  skinned and chopped

90 g/3 oz/6 tbsp butter

4 shallots, finely chopped

2 garlic cloves, crushed

1 carrot, diced

1 leek, finely chopped

300 ml/½ pint/1¼ cups
  dry (hard) cider

300 ml/½ pint/1¼ cups
  medium sweet cider

2 tsp anchovy essence (extract)

1 tbsp tarragon vinegar

450 g/1 lb dried spaghetti

1 tbsp olive oil

salt and pepper

chopped fresh parsley, to garnish

crusty brown bread, to serve

1 Season the flour with salt and pepper. Sprinkle 25 g/1 oz/¼ cup of the seasoned flour on to a shallow plate. Press the fish pieces into the seasoned flour to coat thoroughly.

2 Melt the butter in a flameproof casserole. Add the fish fillets, shallots, garlic, carrot and leek and cook over a low heat, stirring frequently, for about 10 minutes.

3 Sprinkle over the remaining seasoned flour and cook, stirring constantly, for 2 minutes. Gradually stir in the cider, anchovy essence (extract) and tarragon vinegar. Bring to the boil and simmer over a low heat for 35 minutes. Alternatively, bake in a preheated oven at 180°C/350°F/Gas 4 for 30 minutes.

4 About 15 minutes before the end of the cooking time, bring a large pan of lightly salted water to the boil. Add the spaghetti and olive oil and cook for about 12 minutes, until tender but still firm to the bite. Drain the pasta thoroughly and transfer to a large serving dish.

5 Arrange the fish on top of the spaghetti and pour over the sauce. Garnish with chopped parsley and serve immediately with warm, crusty brown bread.

Sole Fillets in Marsala

A rich wine and cream sauce makes this an excellent dinner party dish. Make the stock the day before to cut down on the preparation time.

NUTRITIONAL INFORMATION

Calories 474   Sugars 3g
Protein . . . . .47g   Fat 28g
Carbohydrate . . . .3g   Saturates 14g

1¼ HOURS   1½ HOURS

SERVES 4

I N G R E D I E N T S

1 tbsp peppercorns, lightly crushed

8 sole fillets

100 ml/3½ fl oz/⅓ cup Marsala

150 ml/¼ pint/⅔ cup double (heavy) cream

S T O C K

600 ml/1 pint/2½ cups water

bones and skin from the sole fillets

1 onion, peeled and halved

1 carrot, peeled and halved

3 fresh bay leaves

S A U C E

1 tbsp olive oil

15 g/½ oz/1 tbsp butter

4 shallots, finely chopped

100 g/3½ oz baby button mushrooms, wiped and halved

1 To make the stock, place the water, fish bones and skin, onion, carrot and bay leaves in a large saucepan and bring to the boil.

2 Reduce the heat and leave the mixture to simmer for 1 hour or until the stock has reduced to about 150 ml/¼ pint/⅔ cup. Drain the stock through a fine sieve (strainer), discarding the bones and vegetables, and set aside.

3 To make the sauce, heat the oil and butter in a frying pan (skillet). Add the shallots and cook, stirring, for 2–3 minutes or until just softened.

4 Add the mushrooms to the frying pan (skillet) and cook, stirring, for a further 2–3 minutes or until they are just beginning to brown.

5 Add the peppercorns and sole fillets to the frying pan (skillet) in batches. Fry the sole fillets for 3–4 minutes on each side or until golden brown. Remove the fish with a perforated spoon, set aside and keep warm while you cook the remainder.

6 When all the fillets have been cooked and removed from the pan, pour the wine and stock into the pan and leave to simmer for 3 minutes. Increase the heat and boil the mixture in the pan for about 5 minutes or until the sauce has reduced and thickened.

7 Pour in the cream and heat through. Pour the sauce over the fish and serve with the cooked vegetables of your choice.

Grilled (Broiled) Stuffed Sole

A delicious stuffing of sun-dried tomatoes and fresh lemon thyme are used to stuff whole sole.

NUTRITIONAL INFORMATION

Calories	207	Sugars	.......0.2g
Protein	........24g	Fat	..........10g
Carbohydrate	....8g	Saturates	.......4g

  25 MINS   20 MINS

SERVES 4

INGREDIENTS

1 tbsp olive oil

25 g/1 oz/2 tbsp butter

1 small onion, finely chopped

1 garlic clove, chopped

3 sun-dried tomatoes, chopped

2 tbsp lemon thyme

50 g/1¾ oz breadcrumbs

1 tbsp lemon juice

4 small whole sole, gutted and cleaned

salt and pepper

lemon wedges, to garnish

fresh green salad leaves, to serve

1 Heat the oil and butter in a frying pan (skillet) until it just begins to froth.

2 Add the onion and garlic to the frying pan (skillet) and cook, stirring, for 5 minutes until just softened.

3 To make the stuffing, mix the tomatoes, thyme, breadcrumbs and lemon juice in a bowl, and season.

4 Add the stuffing mixture to the pan, and stir to mix.

5 Using a sharp knife, pare the skin from the bone inside the gut hole of the fish to make a pocket. Spoon the tomato and herb stuffing into the pocket.

6 Cook the fish, under a preheated grill (broiler), for 6 minutes on each side or until golden brown.

7 Transfer the stuffed fish to serving plates and garnish with lemon wedges. Serve immediately with fresh green salad leaves.

COOK'S TIP

Lemon thyme (*Thymus* x *citriodorus*) has a delicate lemon scent and flavour. Ordinary thyme can be used instead, but mix it with 1 teaspoon of lemon rind to add extra flavour.

Lemon Sole & Haddock Ravioli

This delicate-tasting dish is surprisingly satisfying for even the hungriest appetites. Prepare the Italian Red Wine Sauce well in advance.

NUTRITIONAL INFORMATION

Calories 977   Sugars 7g
Protein ....67g   Fat 40g
Carbohydrate ...93g   Saturates 17g

9¾ HOURS   25 MINS

SERVES 4

INGREDIENTS

450 g/1 lb lemon sole fillets, skinned

450 g/1 lb haddock fillets, skinned

3 eggs beaten

450 g/1 lb cooked potato gnocchi

175 g/6 oz/3 cups fresh breadcrumbs

50 ml/2 fl oz/¼ cup double
(heavy) cream

450 g/1 lb basic pasta dough

300 ml/½ pint/1¼ cups Italian Red Wine
Sauce (see page 15)

60 g/2 oz/⅔ cup freshly grated
Parmesan cheese

salt and pepper

1 Flake the lemon sole and haddock fillets with a fork and transfer the flesh to a large mixing bowl.

2 Mix the eggs, cooked potato gnocchi, breadcrumbs and cream in a bowl until thoroughly combined. Add the fish to the bowl containing the gnocchi and season the mixture with salt and pepper to taste.

3 Roll out the pasta dough on to a lightly floured surface and cut out 7.5 cm/3 inch rounds using a plain cutter.

4 Place a spoonful of the fish stuffing on each round. Dampen the edges slightly and fold the pasta rounds over, pressing together to seal.

5 Bring a large saucepan of lightly salted water to the boil. Add the ravioli and cook for 15 minutes.

6 Drain the ravioli, using a slotted spoon, and transfer to a large serving dish. Pour over the Italian Red Wine Sauce, sprinkle over the Parmesan cheese and serve immediately.

COOK'S TIP

For square ravioli, divide the dough in two. Wrap half in cling film; thinly roll out the other half. Cover; roll out the remaining dough. Pipe the filling at regular intervals and brush the spaces in between with water or beaten egg. Lift the second sheet of dough into position with a rolling pin and press between the filling to seal. Cut with a ravioli cutter or a knife.

Trout in Red Wine

This recipe from Trentino is best when the fish are freshly caught, but it is a good way to cook any trout, giving it an interesting flavour.

NUTRITIONAL INFORMATION

Calories 489   Sugars 0.6g
Protein . . . . .48g   Fat 27g
Carbohydrate . . .0.6g   Saturates 14g

20 MINS   45 MINS

SERVES 4

INGREDIENTS

4 fresh trout, about 300 g/10 oz each

250 ml/9 fl oz/1 cup red or
    white wine vinegar

300 ml/½ pint/1¼ cups red or
    dry white wine

150 ml/¼ pint/⅔ cup water

1 carrot, sliced

2–4 bay leaves

thinly pared rind of 1 lemon

1 small onion, sliced very thinly

4 sprigs fresh parsley

4 sprigs fresh thyme

1 tsp black peppercorns

6–8 whole cloves

90 g/3 oz/6 tbsp butter

1 tbsp chopped fresh mixed herbs

salt and pepper

TO GARNISH

sprigs of herbs

lemon slices

1 Gut the trout but leave their heads on. Dry on paper towels and lay the fish head to tail in a shallow container or baking tin (pan) large enough to hold them.

2 Bring the wine vinegar to the boil and pour slowly all over the fish. Leave the fish to marinate in the refrigerator for about 20 minutes.

3 Meanwhile, put the wine, water, carrot, bay leaves, lemon rind, onion, herbs, peppercorns and cloves into a pan with a good pinch of sea salt and heat gently.

4 Drain the fish thoroughly, discarding the vinegar. Place the fish in a fish kettle or large frying pan (skillet) so they touch. When the wine mixture boils, strain gently over the fish so they are about half covered. Cover the pan and simmer very gently for 15 minutes.

5 Carefully remove the fish from the pan, draining off as much of the liquid as possible, and arrange on a serving dish. Keep warm.

6 Boil the cooking liquid until reduced to about 4–6 tbsp. Melt the butter in a pan and strain in the cooking liquor. Season and spoon the sauce over the fish. Garnish and serve.

Trout with Smoked Bacon

Most trout available nowadays is farmed rainbow trout, however, if you can, buy wild brown trout for this recipe.

NUTRITIONAL INFORMATION

Calories .... .802   Sugars 8g
Protein .... 68g   Fat .... .36g
Carbohydrate ...54g   Saturates 10g

35 MINS   25 MINS

SERVES 4

INGREDIENTS

butter, for greasing

4 x 275 g/9½ oz trout, gutted and cleaned

12 anchovies in oil, drained and chopped

2 apples, peeled, cored and sliced

4 fresh mint sprigs

juice of 1 lemon

12 slices rindless smoked fatty bacon

450 g/1 lb dried tagliatelle

1 tbsp olive oil

salt and pepper

TO GARNISH

2 apples, cored and sliced

4 fresh mint sprigs

1 Grease a deep baking tray (cookie sheet) with butter.

2 Open up the cavities of each trout and rinse with warm salt water.

3 Season each cavity with salt and pepper. Divide the anchovies, sliced apples and mint sprigs between each of the cavities. Sprinkle the lemon juice into each cavity.

4 Carefully cover the whole of each trout, except the head and tail, with three slices of smoked bacon in a spiral.

5 Arrange the trout on the baking tray (cookie sheet) with the loose ends of bacon tucked underneath. Season with pepper and bake in a preheated oven at 200°C/400°F/Gas Mark 6 for 20 minutes, turning the trout over after 10 minutes.

6 Meanwhile, bring a large pan of lightly salted water to the boil. Add the tagliatelle and olive oil and cook for about 12 minutes, until tender but still firm to the bite. Drain the pasta and transfer to a large, warm serving dish.

7 Remove the trout from the oven and arrange on the tagliatelle. Garnish with sliced apples and fresh mint sprigs and serve immediately.

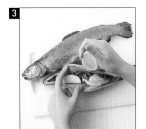

Fillets of Red Mullet & Pasta

This simple recipe perfectly complements the sweet flavour and delicate texture of the fish.

NUTRITIONAL INFORMATION

Calories	457	Sugars	.........3g
Protein	........39g	Fat	..........12g
Carbohydrate	...44g	Saturates	.......5g

 15 MINS   1 HOUR

SERVES 4

INGREDIENTS

1 kg/2 lb 4 oz red mullet fillets

300 ml/½ pint/1¼ cups dry white wine

4 shallots, finely chopped

1 garlic clove, crushed

3 tbsp finely chopped mixed fresh herbs

finely grated rind and juice of 1 lemon

pinch of freshly grated nutmeg

3 anchovy fillets, roughly chopped

2 tbsp double (heavy) cream

1 tsp cornflour (cornstarch)

450 g/1 lb dried vermicelli

1 tbsp olive oil

salt and pepper

TO GARNISH

1 fresh mint sprig

lemon slices

lemon rind

1 Put the red mullet fillets in a large casserole. Pour over the wine and add the shallots, garlic, herbs, lemon rind and juice, nutmeg and anchovies. Season. Cover and bake in a preheated oven at 180°C/350°F/Gas Mark 4 for 35 minutes.

2 Transfer the mullet to a warm dish. Set aside and keep warm.

3 Pour the cooking liquid into a pan and bring to the boil. Simmer for 25 minutes, until reduced by half. Mix the cream and cornflour (cornstarch) and stir into the sauce to thicken.

4 Meanwhile, bring a pan of lightly salted water to the boil. Add the vermicelli and oil and cook for 8–10 minutes, until tender but still firm to the bite. Drain the pasta and transfer to a warm serving dish.

5 Arrange the red mullet fillets on top of the vermicelli and pour over the sauce. Garnish with a fresh mint sprig, slices of lemon and strips of lemon rind and serve immediately.

Sardinian Red Mullet

Red mullet has a beautiful pink skin, which is enhanced in this dish by being cooked in red wine and orange juice.

NUTRITIONAL INFORMATION

Calories 287	Sugars 15g	
Protein 31g	Fat 9g	
Carbohydrate ...15g	Saturates 1g	

2½ HOURS   25 MINS

SERVES 4

INGREDIENTS

50 g/1¾ oz sultanas

150 ml/¼ pint/⅔ cup red wine

2 tbsp olive oil

2 medium onions, sliced

1 courgette (zucchini), cut into
5 cm/2 inch sticks

2 oranges

2 tsp coriander seeds, lightly crushed

4 red mullet, boned and filleted

50 g/1¾ oz can anchovy fillets, drained

2 tbsp chopped, fresh oregano

COOK'S TIP

Red mullet is usually available all year round – frozen, if not fresh – from your fishmonger or supermarket. If you cannot get hold of it try using telapia. This dish can also be served warm, if you prefer.

1 Place the sultanas in a bowl. Pour over the red wine and leave to soak for about 10 minutes.

2 Heat the oil in a large frying pan (skillet). Add the onions and sauté for 2 minutes.

3 Add the courgettes (zucchini) to the pan and fry for a further 3 minutes or until tender.

4 Using a zester, pare long, thin strips from one of the oranges. Using a sharp knife, remove the skin from both of the oranges, then segment the oranges by slicing between the lines of pith.

5 Add the orange zest to the frying pan (skillet) with the coriander seeds, red wine, sultanas, red mullet and anchovies to the pan and leave to simmer for 10–15 minutes or until the fish is cooked through.

6 Stir in the oregano, set aside and leave to cool. Place the mixture in a large bowl and leave to chill, covered, in the refrigerator for at least 2 hours to allow the flavours to mingle. Transfer to serving plates and serve.

Charred Tuna Steaks

Tuna has a firm flesh, which is ideal for barbecuing (grilling), but it can be a little dry unless it is marinated first.

NUTRITIONAL INFORMATION

Calories 153   Sugars 1g
Protein ....29g   Fat 3g
Carbohydrate ....1g   Saturates 1g

 2 HOURS   15 MINS

SERVES 4

I N G R E D I E N T S

4 tuna steaks

3 tbsp soy sauce

1 tbsp Worcestershire sauce

1 tsp wholegrain mustard

1 tsp caster (superfine) sugar

1 tbsp sunflower oil

green salad, to serve

TO GARNISH

flat-leaf parsley

lemon wedges

1 Place the tuna steaks in a shallow dish.

2 Mix together the soy sauce, Worcestershire sauce, mustard, sugar and oil in a small bowl.

3 Pour the marinade over the tuna steaks.

4 Gently turn over the tuna steaks, using your fingers or a fork. Make sure that the fish steaks are well coated with the marinade.

5 Cover and place the tuna steaks in the refrigerator. Leave to chill for between 30 minutes and 2 hours.

6 Barbecue (grill) the marinated fish over hot coals for 10–15 minutes, turning once.

7 Baste frequently with any of the marinade that is left in the dish.

8 Garnish with flat-leaf parsley and lemon wedges. Serve with a fresh green salad.

COOK'S TIP

If a marinade contains soy sauce, the marinating time should be limited, usually to 2 hours. If allowed to marinate for too long, the fish will dry out and become tough.

Poached Salmon with Penne

Fresh salmon and pasta in a mouth-watering lemon and watercress sauce – a wonderful summer evening treat.

NUTRITIONAL INFORMATION

Calories 968	Sugars 3g	
Protein 59g	Fat 58g	
Carbohydrate ...49g	Saturates 19g	

10 MINS   30 MINS

SERVES 4

INGREDIENTS

4 x 275 g/9½ oz fresh salmon steaks

60 g/2 oz/4 tbsp butter

175 ml/6 fl oz/¾ cup dry white wine

sea salt

8 peppercorns

fresh dill sprig

fresh tarragon sprig

1 lemon, sliced

450 g/1 lb dried penne

2 tbsp olive oil

lemon slices and fresh watercress,
　to garnish

LEMON & WATERCRESS SAUCE

25 g/1 oz/2 tbsp butter

25 g/1 oz/¼ cup plain (all-purpose) flour

150 ml/¼ pint/⅝ cup warm milk

juice and finely grated rind of 2 lemons

60 g/2 oz watercress, chopped

salt and pepper

1 Put the salmon in a large, non-stick pan. Add the butter, wine, a pinch of sea salt, the peppercorns, dill, tarragon and lemon. Cover, bring to the boil, and simmer for 10 minutes.

2 Using a fish slice, carefully remove the salmon. Strain and reserve the cooking liquid. Remove and discard the salmon skin and centre bones. Place on a warm dish, cover and keep warm.

3 Meanwhile, bring a saucepan of salted water to the boil. Add the penne and 1 tbsp of the oil and cook for 8–10 minutes, until tender but still firm to the bite. Drain and sprinkle over the remaining olive oil. Place on a warm serving dish, top with the salmon steaks and keep warm.

4 To make the sauce, melt the butter and stir in the flour for 2 minutes. Stir in the milk and about 7 tbsp of the reserved cooking liquid. Add the lemon juice and rind and cook, stirring, for a further 10 minutes.

5 Add the watercress to the sauce, stir gently and season to taste with salt and pepper.

6 Pour the sauce over the salmon and penne, garnish with slices of lemon and fresh watercress and serve.

Salmon Lasagne Rolls

Sheets of green lasagne are filled with a mixture of fresh salmon and oyster mushrooms. This recipe has been adapted for the microwave.

NUTRITIONAL INFORMATION

Calories 352   Sugars 5g
Protein . . . . .19g   Fat 19g
Carbohydrate . . .25g   Saturates 9g

  🕐 🕐 🕐

🍲 20 MINS   🕐 35 MINS

SERVES 4

I N G R E D I E N T S

8 sheets green lasagne

1 onion, sliced

15 g/½ oz/1 tbsp butter

½ red (bell) pepper, chopped

1 courgette (zucchini), diced

1 tsp chopped ginger root

125 g/4½ oz oyster mushrooms, preferably
    yellow, chopped coarsely

225 g/8 oz fresh salmon fillet, skinned, and
    cut into chunks

2 tbsp dry sherry

2 tsp cornflour (cornstarch)

20 g/¾ oz/3 tbsp plain (all-purpose) flour

20 g/¾ oz/1½ tbsp butter

300 ml/½ pint/1¼ cups milk

25 g/1 oz/¼ cup Cheddar cheese, grated

15 g/½ oz/¼ cup fresh white breadcrumbs

salt and pepper

salad leaves, to serve

1 Place the lasagne sheets in a large shallow dish. Cover with plenty of boiling water. Cook on HIGH power for 5 minutes. Leave to stand, covered, for a few minutes before draining. Rinse in cold water and lay the sheets out on a clean work surface.

2 Put the onion and butter into a bowl. Cover and cook on HIGH power for 2 minutes. Add the (bell) pepper, courgette (zucchini) and ginger root. Cover and cook on HIGH power for 3 minutes.

3 Add the mushrooms and salmon to the bowl. Mix the sherry into the cornflour (cornstarch) then stir into the bowl. Cover and cook on HIGH power for 4 minutes until the fish flakes when tested with a fork. Season to taste.

4 Whisk the flour, butter and milk in a bowl. Cook on HIGH power for 3–4 minutes, whisking every minute, to give a sauce of coating consistency. Stir in half the cheese and season with salt and pepper to taste.

5 Spoon the salmon filling in equal quantities along the shorter side of each lasagne sheet. Roll up to enclose the filling. Arrange in a lightly oiled large rectangular dish. Pour over the sauce and sprinkle over the remaining cheese and the breadcrumbs.

6 Cook on HIGH power for 3 minutes until heated through. If possible, lightly brown under a preheated grill (broiler) before serving. Serve with salad.

Tuna with Roast (Bell) Peppers

Fresh tuna will be either a small bonito fish or steaks from a skipjack.
The more delicately flavoured fish have a paler flesh.

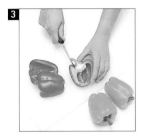

NUTRITIONAL INFORMATION

Calories 428   Sugars 5g
Protein ....60g   Fat 19g
Carbohydrate ....5g   Saturates 3g

20 MINS   30 MINS

SERVES 4

I N G R E D I E N T S

4 tuna steaks, about 250 g/9 oz each

3 tbsp lemon juice

1 litre/1¾ pints/4 cups water

6 tbsp olive oil

2 orange (bell) peppers

2 red (bell) peppers

12 black olives

1 tsp balsamic vinegar

salt and pepper

1 Put the tuna steaks into a bowl with the lemon juice and water. Leave for 15 minutes.

2 Drain and brush the steaks all over with olive oil and season well with salt and pepper.

3 Halve, core and deseed the (bell) peppers. Put them over a hot barbecue (grill) and cook for 12 minutes until they are charred all over. Put them into a plastic bag and seal it.

4 Meanwhile, cook the tuna over a hot barbecue (grill) for 12–15 minutes, turning once.

5 When the (bell) peppers are cool enough to handle, peel them and cut each piece into 4 strips. Toss them with the remaining olive oil, olives and balsamic vinegar.

6 Serve the tuna steaks piping hot, with the roasted (bell) pepper salad.

COOK'S TIP

Red, orange and yellow (bell) peppers can also be peeled by cooking them in a hot oven for 30 minutes, turning them frequently, or roasting them straight over a naked gas flame, again turning them frequently. In both methods, deseed the (bell) peppers after peeling.

Spaghetti al Tonno

The classic Italian combination of pasta and tuna is enhanced in this recipe with a delicious parsley sauce.

NUTRITIONAL INFORMATION

Calories ....1065 Sugars 3g
Protein ....27g Fat 85g
Carbohydrate ...52g Saturates 18g

10 MINS   15 MINS

SERVES 4

INGREDIENTS

200 g/7 oz can tuna, drained

60 g/2 oz can anchovies, drained

250 ml/9 fl oz/1⅛ cups olive oil

60 g/2 oz/1 cup roughly chopped
  flat leaf parsley

150 ml/¼ pint/⅔ cup crème fraîche

450 g/1 lb dried spaghetti

25 g/1 oz/2 tbsp butter

salt and pepper

black olives, to garnish

crusty bread, to serve

1 Remove any bones from the tuna. Put the tuna into a food processor or blender, together with the anchovies, 225 ml/ 8 fl oz/1 cup of the olive oil and the flat leaf parsley. Process until the sauce is very smooth.

VARIATION

If liked, you could add 1–2 garlic cloves to the sauce, substitute 25 g/1 oz/½ cup chopped fresh basil for half the parsley and garnish with capers instead of black olives.

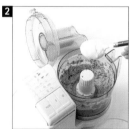

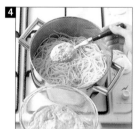

2 Spoon the crème fraîche into the food processor or blender and process again for a few seconds to blend thoroughly. Season with salt and pepper to taste.

3 Bring a large pan of lightly salted water to the boil. Add the spaghetti and the remaining olive oil and cook for 8–10 minutes until tender, but still firm to the bite.

4 Drain the spaghetti, return to the pan and place over a medium heat. Add the butter and toss well to coat. Spoon in the sauce and quickly toss into the spaghetti, using 2 forks.

5 Remove the pan from the heat and divide the spaghetti between 4 warm individual serving plates. Garnish with the olives and serve immediately with warm, crusty bread.

Baked Red Snapper

You can substitute other whole fish for the snapper, or use cutlets of cod or halibut.

NUTRITIONAL INFORMATION

Calories . . . . .519 Sugars 12g
Protein . . . . .61g Fat 23g
Carbohydrate . . .18g Saturates 3g

🍞 🍞 🍞

🧊 20 MINS   🕐 50 MINS

SERVES 4

I N G R E D I E N T S

1 red snapper, about 1.25 kg/2 lb 12 oz, cleaned

juice of 2 limes, or 1 lemon

4-5 sprigs of thyme or parsley

3 tbsp olive oil

1 large onion, chopped

2 garlic cloves, finely chopped

1 x 425 g/15 oz can chopped tomatoes

2 tbsp tomato purée (paste)

2 tbsp red wine vinegar

5 tbsp low-fat yogurt

2 tbsp chopped parsley

2 tsp dried oregano

6 tbsp dry breadcrumbs

60 g/2 oz/¼ cup low-fat yogurt cheese, crumbled

salt and pepper

S A L A D

1 small lettuce, thickly sliced

10-12 young spinach leaves, torn

½ small cucumber, sliced and quartered

4 spring onions (scallions), thickly sliced

3 tbsp chopped parsley

2 tbsp olive oil

2 tbsp plain low-fat yogurt

1 tbsp red wine vinegar

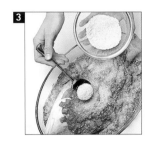

1 Sprinkle the lime or lemon juice inside and over the fish and season. Place the herbs inside the fish.

2 Heat the oil in a pan and fry the onion until translucent. Stir in the garlic and cook for 1 minute, then add the chopped tomatoes, tomato purée (paste) and vinegar. Simmer, uncovered, for 5 minutes. Allow the sauce to cool, then stir in the yogurt, parsley and oregano.

3 Pour half of the sauce into an ovenproof dish just large enough for the fish. Add the fish and then pour the remainder of the sauce over it, and sprinkle with breadcrumbs. Bake uncovered for 30-35 minutes. Sprinkle the cheese over the fish and serve with lime wedges and dill sprigs.

4 Arrange the salad ingredients in a bowl. Whisk the oil, yogurt and vinegar and pour over the salad.

Salmon with Caper Sauce

The richness of salmon is beautifully balanced by the tangy capers in this creamy herb sauce.

NUTRITIONAL INFORMATION

Calories . . . . . . .302 Sugars 0g
Protein . . . . .21g Fat 24g
Carbohydrate . . . .1g Saturates 9g

5 MINS   25 MINS

SERVES 4

INGREDIENTS

4 salmon fillets, skinned

1 fresh bay leaf

few black peppercorns

1 tsp white wine vinegar

150 ml/¼ pint/⅔ cup fish stock

3 tbsp double (heavy) cream

1 tbsp capers

1 tbsp chopped fresh dill

1 tbsp chopped fresh chives

1 tsp cornflour (cornstarch)

2 tbsp skimmed milk

salt and pepper

new potatoes, to serve

TO GARNISH

fresh dill sprigs

chive flowers

1 Lay the salmon fillets in a shallow ovenproof dish. Add the bay leaf, peppercorns, vinegar and stock.

2 Cover with foil and bake in a preheated oven at 180°C/350°F/Gas Mark 4 for 15–20 minutes until the flesh is opaque and flakes easily when tested with a fork.

3 Transfer the fish to warmed serving plates, cover and keep warm.

4 Strain the cooking liquid into a saucepan. Stir in the cream, capers, dill and chives and seasoning to taste.

5 Blend the cornflour (cornstarch) with the milk. Add to the saucepan and heat, stirring, until thickened slightly. Boil for 1 minute.

6 Spoon the sauce over the salmon, garnish with dill sprigs and chive flowers.

7 Serve with new potatoes.

COOK'S TIP

Ask the fishmonger to skin the fillets for you. The cooking time for the salmon will depend on the thickness of the fish: the thin tail end of the salmon takes the least time to cook.

Marinated Fish

Marinating fish, for even a short period, adds a subtle flavour to the flesh and makes even simply grilled (broiled) or fried fish delicious.

NUTRITIONAL INFORMATION

Calories 361   Sugars 0g
Protein . . . . .26g   Fat 29g
Carbohydrate . . . .0g   Saturates 5g

45 MINS   15 MINS

SERVES 4

INGREDIENTS

4 whole mackerel, cleaned and gutted

4 tbsp chopped marjoram

2 tbsp extra virgin olive oil

finely grated rind and juice of 1 lime

2 garlic cloves, crushed

salt and pepper

1 Under gently running water, scrape the mackerel with the blunt side of a knife to remove any scales.

2 Using a sharp knife, make a slit in the stomach of the fish and cut horizontally along until the knife will go no further very easily. Gut the fish and rinse under water. You may prefer to remove the heads before cooking, but it is not necessary.

3 Using a sharp knife, cut 4–5 diagonal slashes on each side of the fish. Place the fish in a shallow, non-metallic dish.

4 To make the marinade, mix together the marjoram, olive oil, lime rind and juice, garlic and salt and pepper in a bowl.

5 Pour the mixture over the fish. Leave to marinate in the refrigerator for about 30 minutes.

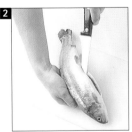

6 Cook the mackerel, under a preheated grill (broiler), for 5–6 minutes on each side, brushing occasionally with the reserved marinade, until golden.

7 Transfer the fish to serving plates. Pour over any remaining marinade before serving.

COOK'S TIP

If the lime is too hard to squeeze, microwave on high power for 30 seconds to release the juice. This dish is also excellent cooked on the barbecue (grill).

Macaroni & Seafood Bake

This adaptation of an eighteenth-century Italian dish is baked until it is golden brown and sizzling, then cut into wedges like a cake.

NUTRITIONAL INFORMATION

Calories	478	Sugars	.........6g
Protein	........27g	Fat	..........17g
Carbohydrate	...57g	Saturates	.......7g

 30 MINS   50 MINS

SERVES 4

INGREDIENTS

350 g/12 oz/3 cups dried
    short-cut macaroni

1 tbsp olive oil, plus extra for brushing

90 g/3 oz/6 tbsp butter, plus extra
    for greasing

2 small fennel bulbs, thinly sliced and
    fronds reserved

175 g/6 oz mushrooms, thinly sliced

175 g/6 oz peeled, cooked prawns (shrimp)

pinch of cayenne pepper

300 ml/½ pint/1¼ cups Béchamel Sauce
    (see page 14)

60 g/2 oz/⅔ cup freshly grated
    Parmesan cheese

2 large tomatoes, sliced

1 tsp dried oregano

salt and pepper

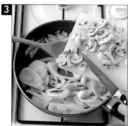

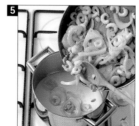

1 Bring a saucepan of salted water to the boil. Add the pasta and oil and cook for 8–10 minutes until tender, but still firm to the bite. Drain the pasta and return to the pan.

2 Add 25 g/1 oz/2 tbsp of the butter to the pasta, cover, shake the pan and keep warm.

3 Melt the remaining butter in a saucepan. Fry the fennel for 3–4 minutes. Stir in the mushrooms and fry for a further 2 minutes.

4 Stir in the prawns (shrimp), then remove the pan from the heat.

5 Stir the cayenne pepper and prawn mixture into the Béchamel Sauce.

6 Pour into a greased ovenproof dish and spread evenly. Sprinkle over the Parmesan cheese and arrange the tomato slices in a ring around the edge. Brush the tomatoes with olive oil and then sprinkle over the oregano.

7 Bake in a preheated oven at 180°C/ 350°F/Gas Mark 4 for 25 minutes, until golden brown. Serve immediately.

Seafood Pizza

Make a change from the standard pizza toppings – this dish is piled high with seafood baked with a red (bell) pepper and tomato sauce.

NUTRITIONAL INFORMATION

Calories 248   Sugars 7g
Protein . . . . .27g   Fat 6g
Carbohydrate . . .22g   Saturates 2g

25 MINS   55 MINS

SERVES 4

INGREDIENTS

145 g/5 oz standard pizza base mix

4 tbsp chopped fresh dill or 2 tbsp dried dill

fresh dill, to garnish

SAUCE

1 large red (bell) pepper

400 g/14 oz can chopped tomatoes with onion and herbs

3 tbsp tomato purée (paste)

salt and pepper

TOPPING

350 g/12 oz assorted cooked seafood, thawed if frozen

1 tbsp capers in brine, drained

25 g/1 oz pitted black olives in brine, drained

25 g/1 oz low-fat Mozzarella cheese, grated

1 tbsp grated, fresh Parmesan cheese

1 Preheat the oven to 200°C/400°F/Gas Mark 6. Place the pizza base mix in a bowl and stir in the dill. Make the dough according to the instructions on the packet.

2 Press the dough into a round measuring 25.5 cm/10 inches across on a baking sheet lined with baking parchment. Set aside to prove (rise).

3 Preheat the grill (broiler) to hot. To make the sauce, halve and deseed the (bell) pepper and arrange on a grill (broiler) rack. Cook for 8–10 minutes until softened and charred. Leave to cool slightly, peel off the skin and chop the flesh.

4 Place the tomatoes and (bell) pepper in a saucepan. Bring to the boil and simmer for 10 minutes. Stir in the tomato purée (paste) and season to taste.

5 Spread the sauce over the pizza base and top with the seafood. Sprinkle over the capers and olives, top with the cheeses and bake for 25–30 minutes.

6 Garnish with sprigs of dill and serve hot.

Mediterranean Fish Stew

Popular in fishing ports around Europe, gentle stewing is an excellent way to maintain the flavour and succulent texture of fish and shellfish.

NUTRITIONAL INFORMATION

Calories	533	Sugars	........11g
Protein	........71g	Fat	..........10g
Carbohydrate	...30g	Saturates	......2g

1¼ HOURS   25 MINS

SERVES 4

INGREDIENTS

2 tsp olive oil

2 red onions, sliced

2 garlic cloves, crushed

2 tbsp red wine vinegar

2 tsp caster (superfine) sugar

300 ml/½ pint/1¼ cups Fish Stock
   (see page 16)

300 ml/½ pint/1¼ cups dry red wine

2 × 400 g/14 oz cans chopped tomatoes

225 g/8 oz baby aubergines (eggplant),
   quartered

225 g/8 oz yellow courgettes (zucchini),
   quartered or sliced

1 green (bell) pepper, sliced

1 tbsp chopped fresh rosemary

500 g/1 lb 2 oz halibut fillet, skinned and
   cut into 2.5 cm/1 inch cubes

750 g/1 lb 10 oz fresh mussels, prepared

225 g/8 oz baby squid, cleaned, trimmed
   and sliced into rings

225 g/8 oz fresh tiger prawns (shrimp),
   peeled and deveined

salt and pepper

4 slices toasted French bread rubbed with a
   cut garlic clove

lemon wedges, to serve

1 Heat the oil in a large non-stick saucepan and fry the onions and garlic gently for 3 minutes.

2 Stir in the vinegar and sugar and cook for a further 2 minutes.

3 Stir in the stock, wine, canned tomatoes, aubergines (eggplant) courgettes (zucchini), (bell) pepper and rosemary. Bring to the boil and simmer, uncovered, for 10 minutes.

4 Add the halibut, mussels and squid. Mix well and simmer, covered, for 5 minutes until the fish is opaque.

5 Stir in the prawns (shrimp) and continue to simmer, covered, for a further 2–3 minutes until the prawns (shrimp) are pink and cooked through.

6 Discard any mussels which haven't opened and season to taste.

7 To serve, put a slice of the prepared garlic bread in the base of each warmed serving bowl and ladle the stew over the top. Serve with lemon wedges.

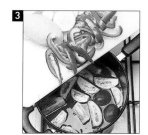

Smoky Fish Pie

This flavoursome and colourful fish pie is perfect for a light supper. The addition of smoked salmon gives it a touch of luxury.

NUTRITIONAL INFORMATION

Calories 523   Sugars 15g
Protein . . . . .58g   Fat 6g
Carbohydrate . . .63g   Saturates 2g

15 MINS   1 HOUR

SERVES 4

I N G R E D I E N T S

900 g/2 lb smoked haddock or cod fillets

600 ml/1 pint/2½ cups skimmed milk

2 bay leaves

115 g/4 oz button mushrooms, quartered

115 g/4 oz frozen peas

115 g/4 oz frozen sweetcorn kernels

675 g/1½ lb potatoes, diced

5 tbsp low-fat natural (unsweetened) yogurt

4 tbsp chopped fresh parsley

60 g/2 oz smoked salmon, sliced into thin strips

3 tbsp cornflour (cornstarch)

25 g/1 oz smoked cheese, grated

salt and pepper

1 Preheat the oven to 200°C/400°F/Gas Mark 6. Place the fish in a pan and add the milk and bay leaves. Bring to the boil, cover and then simmer for 5 minutes.

2 Add the mushrooms, peas and sweetcorn, bring back to a simmer, cover and cook for 5–7 minutes. Leave to cool.

3 Place the potatoes in a saucepan, cover with water, boil and cook for 8 minutes. Drain well and mash with a fork or a potato masher. Stir in the yogurt, parsley and seasoning. Set aside.

4 Using a slotted spoon, remove the fish from the pan. Flake the cooked fish away from the skin and place in an ovenproof gratin dish. Reserve the cooking liquid.

5 Drain the vegetables, reserving the cooking liquid, and gently stir into the fish with the salmon strips.

6 Blend a little cooking liquid into the cornflour (cornstarch) to make a paste. Transfer the rest of the liquid to a saucepan and add the paste. Heat through, stirring, until thickened. Discard the bay leaves and season to taste. Pour the sauce over the fish and vegetables and mix. Spoon over the mashed potato so that the fish is covered, sprinkle with cheese and bake for 25–30 minutes.

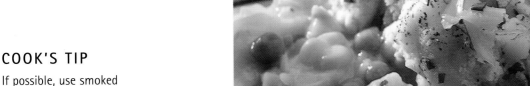

COOK'S TIP

If possible, use smoked haddock or cod that has not been dyed bright yellow or artificially flavoured to give the illusion of having been smoked.

Smoked Fish Lasagne

Use smoked cod or haddock in this delicious lasagne. It's a great way to make a little go a long way.

NUTRITIONAL INFORMATION

Calories	483	Sugars	.........8g
Protein	........36g	Fat	..........24g
Carbohydrate	...32g	Saturates	......12g

 20 MINS 🕐 1¼ HOURS

SERVES 4

INGREDIENTS

2 tsp olive or vegetable oil

1 garlic clove, crushed

1 small onion, chopped finely

125 g/4½ oz mushrooms, sliced

400 g/14 oz can chopped tomatoes

1 small courgette (zucchini), sliced

150 ml/¼ pint/⅔ cup vegetable stock
  or water

25 g/1 oz/2 tbsp butter or margarine

300 ml/½ pint/1¼ cups skimmed milk

25 g/1 oz/¼ cup plain (all-purpose) flour

125 g/4 oz/1 cup grated mature (sharp)
  Cheddar cheese

1 tbsp chopped fresh parsley

125 g/4½ oz (6 sheets) pre-cooked lasagne

350 g/12 oz skinned and boned smoked
  cod or haddock, cut into chunks

salt and pepper

fresh parsley sprigs to garnish

1 Heat the oil in a saucepan and fry the garlic and onion for about 5 minutes. Add the mushrooms and cook for 3 minutes, stirring.

2 Add the tomatoes, courgette (zucchini) and stock or water and simmer, uncovered, for 15–20 minutes until the vegetables are soft. Season.

3 Put the butter or margarine, milk and flour into a small saucepan and heat, whisking constantly, until the sauce boils and thickens. Remove from the heat and add half of the cheese and all of the parsley. Stir gently to melt the cheese and season to taste.

4 Spoon the tomato sauce mixture into a large, shallow ovenproof dish and top with half of the lasagne sheets. Scatter the chunks of fish evenly over the top, then pour over half of the cheese sauce. Top with the remaining lasagne sheets and then spread the rest of the cheese sauce on top. Sprinkle with the remaining cheese.

5 Bake in a preheated oven at 190°C/375°F/Gas Mark 5 for 40 minutes, until the top is golden brown and bubbling. Garnish with parsley sprigs and serve hot.

Stuffed Squid

Whole squid are stuffed with a mixture of fresh herbs and sun-dried tomatoes and then cooked in a wine sauce.

NUTRITIONAL INFORMATION

Calories ....276 Sugars 1g
Protein ....23g Fat 8g
Carbohydrate ...20g Saturates 1g

 25 MINS   35 MINS

SERVES 4

INGREDIENTS

8 squid, cleaned and gutted but left whole
   (ask your fishmonger to do this)
6 canned anchovies, chopped
2 garlic cloves, chopped
2 tbsp rosemary, stalks removed and
   leaves chopped
2 sun-dried tomatoes, chopped
150 g/5½ oz breadcrumbs
1 tbsp olive oil
1 onion, finely chopped
200 ml/7 fl oz/¾ cup white wine
200 ml/7 fl oz/¾ cup fish stock
cooked rice, to serve

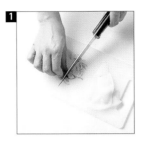

1 Remove the tentacles from the body of the squid and chop the flesh finely.

2 Grind the anchovies, garlic, rosemary and tomatoes to a paste in a mortar and pestle.

3 Add the breadcrumbs and the chopped squid tentacles and mix. If the mixture is too dry to form a thick paste at this point, add 1 teaspoon of water.

4 Spoon the paste into the body sacs of the squid then tie a length of cotton around the end of each sac to fasten

them. Do not overfill the sacs, because they will expand during cooking.

5 Heat the oil in a frying pan (skillet). Add the onion and cook, stirring, for 3–4 minutes or until golden.

6 Add the stuffed squid to the pan and cook for 3–4 minutes or until brown all over.

7 Add the wine and stock and bring to the boil. Reduce the heat, cover and then leave to simmer for 15 minutes.

8 Remove the lid and cook for a further 5 minutes or until the squid is tender and the juices reduced. Serve with plenty of cooked rice.

Pasta & Prawn (Shrimp) Parcels

This is the ideal dish when you have unexpected guests because the parcels can be prepared in advance, then put in the oven when you are ready to eat.

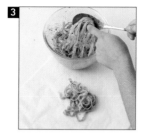

NUTRITIONAL INFORMATION

Calories	640	Sugars	.........1g
Protein	........50g	Fat	..........29g
Carbohydrate	...42g	Saturates	.......4g

15 MINS   30 MINS

SERVES 4

I N G R E D I E N T S

450 g/1 lb dried fettuccine

150 ml/¼ pint/⅝ cup Pesto Sauce
  (Shop bought)

4 tsp extra virgin olive oil

750 g/1 lb 10 oz large raw prawns (shrimp),
  peeled and deveined

2 garlic cloves, crushed

125 ml/4 fl oz/½ cup dry white wine

salt and pepper

1 Cut out 4 x 30 cm/12 inch squares of greaseproof paper.

2 Bring a large saucepan of lightly salted water to the boil. Add the fettuccine and cook for 2–3 minutes, until just softened. Drain and set aside.

3 Mix together the fettuccine and half of the Pesto Sauce. Spread out the paper squares and put 1 tsp olive oil in the middle of each. Divide the fettuccine between the the squares, then divide the prawns (shrimp) and place on top of the fettuccine.

4 Mix together the remaining Pesto Sauce and the garlic and spoon it over the prawns (shrimp). Season each parcel with salt and black pepper and sprinkle with the white wine.

5 Dampen the edges of the greaseproof paper and wrap the parcels loosely, twisting the edges to seal.

6 Place the parcels on a baking tray (cookie sheet) and bake in a preheated oven at 200°C/400°F/Gas Mark 6 for 10–15 minutes. Transfer the parcels to 4 individual serving plates and serve.

COOK'S TIP

Traditionally, these parcels are designed to look like money bags. The resemblance is more effective with greaseproof paper than with foil.

Pan-Fried Prawns (Shrimp)

A luxurious dish which makes an impressive starter or light meal. Prawns (shrimp) and garlic are a winning combination.

NUTRITIONAL INFORMATION

Calories 455	Sugars 0g	
Protein 6g	Fat 37g	
Carbohydrate 0g	Saturates 18g	

 10 MINS   5 MINS

SERVES 4

I N G R E D I E N T S

4 garlic cloves

20–24 unshelled large raw prawns (shrimp)

125 g/4½ oz/8 tbsp butter

4 tbsp olive oil

6 tbsp brandy

salt and pepper

2 tbsp chopped fresh parsley

T O   S E R V E

lemon wedges

ciabatta bread

1 Using a sharp knife, peel and slice the garlic.

2 Wash the prawns (shrimp) and pat dry using paper towels.

3 Melt the butter with the oil in a large frying pan (skillet), add the garlic and prawns (shrimp), and fry over a high heat, stirring, for 3–4 minutes until the prawns (shrimp) are pink.

4 Sprinkle with brandy and season with salt and pepper to taste. Sprinkle with parsley and serve immediately with lemon wedges and ciabatta bread, if desired.

Pasta Shells with Mussels

Serve this aromatic seafood dish to family and friends who admit to a love of garlic.

NUTRITIONAL INFORMATION

Calories	686	Sugars	.........2g
Protein	........30g	Fat	..........45g
Carbohydrate	...36g	Saturates	......27g

15 MINS   25 MINS

SERVES 6

I N G R E D I E N T S

1.25 kg/2 lb 12 oz mussels

225 ml/8 fl oz/1 cup dry white wine

2 large onions, chopped

115 g/4 oz/½ cup unsalted butter

6 large garlic cloves, finely chopped

5 tbsp chopped fresh parsley

300 ml/½ pint/1¼ cups double
 (heavy) cream

400 g/14 oz dried pasta shells

1 tbsp olive oil

salt and pepper

crusty bread, to serve

1 Scrub and debeard the mussels under cold running water. Discard any mussels that do not close immediately when sharply tapped. Put the mussels into a large saucepan, together with the wine and half of the onions. Cover and cook over a medium heat, shaking the pan frequently, for 2–3 minutes, or until the shells open.

2 Remove the pan from the heat. Drain the mussels and reserve the cooking liquid. Discard any mussels that have not opened. Strain the cooking liquid through a clean cloth into a glass jug (pitcher) or bowl and reserve.

3 Melt the butter in a pan over a medium heat. Add the remaining onion and fry until translucent. Stir in the garlic and cook for 1 minute. Gradually stir in the reserved cooking liquid. Stir in the parsley and cream and season to taste with salt and pepper. Bring to simmering point over a low heat.

4 Meanwhile, bring a large pan of lightly salted water to the boil. Add the pasta and oil and cook for 8–10 minutes until just tender, but still firm to the bite. Drain the pasta, return to the pan, cover and keep warm.

5 Reserve a few mussels for the garnish and remove the remainder from their shells. Stir the shelled mussels into the cream sauce and warm briefly.

6 Transfer the pasta to a serving dish. Pour over the sauce and toss to coat. Garnish with the reserved mussels.

Farfallini Buttered Lobster

This is one of those dishes that looks almost too lovely to eat – but you should!

NUTRITIONAL INFORMATION

Calories	686	Sugars	.........1g
Protein	........45g	Fat	..........36g
Carbohydrate	...44g	Saturates	......19g

  30 MINS   🕐 25 MINS

SERVES 4

INGREDIENTS

2 x 700 g/1 lb 9 oz lobsters, split into halves

juice and grated rind of 1 lemon

115 g/4 oz/½ cup butter

4 tbsp fresh white breadcrumbs

2 tbsp brandy

5 tbsp double (heavy) cream or crème fraîche

450 g/1 lb dried farfallini

1 tbsp olive oil

60 g/2 oz/⅔ cup freshly grated Parmesan cheese

salt and pepper

TO GARNISH

1 kiwi fruit, sliced

4 unpeeled, cooked king prawns (shrimp)

fresh dill sprigs

1 Carefully discard the stomach sac, vein and gills from each lobster. Remove all the meat from the tail and chop. Crack the claws and legs, remove the meat and chop. Transfer the meat to a bowl and add the lemon juice and grated lemon rind.

2 Clean the shells thoroughly and place in a warm oven at 170°C/325°/Gas Mark 3 to dry out.

3 Melt 25 g/1 oz/2 tbsp of the butter in a frying pan (skillet). Add the breadcrumbs and fry for about 3 minutes, until crisp and golden brown.

4 Melt the remaining butter in a saucepan. Add the lobster meat and heat through gently. Add the brandy and cook for a further 3 minutes, then add the cream or crème fraîche (unsweetened yogurt) and season to taste with salt and pepper.

5 Meanwhile, bring a large pan of lightly salted water to the boil. Add the farfallini and olive oil and cook for 8–10 minutes, until tender but still firm to the bite. Drain and spoon the pasta into the clean lobster shells.

6 Top with the buttered lobster and sprinkle with a little grated Parmesan cheese and the breadcrumbs. Grill (broil) for 2–3 minutes, until golden brown.

7 Transfer the lobster shells to a warm serving dish, garnish with the lemon slices, kiwi fruit, king prawns (shrimp) and dill sprigs and serve immediately.

Vermicelli with Clams

A quickly-cooked recipe that transforms store-cupboard ingredients into a dish with style.

NUTRITIONAL INFORMATION

Calories ....520 Sugars 2g
Protein ....26g Fat 13g
Carbohydrate ....71g Saturates 4g

10 MINS   25 MINS

SERVES 4

I N G R E D I E N T S

400 g/14 oz dried vermicelli, spaghetti or
    other long pasta

2 tbsp olive oil

25 g/1 oz/2 tbsp butter

2 onions, chopped

2 garlic cloves, chopped

2 x 200 g/7 oz jars clams in brine

125 ml/4 fl oz/½ cup white wine

4 tbsp chopped fresh parsley

½ tsp dried oregano

pinch of freshly grated nutmeg

salt and pepper

TO GARNISH

2 tbsp Parmesan cheese shavings

fresh basil sprigs

1 Bring a large pan of lightly salted water to the boil. Add the pasta and half of the olive oil and cook for 8–10 minutes until tender, but still firm to the bite. Drain, return to the pan and add the butter. Cover the pan, shake well and keep warm.

2 Heat the remaining oil in a pan over a medium heat. Add the onions and fry until they are translucent. Stir in the garlic and cook for 1 minute.

3 Strain the liquid from 1 jar of clams and add the liquid to the pan, with the wine. Stir, bring to simmering point and simmer for 3 minutes. Drain the second jar of clams and discard the liquid.

4 Add the clams, parsley and oregano to the pan and season with pepper and nutmeg. Lower the heat and cook until the sauce is heated through.

5 Transfer the pasta to a warm serving dish and pour over the sauce. Sprinkle with the Parmesan cheese, garnish with the basil and serve immediately.

COOK'S TIP

There are many different types of clams found along almost every coast in the world. Those traditionally used in this dish are the tiny ones – only 2.5-5 cm/1-2 inches across – known in Italy as vongole.

Baked Scallops & Pasta

This is another tempting seafood dish where the eye is delighted as much as the taste-buds.

NUTRITIONAL INFORMATION

Calories	725	Sugars	.........2g
Protein	........38g	Fat	..........48g
Carbohydrate	...38g	Saturates	......25g

🍞 🍞 🍞

🧈 20 MINS   🕐 30 MINS

SERVES 4

I N G R E D I E N T S

12 scallops

3 tbsp olive oil

350 g/12 oz/3 cups small, dried wholemeal (whole wheat) pasta shells

150 ml/¼ pint/⅔ cup fish stock

1 onion, chopped

juice and finely grated rind of 2 lemons

150 ml/¼ pint/⅔ cup double (heavy) cream

225 g/8 oz/2 cups grated Cheddar cheese

salt and pepper

crusty brown bread, to serve

1 Remove the scallops from their shells. Scrape off the skirt and the black intestinal thread. Reserve the white part (the flesh) and the orange part (the coral or roe). Very carefully ease the flesh and coral from the shell with a short, but very strong knife.

2 Wash the shells thoroughly and dry them well. Put the shells on a baking tray (cookie sheet), sprinkle lightly with two thirds of the olive oil and set aside.

3 Meanwhile, bring a large saucepan of lightly salted water to the boil. Add the pasta shells and remaining olive oil and cook for 8–10 minutes or until tender, but still firm to the bite. Drain well and

spoon about 25 g/1 oz of pasta into each scallop shell.

4 Put the scallops, fish stock, lemon rind and onion in an ovenproof dish and season to taste with pepper. Cover with foil and bake in a preheated oven at 180°C/350°F/Gas Mark 4 for 8 minutes.

5 Remove the dish from the oven. Remove the foil and, using a slotted spoon, transfer the scallops to the shells.

Add 1 tablespoon of the cooking liquid to each shell, together with a drizzle of lemon juice and a little cream, and top with the grated cheese.

6 Increase the oven temperature to 230°C/450°F/Gas Mark 8 and return the scallops to the oven for a further 4 minutes.

7 Serve the scallops in their shells with crusty brown bread and butter.

Meat

Italians have their very own special way of butchering meat, producing very different cuts. Most meat is sold ready-boned and often cut straight across the grain. Veal is a great favourite and widely available. Pork is also popular, with roast pig being the traditional dish of Umbria. Suckling pig is roasted with lots of fresh herbs,

especially rosemary, until the skin is crisp and brown. Lamb is often served for special occasions, cooked on a spit or roasted in the oven with wine, garlic and herbs; and the very small cutlets from young lambs feature widely, especially in Rome. Offal plays an important role, too, with liver, brains, sweetbreads, tongue, heart, tripe and kidneys always available. Whatever your favourite Italian meat dish is, it's sure to be included in this chapter.

Beef in Barolo

Barolo is a famous wine from the Piedmont area of Italy. Its mellow flavour is the key to this dish, so don't stint on the quality of the wine.

NUTRITIONAL INFORMATION

Calories 744   Sugars 1g
Protein . . . . .66g   Fat 43g
Carbohydrate . . . .1g   Saturates 16g

15 MINS   2¼ HOURS

SERVES 4

INGREDIENTS

4 tbsp oil

1 kg/2 lb 4 oz piece boned rolled rib of
    beef, or piece of silverside (round)

2 garlic cloves, crushed

4 shallots, sliced

1 tsp chopped fresh rosemary

1 tsp chopped fresh oregano

2 celery stalks, sliced

1 large carrot, diced

2 cloves

1 bottle Barolo wine

freshly grated nutmeg

salt and pepper

cooked vegetables, such as broccoli, carrots
    and new potatoes, to serve

1 Heat the oil in a flameproof casserole and brown the meat all over. Remove the meat from the casserole.

2 Add the garlic, shallots, herbs, celery, carrot and cloves and fry for 5 minutes.

3 Replace the meat on top of the vegetables. Pour in the wine. Cover the casserole and simmer gently for about 2 hours until tender. Remove the meat from the casserole, slice and keep warm.

4 Rub the contents of the pan through a sieve (strainer) or purée in a blender, adding a little hot beef stock if necessary. Season with nutmeg, salt and pepper.

5 Serve the meat with the sauce and accompanied by cooked vegetables, such as broccoli, carrots and new potatoes, if wished.

Rich Beef Stew

This slow-cooked beef stew is flavoured with oranges, red wine and porcini mushrooms.

NUTRITIONAL INFORMATION

Calories ....388 Sugars 15g
Protein ....30g Fat 21g
Carbohydrate ...16g Saturates 9g

45 MINS   1¾ HOURS

SERVES 4

INGREDIENTS

1 tbsp oil

15 g/½ oz/1 tbsp butter

225 g/8 oz baby onions, peeled and halved

600 g/1 lb 5 oz stewing steak, diced into
    4 cm/1½ inch chunks

300 ml/½ pint/1¼ cup beef stock

150 ml/¼ pint/⅔ cup red wine

4 tbsp chopped oregano

1 tbsp sugar

1 orange

25 g/1 oz porcini or other dried mushrooms

225 g/8 oz fresh plum tomatoes

cooked rice or potatoes, to serve

1 Heat the oil and butter in a large frying pan (skillet). Add the onions and sauté for 5 minutes or until golden. Remove the onions with a perforated spoon, set aside and keep warm.

2 Add the beef to the pan and cook, stirring, for 5 minutes or until browned all over.

3 Return the onions to the frying pan (skillet) and add the stock, wine, oregano and sugar, stirring to mix well. Transfer the mixture to an ovenproof casserole dish.

4 Pare the rind from the orange and cut it into strips. Slice the orange flesh into rings. Add the orange rings and the rind to the casserole. Cook in a preheated oven, at 180°C/350°F/Gas Mark 4, for 1¼ hours.

5 Soak the porcini mushrooms for 30 minutes in a small bowl containing 4 tablespoons of warm water.

6 Peel and halve the tomatoes. Add the tomatoes, porcini mushrooms and their soaking liquid to the casserole. Cook for a further 20 minutes until the beef is tender and the juices thickened. Serve with cooked rice or potatoes.

Beef Olives in Rich Gravy

Wafer-thin slices of tender beef with a rich garlic and bacon stuffing, flavoured with the tang of orange.

NUTRITIONAL INFORMATION

Calories	379	Sugars	.........4g
Protein	........26g	Fat	..........24g
Carbohydrate	....4g	Saturates	.......8g

20 MINS   20 MINS

SERVES 4

INGREDIENTS

8 ready prepared beef olives

4 tbsp chopped fresh parsley

4 garlic cloves, chopped finely

125 g/4½ oz smoked streaky bacon, rinded and chopped finely

grated rind of ½ small orange

2 tbsp olive oil

300 ml/½ pint/1¼ cups dry red wine

1 bay leaf

1 tsp sugar

60 g/2 oz pitted black olives, drained

salt and pepper

TO GARNISH

orange slices

chopped fresh parsley

1 Unroll the beef olives and flatten out as thinly as possible using a meat tenderizer or mallet. Trim the edges to neaten them.

2 Mix together the parsley, garlic, bacon, orange rind and salt and pepper to taste. Spread this mixture evenly over each beef olive.

3 Roll up each beef olive tightly, then secure with a cocktail stick (toothpick).

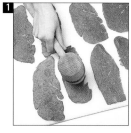

Heat the oil in a frying pan (skillet) and fry the beef on all sides for 10 minutes.

4 Drain the beef olives, reserving the pan juices, and keep warm. Pour the wine into the juices, add the bay leaf, sugar and seasoning. Bring to the boil and boil rapidly for 5 minutes to reduce slightly, stirring.

5 Return the cooked beef to the pan along with the black olives and heat through for a further 2 minutes. Discard the bay leaf and cocktail sticks (toothpicks).

6 Transfer the beef olives and gravy to a serving dish, and serve garnished with orange slices and parsley.

Creamed Strips of Sirloin

This quick and easy dish tastes superb and would make a delicious treat for a special occasion.

NUTRITIONAL INFORMATION

Calories 796   Sugars 2g
Protein . . . . .29g   Fat 63g
Carbohydrate . . .26g   Saturates 39g

15 MINS   30 MINS

SERVES 4

I N G R E D I E N T S

75 g/2¾ oz/6 tbsp butter

450 g/1 lb sirloin steak, trimmed
    and cut into thin strips

175 g/6 oz button mushrooms, sliced

1 tsp mustard

pinch of freshly grated root ginger

2 tbsp dry sherry

150 ml/¼ pint/⅔ cup double (heavy) cream

salt and pepper

4 slices hot toast, cut into triangles,
    to serve

P A S T A

450 g/1 lb dried rigatoni

2 tbsp olive oil

2 fresh basil sprigs

115 g/4 oz/8 tbsp butter

COOK'S TIP

Dried pasta will keep for up to 6 months. Keep it in the packet and reseal it once you have opened it, or transfer the pasta to an airtight jar.

1 Melt the butter in a large frying pan (skillet) and gently fry the steak over a low heat, stirring frequently, for 6 minutes. Using a slotted spoon, transfer the steak to an ovenproof dish and keep warm.

2 Add the sliced mushrooms to the frying pan (skillet) and cook for 2–3 minutes in the juices remaining in the pan. Add the mustard, ginger, salt and pepper. Cook for 2 minutes, then add the sherry and cream. Cook for a further 3 minutes, then pour the cream sauce over the steak.

3 Bake the steak and cream mixture in a preheated oven, at 190°C/375°F/Gas Mark 5, for 10 minutes.

4 Meanwhile, cook the pasta. Bring a large saucepan of lightly salted water to the boil. Add the rigatoni, olive oil and 1 of the basil sprigs and boil rapidly for 10 minutes, until tender but still firm to the bite. Drain the pasta and transfer to a warm serving plate. Toss the pasta with the butter and garnish with a sprig of basil.

5 Serve the creamed steak strips with the pasta and triangles of warm toast.

Beef & Spaghetti Surprise

This delicious Sicilian recipe originated as a handy way of using up leftover cooked pasta.

NUTRITIONAL INFORMATION

Calories	797	Sugars	.........7g
Protein	........31g	Fat	..........60g
Carbohydrate	...35g	Saturates	......16g

 30 MINS   1½ HOURS

SERVES 4

INGREDIENTS

150 ml/¼ pint/⅔ cup olive oil, plus extra
   for brushing

2 aubergines (eggplants)

350 g/12 oz/3 cups minced (ground) beef

1 onion, chopped

2 garlic cloves, crushed

2 tbsp tomato purée (paste)

400 g/14 oz can chopped tomatoes

1 tsp Worcestershire sauce

1 tsp chopped fresh marjoram or oregano
   or ½ tsp dried marjoram or oregano

60 g/2 oz/½ cup stoned (pitted) black
   olives, sliced

1 green, red or yellow (bell) pepper, cored,
   seeded and chopped

175 g/6 oz dried spaghetti

115 g/4 oz/1 cup freshly grated
   Parmesan cheese

salt and pepper

fresh oregano or parsley sprigs,
   to garnish

1 Brush a 20 cm/8 inch loose-based round cake tin (pan) with oil, line the base with baking parchment and brush with oil.

2 Slice the aubergines (eggplants). Heat a little oil in a pan and fry the aubergines (eggplant), in batches, for 3–4 minutes or until browned on both sides. Add more oil, as necessary. Drain on kitchen paper (paper towels).

3 Put the minced (ground) beef, onion and garlic in a saucepan and cook over a medium heat, stirring occasionally, until browned. Add the tomato purée (paste), tomatoes, Worcestershire sauce, marjoram or oregano and salt and pepper to taste. Leave to simmer, stirring occasionally, for 10 minutes. Add the olives and (bell) pepper and cook for a further 10 minutes.

4 Bring a pan of salted water to the boil. Add the spaghetti and 1 tbsp oil and cook for 8–10 minutes until tender, but still firm to the bite. Drain and turn the spaghetti into a bowl. Add the meat mixture and cheese and toss with 2 forks.

5 Arrange aubergine (eggplant) slices over the base and up the sides of the tin (pan). Add the spaghetti, pressing down firmly, and then cover with the rest of the aubergine (eggplant) slices. Bake in a preheated oven at 200°C/400°F/Gas Mark 6 for 40 minutes. Leave to stand for 5 minutes, then invert on to a serving dish. Discard the baking parchment. Garnish with the fresh herbs and serve.

Beef & Potato Ravioli

In this recipe the 'pasta' dough is made with potatoes instead of flour. The small round ravioli are filled with a rich bolognese sauce.

NUTRITIONAL INFORMATION

Calories	618	Sugars	........4g
Protein	........16g	Fat	..........31g
Carbohydrate	...74g	Saturates	......12g

30 MINS   50 MINS

SERVES 4

INGREDIENTS

FILLING

1 tbsp vegetable oil

125 g/4½ oz ground beef

1 shallot, diced

1 garlic clove, crushed

1 tbsp plain (all-purpose) flour

1 tbsp tomato purée (paste)

150 ml/¼ pint/⅔ cup beef stock

1 celery stick, chopped

2 tomatoes, peeled and diced

2 tsp chopped fresh basil

salt and pepper

RAVIOLI

450 g/1 lb floury (mealy) potatoes, diced

3 small egg yolks

3 tbsp olive oil

175 g/6 oz/1½ cups plain (all-purpose) flour

60 g/2 oz/¼ cup butter, for frying

shredded basil leaves, to garnish

1 To make the filling, heat the vegetable oil in a pan and fry the beef for 3-4 minutes, breaking it up with a spoon.

2 Add the shallots and garlic to the pan and cook for 2-3 minutes, or until the shallots have softened.

3 Stir in the flour and tomato purée (paste) and cook for 1 minute. Stir in the beef stock, celery, tomatoes and chopped fresh basil. Season to taste with salt and pepper.

4 Cook the mixture over a low heat for 20 minutes. Remove from the heat and leave to cool.

5 To make the ravioli, cook the potatoes in a pan of boiling water for 10 minutes until cooked.

6 Mash the potatoes and place them in a mixing bowl. Blend in the egg yolks and oil. Season with salt and pepper, then stir in the flour and mix to form a dough.

7 On a lightly floured surface, divide the dough into 24 pieces and shape into flat rounds. Spoon the filling on to one half of each round and fold the dough over to encase the filling, pressing down to seal the edges.

8 Melt the butter in a frying pan (skillet) and cook the ravioli for 6-8 minutes, turning once, until golden. Serve hot, garnished with shredded basil leaves.

Beef & Pasta Bake

The combination of Italian and Indian ingredients makes a surprisingly delicious recipe. Marinate the steak in advance to save time.

NUTRITIONAL INFORMATION

Calories 1050   Sugars 4g
Protein . . . . .47g   Fat 81g
Carbohydrate . . .37g   Saturates 34g

6¼ HOURS   1¼ HOURS

SERVES 4

INGREDIENTS

900g/2 lb steak, cut into cubes

150 ml/¼ pint/⅔ cup beef stock

450g/1 lb dried macaroni

300 ml/½ pint/1¼ cups double
    (heavy) cream

½ tsp garam masala

salt

fresh coriander (cilantro) and flaked
    (slivered) almonds, to garnish

KORMA PASTE

60 g/2 oz/½ cup blanched almonds

6 garlic cloves

2.5 cm/1 inch piece fresh root ginger,
    coarsely chopped

6 tbsp beef stock

1 tsp ground cardamom

4 cloves, crushed

1 tsp cinnamon

2 large onions, chopped

1 tsp coriander seeds

2 tsp ground cumin seeds

pinch of cayenne pepper

6 tbsp of sunflower oil

1 To make the korma paste, grind the almonds finely using a pestle and mortar. Put the ground almonds and the rest of the korma paste ingredients into a food processor or blender and process to make a very smooth paste.

2 Put the steak in a shallow dish and spoon over the korma paste, turning to coat the steak well. Leave in the refrigerator to marinate for 6 hours.

3 Transfer the steak and korma paste to a large saucepan, and simmer over a low heat, adding a little beef stock if required, for 35 minutes.

4 Meanwhile, bring a large saucepan of lightly salted water to the boil. Add the macaroni and cook for 10 minutes until tender, but still firm to the bite. Drain the pasta thoroughly and transfer to a deep casserole. Add the steak, double (heavy) cream and garam masala.

5 Bake in a preheated oven at 200°C/ 400°F/Gas Mark 6 for 30 minutes. Remove the casserole from the oven and allow to stand for about 10 minutes. Garnish the bake with fresh coriander (cilantro) and serve.

Fresh Spaghetti & Meatballs

This well-loved Italian dish is famous across the world. Make the most of it by using high-quality steak for the meatballs.

NUTRITIONAL INFORMATION

Calories . . . . . . .665 Sugars 9g
Protein . . . . .39g Fat 24g
Carbohydrate . . .77g Saturates 8g

45 MINS   1¼ HOURS

SERVES 4

INGREDIENTS

150 g/5½ oz/2½ cups brown breadcrumbs

150 ml/¼ pint/⅔ cup milk

25 g/1 oz/2 tbsp butter

25 g/1 oz/¼ cup wholemeal
    (whole-wheat) flour

200 ml/7 fl oz/⅞ cup beef stock

400 g/14 oz can chopped tomatoes

2 tbsp tomato purée (paste)

1 tsp sugar

1 tbsp finely chopped fresh tarragon

1 large onion, chopped

450 g/1 lb/4 cups minced steak

1 tsp paprika

4 tbsp olive oil

450 g/1 lb fresh spaghetti

salt and pepper

fresh tarragon sprigs, to garnish

1 Place the breadcrumbs in a bowl, add the milk and set aside to soak for about 30 minutes.

2 Melt half of the butter in a pan. Add the flour and cook, stirring constantly, for 2 minutes. Gradually stir in the beef stock and cook, stirring constantly, for a further 5 minutes. Add the tomatoes, tomato purée (paste), sugar and tarragon. Season well and simmer for 25 minutes.

3 Mix the onion, steak and paprika into the breadcrumbs and season to taste. Shape the mixture into 14 meatballs.

4 Heat the oil and remaining butter in a frying pan (skillet) and fry the meatballs, turning, until brown all over. Place in a deep casserole, pour over the tomato sauce, cover and bake in a preheated oven, at 180°C/ 350°F/Gas Mark 4, for 25 minutes.

5 Bring a large saucepan of lightly salted water to the boil. Add the fresh spaghetti, bring back to the boil and cook for about 2–3 minutes or until tender, but still firm to the bite.

6 Meanwhile, remove the meatballs from the oven and allow them to cool for 3 minutes. Serve the meatballs and their sauce with the spaghetti, garnished with tarragon sprigs.

Meatballs in Red Wine Sauce

A different twist is given to this traditional pasta dish with a rich, but subtle sauce.

45 MINS   1½ HOURS

SERVES 4

I N G R E D I E N T S

150 ml/¼ pint/⅔ cup milk

150 g/5½ oz/2 cups white breadcrumbs

25 g/1 oz/2 tbsp butter

9 tbsp olive oil

225 g/8 oz/3 cups sliced
   oyster mushrooms

25 g/1 oz/¼ cup wholemeal
(whole-wheat) flour

200 ml/7 fl oz/⅞ cup beef stock

150 ml/¼ pint/⅔ cup red wine

4 tomatoes, skinned and chopped

1 tbsp tomato purée (paste)

1 tsp brown sugar

1 tbsp finely chopped fresh basil

12 shallots, chopped

450 g/1 lb/4 cups minced (ground) steak

1 tsp paprika

450 g/1 lb dried egg tagliarini

salt and pepper

fresh basil sprigs, to garnish

1 Pour the milk into a bowl and soak the breadcrumbs in the milk for 30 minutes.

2 Heat half of the butter and 4 tbsp of the oil in a pan. Fry the mushrooms for 4 minutes, then stir in the flour and cook for 2 minutes. Add the stock and wine and simmer for 15 minutes. Add the tomatoes, tomato purée (paste), sugar and basil. Season and simmer for 30 minutes.

3 Mix the shallots, steak and paprika with the breadcrumbs and season to taste. Shape the mixture into 14 meatballs.

4 Heat 4 tbsp of the remaining oil and the remaining butter in a large frying pan (skillet). Fry the meatballs, turning frequently, until brown all over. Transfer to a deep casserole, pour over the red wine and the mushroom sauce, cover and bake in a preheated oven, at 180°C/350°F/Gas Mark 4, for 30 minutes.

5 Bring a pan of salted water to the boil. Add the pasta and the remaining oil and cook for 8–10 minutes or until tender. Drain and transfer to a serving dish. Remove the casserole from the oven and cool for 3 minutes. Pour the meatballs and sauce on to the pasta, garnish and serve.

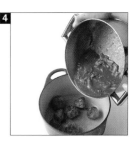

Pork Chops with Sage

The fresh taste of sage is the perfect ingredient to counteract the richness of pork.

NUTRITIONAL INFORMATION

Calories 364   Sugars 5g
Protein ....34g   Fat 19g
Carbohydrate ...14g   Saturates 7g

10 MINS   15 MINS

SERVES 4

INGREDIENTS

2 tbsp flour

1 tbsp chopped fresh sage or 1 tsp dried

4 lean boneless pork chops, trimmed of excess fat

2 tbsp olive oil

15 g/½ oz/1 tbsp butter

2 red onions, sliced into rings

1 tbsp lemon juice

2 tsp caster (superfine) sugar

4 plum tomatoes, quartered

salt and pepper

1 Mix the flour, sage and salt and pepper to taste on a plate. Lightly dust the pork chops on both sides with the seasoned flour.

2 Heat the oil and butter in a frying pan (skillet), add the chops and cook them for 6–7 minutes on each side until cooked through. Drain the chops, reserving the pan juices, and keep warm.

3 Toss the onion in the lemon juice and fry along with the sugar and tomatoes for 5 minutes until tender.

4 Serve the pork with the tomato and onion mixture and a green salad.

Pasta & Pork in Cream Sauce

This unusual and attractive dish is extremely delicious. Make the Italian Red Wine Sauce well in advance to reduce the preparation time.

NUTRITIONAL INFORMATION

Calories	735	Sugars	.........4g
Protein	........31g	Fat	..........52g
Carbohydrate	...37g	Saturates	......19g

8¾ HOURS   35 MINS

SERVES 4

I N G R E D I E N T S

450 g/1 lb pork fillet (tenderloin),
   thinly sliced

4 tbsp olive oil

225 g/8 oz button mushrooms, sliced

200 ml/7 fl oz/⅞ cup Italian Red Wine Sauce
   (see page 15)

1 tbsp lemon juice

pinch of saffron

350 g/12 oz/3 cups dried orecchioni

4 tbsp double (heavy) cream

12 quail eggs (see Cook's Tip)

salt

1 Pound the slices of pork between 2 sheets of cling film until wafer thin, then cut into strips.

2 Heat the olive oil in a large frying pan (skillet), add the pork and stir-fry for 5 minutes. Add the mushrooms to the pan and stir-fry for a further 2 minutes.

3 Pour over the Italian Red Wine Sauce, lower the heat and simmer gently for 20 minutes.

4 Meanwhile, bring a large saucepan of lightly salted water to the boil. Add the lemon juice, saffron and orecchioni and cook for 8–10 minutes, until tender but still firm to the bite. Drain the pasta and keep warm.

5 Stir the cream into the pan with the pork and heat gently for a few minutes.

6 Boil the quail eggs for 3 minutes, cool them in cold water and remove the shells.

7 Transfer the pasta to a large, warm serving plate, top with the pork and the sauce and garnish with the eggs. Serve immediately.

COOK'S TIP

In this recipe, the quail eggs are soft-boiled (soft-cooked). As they are extremely difficult to shell when warm, it is important that they are thoroughly cooled first. Otherwise, they will break up.

Pork with Fennel & Juniper

The addition of juniper and fennel to the pork chops gives an unusual and delicate flavour to this dish.

NUTRITIONAL INFORMATION

Calories ....277 Sugars 0.4g
Protein ....32g Fat 16g
Carbohydrate ...0.4g Saturates 5g

 2¼ HOURS   15 MINS

SERVES 4

INGREDIENTS

½ fennel bulb

1 tbsp juniper berries

about 2 tbsp olive oil

finely grated rind and juice of 1 orange

4 pork chops, each about 150 g/5½ oz

fresh bread and a crisp salad, to serve

1 Finely chop the fennel bulb, discarding the green parts.

2 Grind the juniper berries in a pestle and mortar. Mix the crushed juniper berries with the fennel flesh, olive oil and orange rind.

3 Using a sharp knife, score a few cuts all over each chop.

COOK'S TIP

Juniper berries are most commonly associated with gin, but they are often added to meat dishes in Italy for a delicate citrus flavour. They can be bought dried from most health food shops and some larger supermarkets.

4 Place the pork chops in a roasting tin (pan) or an ovenproof dish. Spoon the fennel and juniper mixture over the chops.

5 Pour the orange juice over the top of each chop, cover and marinate in the refrigerator for about 2 hours.

6 Cook the pork chops, under a preheated grill (broiler), for 10–15 minutes, depending on the thickness of the meat, or until the meat is tender and cooked through, turning occasionally.

7 Transfer the pork chops to serving plates and serve with a crisp, fresh salad and plenty of fresh bread to mop up the cooking juices.

Pork Cooked in Milk

This traditional dish of boned pork cooked with garlic and milk can be served hot or cold.

NUTRITIONAL INFORMATION

Calories	498	Sugars	........15g
Protein	........50g	Fat	..........27g
Carbohydrate	...15g	Saturates	.......9g

 20 MINS   1¾ HOURS

SERVES 4

INGREDIENTS

800 g/1 lb 12 oz leg of pork, boned

1 tbsp oil

25 g/1 oz/2 tbsp butter

1 onion, chopped

2 garlic cloves, chopped

75 g/2¾ oz pancetta, diced

1.2 litres/2 pints/5 cups milk

1 tbsp green peppercorns, crushed

2 fresh bay leaves

2 tbsp marjoram

2 tbsp thyme

1 Using a sharp knife, remove the fat from the pork. Shape the meat into a neat form, tying it in place with a length of string.

2 Heat the oil and butter in a large pan. Add the onion, garlic and pancetta to the pan and cook for 2–3 minutes.

3 Add the pork to the pan and cook, turning occasionally, until it is browned all over.

4 Pour over the milk, add the peppercorns, bay leaves, marjoram and thyme and cook over a low heat for 1¼–1½ hours or until tender. Watch the

 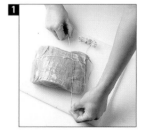 

liquid carefully for the last 15 minutes of cooking time because it tends to reduce very quickly and will then burn. If the liquid reduces and the pork is still not tender, add another 100 ml/3½ fl oz milk and continue cooking. Reserve the cooking liquid (as the milk reduces naturally in this dish, it forms a thick and creamy sauce, which curdles slightly but tastes very delicious).

5 Remove the pork from the saucepan. Using a sharp knife, cut the meat into slices. Transfer the pork slices to serving plates and serve immediately with the reserved cooking liquid.

Pork with Lemon & Garlic

This is a simplified version of a traditional dish from the Marche region of Italy. Pork fillet pockets are stuffed with ham (prosciutto) and herbs.

NUTRITIONAL INFORMATION

Calories 428   Sugars 2g
Protein ....31g   Fat 32g
Carbohydrate ....4g   Saturates 4g

25 MINS   1 HOUR

SERVES 4

INGREDIENTS

450 g/1 lb pork fillet

50 g/1¾ oz chopped almonds

2 tbsp olive oil

100 g/3½ oz raw Parma ham (prosciutto), finely chopped

2 garlic cloves, chopped

1 tbsp fresh oregano, chopped

finely grated rind of 2 lemons

4 shallots, finely chopped

200 ml/7 fl oz/¾ cup ham or chicken stock

1 tsp sugar

1 Using a sharp knife, cut the pork fillet into 4 equal pieces. Place the pork between sheets of greaseproof paper and pound each piece with a meat mallet or the end of a rolling pin to flatten it.

2 Cut a horizontal slit in each piece of pork to make a pocket.

3 Place the almonds on a baking tray (cookie sheet). Lightly toast the almonds under a medium-hot grill (broiler) for 2–3 minutes or until golden.

4 Mix the almonds with 1 tbsp oil, ham (prosciutto), garlic, oregano and the finely grated rind from 1 lemon. Spoon the mixture into the pockets of the pork.

5 Heat the remaining oil in a large frying pan (skillet). Add the shallots and cook for 2 minutes.

6 Add the pork to the frying pan (skillet) and cook for 2 minutes on each side or until browned all over.

7 Add the ham or chicken stock to the pan, bring to the boil, cover and leave to simmer for 45 minutes or until the pork is tender. Remove the meat from the pan, set aside and keep warm.

8 Add the lemon rind and sugar to the pan, boil for 3–4 minutes or until reduced and syrupy. Pour the lemon sauce over the pork fillets and serve immediately.

Pork Stuffed with Prosciutto

This sophisticated roast with Mediterranean flavours is ideal served with a pungent olive paste.

NUTRITIONAL INFORMATION

Calories 427   Sugars 0g
Protein ....31g   Fat 34g
Carbohydrate ...0.2g   Saturates 7g

🥗 25 MINS   🕐 55 MINS

SERVES 4

INGREDIENTS

500 g/1 lb 2 oz piece of lean pork fillet

small bunch fresh of basil leaves, washed

2 tbsp freshly grated Parmesan

2 tbsp sun-dried tomato paste

6 thin slices Parma ham (prosciutto)

1 tbsp olive oil

salt and pepper

OLIVE PASTE

125 g/4 oz/⅔ cup pitted black olives

4 tbsp olive oil

2 garlic cloves, peeled

1 Trim away excess fat and membrane from the pork fillet. Slice the pork lengthways down the middle, taking care not to cut all the way through.

2 Open out the pork and season the inside. Lay the basil leaves down the centre. Mix the cheese and sun-dried tomato paste and spread over the basil.

3 Press the pork back together. Wrap the ham around the pork, overlapping, to cover. Place on a rack in a roasting tin (pan), seamside down, and brush with oil. Bake in a preheated oven, 190°C/375°F/Gas Mark 5, for 30–40 minutes depending on thickness until cooked through. Allow to stand for 10 minutes.

4 For the olive paste, place all the ingredients in a blender or food processor and blend until smooth. Alternatively, for a coarser paste, finely chop the olives and garlic and mix with the oil.

5 Drain the cooked pork and slice thinly. Serve with the olive paste and a salad.

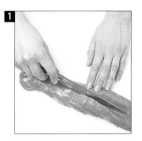

Stuffed Cannelloni

Cannelloni, the thick, round pasta tubes, make perfect containers for close-textured sauces of all kinds.

NUTRITIONAL INFORMATION

Calories 520	Sugars 5g	
Protein 21g	Fat 39g	
Carbohydrate ...23g	Saturates 18g	

30 MINS   1¼ HOURS

SERVES 4

INGREDIENTS

8 dried cannelloni tubes

1 tbsp olive oil

25 g/1 oz/¼ cup freshly grated
  Parmesan cheese

fresh herb sprigs, to garnish

FILLING

25 g/1 oz/2 tbsp butter

300 g/10½ oz frozen spinach, thawed
  and chopped

115 g/4 oz/½ cup ricotta cheese

25 g/1 oz/¼ cup freshly grated
  Parmesan cheese

60 g/2 oz/¼ cup chopped ham

pinch of freshly grated nutmeg

2 tbsp double (heavy) cream

2 eggs, lightly beaten

salt and pepper

SAUCE

25 g/1 oz/2 tbsp butter

25 g/1 oz/¼ cup plain
  (all-purpose) flour

300 ml/½ pint/1¼ cups milk

2 bay leaves

pinch of freshly grated nutmeg

1 To make the filling, melt the butter in a pan and stir-fry the spinach for 2–3 minutes. Remove from the heat and stir in the ricotta and Parmesan cheeses and the ham. Season to taste with nutmeg, salt and pepper. Beat in the cream and eggs to make a thick paste.

2 Bring a pan of lightly salted water to the boil. Add the pasta and the oil and cook for 10–12 minutes, or until almost tender. Drain and set aside to cool.

3 To make the sauce, melt the butter in a pan. Stir in the flour and cook, stirring, for 1 minute. Gradually stir in the milk. Add the bay leaves and simmer, stirring, for 5 minutes. Add the nutmeg and salt and pepper to taste. Remove from the heat and discard the bay leaves.

4 Spoon the filling into a piping bag and fill the cannelloni.

5 Spoon a little sauce into the base of an ovenproof dish. Arrange the cannelloni in the dish in a single layer and pour over the remaining sauce. Sprinkle over the Parmesan cheese and bake in a preheated oven at 190°C/375°F/Gas Mark 5 for 40–45 minutes. Garnish with fresh herb sprigs and serve.

Neapolitan Pork Steaks

An Italian version of grilled pork steaks, this dish is easy to make and delicious to eat.

NUTRITIONAL INFORMATION

Calories 353	Sugars 3g	
Protein 39g	Fat 20g	
Carbohydrate 4g	Saturates 5g	

 10 MINS   25 MINS

SERVES 4

INGREDIENTS

2 tbsp olive oil

1 garlic clove, chopped

1 large onion, sliced

400 g/14 oz can tomatoes

2 tsp yeast extract

4 pork loin steaks, each about 125 g/4½ oz

75 g/2¾ oz black olives, pitted

2 tbsp fresh basil, shredded

freshly grated Parmesan cheese, to serve

1 Heat the oil in a large frying pan (skillet). Add the onions and garlic and cook, stirring, for 3–4 minutes or until they just begin to soften.

2 Add the tomatoes and yeast extract to the frying pan (skillet) and leave to simmer for about 5 minutes or until the sauce starts to thicken.

COOK'S TIP

Parmesan is a mature and exceptionally hard cheese produced in Italy. You only need to add a little as it has a very strong flavour.

3 Cook the pork steaks, under a preheated grill (broiler), for 5 minutes on both sides, until the the meat is cooked through. Set the pork aside and keep warm.

4 Add the olives and fresh shredded basil to the sauce in the frying pan (skillet) and stir quickly to combine.

5 Transfer the steaks to warm serving plates. Top the steaks with the sauce, sprinkle with freshly grated Parmesan cheese and serve immediately.

Pasta & Lamb Loaf

Any dried pasta shape can be used for this delicious recipe. It has been adapted for microwave cooking for convenience.

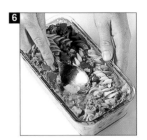

NUTRITIONAL INFORMATION

Calories ....245 Sugars 2g
Protein ....15g Fat 18g
Carbohydrate ....6g Saturates 7g

35 MINS   35 MINS

SERVES 4

INGREDIENTS

15 g/½ oz/1 tbsp butter

½ small aubergine (eggplant), diced

60 g/2 oz multi-coloured fusilli

2 tsp olive oil

225 g/8 oz/1 cup minced (ground) lamb

½ small onion, chopped

½ red (bell) pepper, chopped

1 garlic clove, crushed

1 tsp dried mixed herbs

2 eggs, beaten

2 tbsp single (light) cream

salt and pepper

TO SERVE

salad

pasta sauce of your choice

1 Place the butter in a 500 g/1 lb 2 oz loaf dish. Cook on HIGH power for 30 seconds until melted. Brush over the base and sides of the dish.

2 Sprinkle the aubergine (eggplant) with salt, put in a colander and leave for 20 minutes. Rinse the aubergine (eggplant) well and pat dry with paper towels.

3 Place the pasta in a bowl, add a little salt and enough boiling water to cover by 2.5 cm/1 inch. Cover and cook on HIGH power for 8 minutes, stirring halfway through. Leave to stand, covered, for a few minutes.

4 Place the oil, lamb and onion in a bowl. Cover and cook on HIGH power for 2 minutes.

5 Break up any lumps of meat using a fork. Add the (bell) pepper, garlic, herbs and aubergine (eggplant). Cover and cook on HIGH power for 5 minutes, stirring halfway through.

6 Drain the pasta and add to the lamb with the eggs and cream. Season well. Turn into the loaf dish and pat down using the back of a spoon.

7 Cook on MEDIUM power for 10 minutes until firm to the touch. Leave to stand for 5 minutes before turning out. Serve in slices with a salad and a pasta sauce.

Roman Pan-Fried Lamb

Chunks of tender lamb, pan-fried with garlic and stewed in red wine are a real Roman dish.

NUTRITIONAL INFORMATION

Calories	299	Sugars	.........1g
Protein	........31g	Fat	..........16g
Carbohydrate	....1g	Saturates	.......7g

 15 MINS   🕐 50 MINS

SERVES 4

I N G R E D I E N T S

1 tbsp oil

15 g/½ oz/1 tbsp butter

600 g/1 lb 5 oz lamb (shoulder or leg),
 cut into 2.5 cm/1 inch chunks

4 garlic cloves, peeled

3 sprigs thyme, stalks removed

6 canned anchovy fillets

150 ml/¼ pint/⅔ cup red wine

150 ml/¼ pint/⅔ cup lamb or
 vegetable stock

1 tsp sugar

50 g/1¾ oz black olives, pitted and halved

2 tbsp chopped parsley, to garnish

mashed potato, to serve

1 Heat the oil and butter in a large frying pan (skillet). Add the lamb and cook for 4–5 minutes, stirring, until the meat is browned all over.

2 Using a pestle and mortar, grind together the garlic, thyme and anchovies to make a smooth paste.

3 Add the wine and lamb or vegetable stock to the frying pan (skillet). Stir in the garlic and anchovy paste together with the sugar.

4 Bring the mixture to the boil, reduce the heat, cover and simmer for 30–40 minutes or until the lamb is tender. For the last 10 minutes of the cooking time, remove the lid to allow the sauce to reduce slightly.

5 Stir the olives into the sauce and mix to combine.

6 Transfer the lamb and the sauce to a serving bowl and garnish. Serve with creamy mashed potatoes.

COOK'S TIP

Rome is the capital of Lazio and Italy and has become a focal point for specialities from all over Italy. Food from this region is fairly simple and quick to prepare, all with plenty of herbs and seasonings giving really robust flavours.

Pot Roasted Leg of Lamb

This dish from the Abruzzi uses a slow cooking method which ensures that the meat absorbs the flavourings and becomes very tender.

NUTRITIONAL INFORMATION

Calories	734	Sugars	.........6g
Protein	........71g	Fat	..........42g
Carbohydrate	....7g	Saturates	......15g

 35 MINS   3 HOURS

SERVES 4

I N G R E D I E N T S

1.75 kg/3½ lb leg of lamb

3–4 sprigs fresh rosemary

125 g/4½ oz streaky bacon rashers

4 tbsp olive oil

2–3 garlic cloves, crushed

2 onions, sliced

2 carrots, sliced

2 celery stalks, sliced

300 ml/½ pint/1¼ cups dry white wine

1 tbsp tomato purée (paste)

300 ml/½ pint/1¼ cups stock

350 g/12 oz tomatoes, peeled, quartered
    and deseeded

1 tbsp chopped fresh parsley

1 tbsp chopped fresh oregano or marjoram

salt and pepper

fresh rosemary sprigs, to garnish

1 Wipe the joint of lamb all over, trimming off any excess fat, then season well with salt and pepper, rubbing well in. Lay the sprigs of rosemary over the lamb, cover evenly with the bacon rashers and tie in place with string.

2 Heat the oil in a frying pan (skillet) and fry the lamb for about 10 minutes or until browned all over, turning several times. Remove from the pan.

3 Transfer the oil from the frying pan (skillet) to a large fireproof casserole and fry the garlic and onion together for 3–4 minutes until beginning to soften. Add the carrots and celery and continue to cook for a few minutes longer.

4 Lay the lamb on top of the vegetables and press down to partly submerge. Pour the wine over the lamb, add the tomato purée (paste) and simmer for 3–4 minutes. Add the stock, tomatoes and herbs and seasoning and bring back to the boil for a further 3–4 minutes.

5 Cover the casserole tightly and cook in a moderate oven, 180°C/350°F/Gas Mark 4, for 2–2½ hours until very tender.

6 Remove the lamb from the casserole and if preferred, take off the bacon and herbs along with the string. Keep warm. Strain the juices, skimming off any excess fat, and serve in a jug. The vegetables may be put around the joint or in a serving dish. Garnish with fresh sprigs of rosemary.

Lamb Cutlets with Rosemary

A classic combination of flavours, this dish would make a perfect Sunday lunch. Serve with tomato and onion salad and jacket potatoes.

NUTRITIONAL INFORMATION

Calories ....560 Sugars 1g
Protein ....48g Fat 40g
Carbohydrate ....1g Saturates 13g

 1¼ HOURS   15 MINS

SERVES 4

INGREDIENTS

8 lamb cutlets

5 tbsp olive oil

2 tbsp lemon juice

1 clove garlic, crushed

½ tsp lemon pepper

salt

8 sprigs rosemary

jacket potatoes, to serve

SALAD

4 tomatoes, sliced

4 spring onions (scallion), sliced diagonally

DRESSING

2 tbsp olive oil

1 tbsp lemon juice

1 clove garlic, chopped

¼ tsp fresh rosemary, chopped finely

1 Trim the lamb chops by cutting away the flesh with a sharp knife to expose the tips of the bones.

2 Place the oil, lemon juice, garlic, lemon pepper and salt in a shallow, non-metallic dish and whisk with a fork to combine.

3 Lay the sprigs of rosemary in the dish and place the lamb on top. Leave to marinate for at least 1 hour, turning the lamb cutlets once.

4 Remove the chops from the marinade and wrap a little kitchen foil around the bones to stop them from burning.

5 Place the rosemary sprigs on the rack and place the lamb on top. Barbecue (grill) for 10–15 minutes, turning once.

6 Meanwhile make the salad and dressing. Arrange the tomatoes on a serving dish and scatter the spring onions (scallions) on top. Place all the ingredients for the dressing in a screw-top jar, shake well and pour over the salad. Serve with the lamb cutlets and jacket potatoes.

COOK'S TIP

Choose medium to small baking potatoes if you want to cook jacket potatoes on the barbecue (grill). Scrub them well, prick with a fork and wrap in buttered kitchen foil. Bury them in the hot coals and barbecue (grill) for 50–60 minutes.

Lamb with Olives

This is a very simple dish, and the chilli adds a bit of spiciness. It is quick to prepare and makes an ideal supper dish.

NUTRITIONAL INFORMATION

Calories 577   Sugars 1g
Protein . . . . .62g   Fat 33g
Carbohydrate . . . .1g   Saturates 10g

15 MINS   1½ HOURS

SERVES 4

I N G R E D I E N T S

1.25 kg/2 lb 12 oz boned leg of lamb

90 ml/3 fl oz/⅓ cup olive oil

2 garlic cloves, crushed

1 onion, sliced

1 small red chilli, cored, deseeded and
    chopped finely

175 ml/6 fl oz/¾ cup dry white wine

175 g/6 oz/1 cup pitted black olives

salt

chopped fresh parsley, to garnish

1 Using a sharp knife, cut the lamb into 2.5 cm/1 inch cubes.

2 Heat the oil in a frying pan (skillet) and fry the garlic, onion and chilli for 5 minutes.

3 Add the meat and wine and cook for a further 5 minutes.

4 Stir in the olives, then transfer the mixture to a casserole. Place in a preheated oven, 180°C/350°F/Gas Mark 4, and cook for 1 hour 20 minutes or until the meat is tender. Season with salt to taste, and serve garnished with chopped fresh parsley.

Lamb with Bay & Lemon

These lamb chops quickly become more elegant when the bone is removed to make noisettes.

NUTRITIONAL INFORMATION

Calories . . . . . . .268 Sugars 0.2g
Protein . . . . .24g Fat 16g
Carbohydrate . . .0.2g Saturates 7g

10 MINS   35 MINS

SERVES 4

INGREDIENTS

4 lamb chops

1 tbsp oil

15 g/½ oz/1 tbsp butter

150 ml/¼ pint/⅔ cup white wine

150 ml/¼ pint/⅔ cup lamb or
   vegetable stock

2 bay leaves

pared rind of 1 lemon

salt and pepper

1 Using a sharp knife, carefully remove the bone from each lamb chop, keeping the meat intact. Alternatively, ask the butcher to prepare the lamb noisettes for you.

2 Shape the meat into rounds and secure with a length of string.

3 In a large frying pan (skillet), heat together the oil and butter until the mixture starts to froth.

4 Add the lamb noisettes to the frying pan (skillet) and cook for 2–3 minutes on each side or until browned all over.

5 Remove the frying pan (skillet) fom the heat, drain off all of the excess fat and discard.

6 Return the frying pan (skillet) to the heat. Add the wine, stock, bay leaves and lemon rind to the frying pan (skillet) and cook for 20–25 minutes or until the lamb is tender. Season the lamb noisettes and sauce to taste with a little salt and pepper.

7 Transfer to serving plates. Remove the string from each noisette and serve with the sauce.

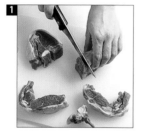

COOK'S TIP

Your local butcher will offer you good advice on how to prepare the lamb noisettes, if you are wary of preparing them yourself.

Barbecued Butterfly Lamb

The appearance of the lamb as it is opened out to cook on the barbecue gives this dish its name. Marinate the lamb in advance if possible.

NUTRITIONAL INFORMATION

Calories ....733 Sugars 6g
Protein ....69g Fat 48g
Carbohydrate ....6g Saturates 13g

6¼ HOURS   1 HOUR

SERVES 4

INGREDIENTS

boned leg of lamb, about 1.8 kg/4 lb

8 tbsp balsamic vinegar

grated rind and juice of 1 lemon

150 ml/¼ pint/⅔ cup sunflower oil

4 tbsp chopped, fresh mint

2 cloves garlic, crushed

2 tbsp light muscovado sugar

salt and pepper

TO SERVE

grilled (broiled) vegetables

green salad leaves

1 Open out the boned leg of lamb so that its shape resembles a butterfly. Thread 2–3 skewers through the meat in order to make it easier to turn on the barbecue (grill).

2 Combine the balsamic vinegar, lemon rind and juice, oil, mint, garlic, sugar and salt and pepper to taste in a non-metallic dish that is large enough to hold the lamb.

3 Place the lamb in the dish and turn it over a few times so that the meat is coated on both sides with the marinade. Leave to marinate for at least 6 hours or preferably overnight, turning occasionally.

4 Remove the lamb from the marinade and reserve the liquid for basting.

5 Place the rack about 15 cm/6 inches above the coals and barbecue (grill) the lamb for about 30 minutes on each side, turning once and basting frequently with the marinade.

6 Transfer the lamb to a chopping board and remove the skewers. Cut the lamb into slices across the grain and serve.

COOK'S TIP

If you prefer, cook the lamb for half the cooking time in a preheated oven at 180°C/350°F/ Gas Mark 4, then finish off on the barbecue (grill).

Saltimbocca

The Italian name for this dish, *saltimbocca*, means 'jump into the mouth'. The stuffed rolls are quick and easy to make and taste delicious.

NUTRITIONAL INFORMATION

Calories .... .303 Sugars 0.3g
Protein ....29g   Fat 17g
Carbohydrate ....1g   Saturates 1g

15 MINS   20 MINS

SERVES 4

INGREDIENTS

4 turkey fillets or 4 veal escalopes, about
　450 g/1 lb in total

100 g/3½ oz Parma ham (prosciutto)

8 sage leaves

1 tbsp olive oil

1 onion, finely chopped

200 ml/7 fl oz/¾ cup white wine

200 ml/7 fl oz/¾ cup chicken stock

1 Place the turkey or veal between sheets of greaseproof paper. Pound the meat with a meat mallet or the end of a rolling pin to flatten it slightly. Cut each escalope in half.

2 Trim the Parma ham (prosciutto) to fit each piece of turkey or veal and place over the meat. Lay a sage leaf on top. Roll up the escalopes and secure with a cocktail stick (toothpick).

3 Heat the oil in a frying pan (skillet) and cook the onion for 3–4 minutes.

Add the turkey or veal rolls to the pan and cook for 5 minutes until browned all over.

4 Pour the white wine and chicken stock into the pan and leave to simmer for 15 minutes if using turkey, and 20 minutes if using veal, or until tender. Serve immediately.

VARIATION

Try a similar recipe called *bocconcini*, meaning 'little mouthfuls'. Follow the same method as given here, but replace the sage leaf with a piece of Gruyère cheese.

Veal in a Rose Petal Sauce

This truly spectacular dish is equally delicious whether you use veal or pork fillet. Make sure the roses are free of blemishes and pesticides.

NUTRITIONAL INFORMATION

Calories 810   Sugars 2g
Protein . . . . .31g   Fat 56g
Carbohydrate . . .49g   Saturates 28g

🥗 10 MINS   🕐 35 MINS

SERVES 4

INGREDIENTS

450 g/1 lb dried fettuccine

7 tbsp olive oil

1 tsp chopped fresh oregano

1 tsp chopped fresh marjoram

175 g/6 oz/¾ cup butter

450 g/1 lb veal fillet, thinly sliced

150 ml/¼ pint/⅔ cup rose petal vinegar

   (see Cook's Tip)

150 ml/¼ pint/⅔ cup fish stock

50 ml/2 fl oz/¼ cup grapefruit juice

50 ml/2 fl oz/¼ cup double

   (heavy) cream

salt

TO GARNISH

12 pink grapefruit segments

12 pink peppercorns

rose petals

fresh herb leaves

1 Bring a large saucepan of lightly salted water to the boil. Add the fettuccine and 1 tablespoon of the oil and cook for 8–10 minutes or until tender, but still firm to the bite. Drain and transfer to a warm serving dish, sprinkle over 2 tablespoons of the olive oil, the oregano and marjoram.

2 Heat 50 g/2 oz/4 tbsp of the butter with the remaining oil in a large frying pan (skillet). Add the veal and cook over a low heat for 6 minutes. Remove the veal from the pan and place on top of the pasta.

3 Add the vinegar and fish stock to the pan and bring to the boil. Boil vigorously until reduced by two thirds. Add the grapefruit juice and cream and simmer over a low heat for 4 minutes. Dice the remaining butter and add to the pan, one piece at a time, whisking constantly until it has been completely incorporated.

4 Pour the sauce around the veal, garnish with grapefruit segments, pink peppercorns, the rose petals (washed) and your favourite herb leaves.

COOK'S TIP

To make rose petal vinegar, infuse the petals of 8 pesticide-free roses in 150 ml/¼ pint/⅔ cup white wine vinegar for 48 hours. Prepare well in advance to reduce the preparation time.

Vitello Tonnato

Veal dishes are the speciality of Lombardy, with this dish being one of the more sophisticated. Serve cold with seasonal salads.

NUTRITIONAL INFORMATION

Calories ....654 Sugars 1g
Protein ....49g Fat 47g
Carbohydrate ....1g Saturates 8g

30 MINS   1¼ HOURS

SERVES 4

INGREDIENTS

750 g/1 lb 10 oz boned leg of veal, rolled

2 bay leaves

10 black peppercorns

2–3 cloves

½ tsp salt

2 carrots, sliced

1 onion, sliced

2 celery stalks, sliced

about 700 ml/1¼ pints/3 cups stock
   or water

150 ml/¼ pint/⅔ cup dry white wine
   (optional)

90 g/3 oz canned tuna fish, well drained

50 g/1½ oz can anchovy fillets, drained

150 ml/¼ pint/⅔ cup olive oil

2 tsp bottled capers, drained

2 egg yolks

1 tbsp lemon juice

salt and pepper

TO GARNISH

capers

lemon wedges

fresh herbs

1 Put the veal in a saucepan with the bay leaves, peppercorns, cloves, salt and vegetables. Add sufficient stock or water and the wine (if using) to barely cover the veal. Bring to the boil, remove any scum from the surface, then cover the pan and simmer gently for about 1 hour or until tender. Leave in the water until cold, then drain thoroughly. If time allows, chill the veal to make it easier to carve.

2 For the tuna sauce: thoroughly mash the tuna with 4 anchovy fillets, 1 tablespoon of oil and the capers. Add the egg yolks and press through a sieve (strainer) or purée in a food processor or liquidizer until smooth.

3 Stir in the lemon juice then gradually whisk in the rest of the oil a few drops at a time until the sauce is smooth and has the consistency of thick cream. Season with salt and pepper to taste.

4 Slice the veal thinly and arrange on a platter in overlapping slices. Spoon the sauce over the veal to cover. Then cover the dish and chill overnight.

5 Before serving, uncover the veal carefully. Arrange the remaining anchovy fillets and the capers in a decorative pattern on top, and then garnish with lemon wedges and sprigs of fresh herbs.

Neapolitan Veal Cutlets

The delicious combination of apple, onion and mushroom perfectly complements the delicate flavour of veal.

NUTRITIONAL INFORMATION

Calories	1071	Sugars	........13g
Protein	........74g	Fat	..........59g
Carbohydrate	...66g	Saturates	......16g

20 MINS   45 MINS

SERVES 4

I N G R E D I E N T S

200 g/7 oz/⅞ cup butter

4 x 250 g/9 oz veal cutlets, trimmed

1 large onion, sliced

2 apples, peeled, cored and sliced

175 g/6 oz button mushrooms

1 tbsp chopped fresh tarragon

8 black peppercorns

1 tbsp sesame seeds

400 g/14 oz dried marille

100 ml/3½ fl oz/scant ½ cup extra virgin
olive oil

175 g/6 oz/¾ cup mascarpone cheese,
broken into small pieces

2 large beef tomatoes, cut in half

leaves of 1 fresh basil sprig

salt and pepper

fresh basil leaves, to garnish

1 Melt 60 g/2 oz/4 tbsp of the butter in a frying pan (skillet). Fry the veal over a low heat for 5 minutes on each side. Transfer to a dish and keep warm.

2 Fry the onion and apples in the pan until lightly browned. Transfer to a dish, place the veal on top and keep warm.

3 Melt the remaining butter in the frying pan (skillet). Gently fry the mushrooms, tarragon and peppercorns over a low heat for 3 minutes. Sprinkle over the sesame seeds.

4 Bring a pan of salted water to the boil. Add the pasta and 1 tbsp of oil. Cook for 8–10 minutes or until tender, but still firm to the bite. Drain; transfer to a plate.

5 Grill (broil) or fry the tomatoes and basil for 2–3 minutes.

6 Top the pasta with the mascarpone cheese and sprinkle over the remaining olive oil. Place the onions, apples and veal cutlets on top of the pasta. Spoon the mushrooms, peppercorns and pan juices on to the cutlets, place the tomatoes and basil leaves around the edge and place in a preheated oven at 150°C/300°F/Gas Mark 2 for 5 minutes.

7 Season to taste with salt and pepper, garnish with fresh basil leaves and serve immediately.

Veal Italienne

This dish is really superb if made with tender veal. However, if veal is unavailable, use pork or turkey escalopes instead.

NUTRITIONAL INFORMATION

Calories 592   Sugars 5g
Protein ....44g   Fat 23g
Carbohydrate ...48g   Saturates 9g

 25 MINS   🕐 1 HR 20 MINS

SERVES 4

INGREDIENTS

60 g/2 oz/¼ cup butter

1 tbsp olive oil

675 g/1½ lb potatoes, cubed

4 veal escalopes, weighing 175 g/6 oz each

1 onion, cut into 8 wedges

2 garlic cloves, crushed

2 tbsp plain (all-purpose) flour

2 tbsp tomato purée (paste)

150 ml/¼ pint/⅔ cup red wine

300 ml/½ pint/1¼ cups chicken stock

8 ripe tomatoes, peeled, seeded and diced

25 g/1 oz stoned (pitted) black olives, halved

2 tbsp chopped fresh basil

salt and pepper

fresh basil leaves, to garnish

1 Heat the butter and oil in a large frying pan (skillet). Add the potato cubes and cook for 5-7 minutes, stirring frequently, until they begin to brown.

2 Remove the potatoes from the pan (skillet) with a perforated spoon and set aside.

3 Place the veal in the frying pan (skillet) and cook for 2-3 minutes on each side until sealed. Remove from the pan and set aside.

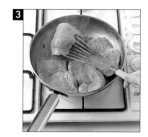

4 Stir the onion and garlic into the pan (skillet) and cook for 2-3 minutes.

5 Add the flour and tomato purée (paste) and cook for 1 minute, stirring. Gradually blend in the red wine and chicken stock, stirring to make a smooth sauce.

6 Return the potatoes and veal to the pan (skillet). Stir in the tomatoes, olives and chopped basil and season with salt and pepper.

7 Transfer to a casserole dish and cook in a preheated oven, 180°C/350°F/Gas Mark 4, for 1 hour or until the potatoes and veal are cooked through. Garnish with basil leaves and serve.

COOK'S TIP

For a quicker cooking time and really tender meat, pound the meat with a meat mallet to flatten it slightly before cooking.

Escalopes & Italian Sausage

Anchovies are often used to enhance flavour, particularly in meat dishes. Either veal or turkey escalopes can be used for this pan-fried dish.

NUTRITIONAL INFORMATION

Calories ....233 Sugars 1g
Protein ....28g Fat 13g
Carbohydrate ....1g Saturates 1g

10 MINS   20 MINS

SERVES 4

INGREDIENTS

1 tbsp olive oil

6 canned anchovy fillets, drained

1 tbsp capers, drained

1 tbsp fresh rosemary, stalks removed

finely grated rind and juice of 1 orange

75 g/2¾ oz Italian sausage, diced

3 tomatoes, skinned and chopped

4 turkey or veal escalopes, each about
    125 g/4½ oz

salt and pepper

crusty bread or cooked polenta, to serve

1 Heat the oil in a large frying pan (skillet). Add the anchovies, capers, fresh rosemary, orange rind and juice, Italian sausage and tomatoes to the pan and cook for 5–6 minutes, stirring occasionally.

2 Meanwhile, place the turkey or veal escalopes between sheets of greasproof paper. Pound the meat with a meat mallet or the end of a rolling pin to flatten it.

3 Add the meat to the mixture in the frying pan (skillet). Season to taste with salt and pepper, cover and cook for 3–5 minutes on each side, slightly longer if the meat is thicker.

4 Transfer to serving plates and serve with fresh crusty bread or cooked polenta, if you prefer.

VARIATION

Try using 4-minute steaks, slightly flattened, instead of the turkey or veal. Cook them for 4–5 minutes on top of the sauce in the pan.

Sausage & Bean Casserole

In this traditional Tuscan dish, Italian sausages are cooked with cannellini beans and tomatoes.

NUTRITIONAL INFORMATION

Calories	609	Sugars	.........7g
Protein	........27g	Fat	..........47g
Carbohydrate	...20g	Saturates	......16g

15 MINS   35 MINS

SERVES 4

INGREDIENTS

8 Italian sausages

1 tbsp olive oil

1 large onion, chopped

2 garlic cloves, chopped

1 green (bell) pepper

225g/8 oz fresh tomatoes, skinned and chopped or 400 g/14 oz can tomatoes, chopped

2 tbsp sun-dried tomato paste

400 g/14 oz can cannellini beans

mashed potato or rice, to serve

1 Using a sharp knife, deseed the (bell) pepper and cut it into thin strips.

2 Prick the Italian sausages all over with a fork. Cook the sausages, under a preheated grill (broiler), for 10–12 minutes, turning occasionally, until brown all over. Set aside and keep warm.

3 Heat the oil in a large frying pan (skillet). Add the onion, garlic and (bell) pepper to the frying pan (skillet) and cook for 5 minutes, stirring occasionally, or until softened.

4 Add the tomatoes to the frying pan (skillet) and leave the mixture to simmer for about 5 minutes, stirring occasionally, or until slightly reduced and thickened.

5 Stir the sun-dried tomato paste, cannellini beans and Italian sausages into the mixture in the frying pan (skillet). Cook for 4–5 minutes or until the mixture is piping hot. Add 4–5 tablespoons of water, if the mixture becomes too dry during cooking.

6 Transfer the Italian sausage and bean casserole to serving plates and serve with mashed potato or cooked rice.

COOK'S TIP

Italian sausages are coarse in texture and have quite a strong flavour. They can be bought in specialist sausage shops, Italian delicatessens and some larger supermarkets. They are replaceable in this recipe only by game sausages.

Liver with Wine Sauce

Liver is popular in Italy and is served in many ways. Tender calf's liver is the best type to use for this recipe, but you could use lamb's liver.

NUTRITIONAL INFORMATION

Calories 435   Sugars 2g
Protein . . . . .30g   Fat 31g
Carbohydrate . . . .4g   Saturates 12g

25 MINS   20 MINS

SERVES 4

INGREDIENTS

4 slices calf's liver or 8 slices lamb's liver, about 500 g/1 lb 2 oz

flour, for coating

1 tbsp olive oil

25 g/1 oz/2 tbsp butter

125 g/4½ oz lean bacon rashers, rinded and cut into narrow strips

1 garlic clove, crushed

1 onion, chopped

1 celery stick, sliced thinly

150 ml/¼ pint/⅔ cup red wine

150 ml/¼ pint/⅔ cup beef stock

good pinch of ground allspice

1 tsp Worcestershire sauce

1 tsp chopped fresh sage or ½ tsp dried sage

3–4 tomatoes, peeled, quartered and deseeded

salt and pepper

fresh sage leaves, to garnish

new potatoes or sauté potatoes, to serve

1 Wipe the liver with kitchen paper (paper towels), season with salt and pepper to taste and then coat lightly in flour, shaking off any excess.

2 Heat the oil and butter in a pan and fry the liver until well sealed on both sides and just cooked through – take care not to overcook. Remove the liver from the pan, cover and keep warm, but do not allow to dry out.

3 Add the bacon to the fat left in the pan, with the garlic, onion and celery. Fry gently until soft.

4 Add the red wine, beef stock, allspice, Worcestershire sauce, sage and salt and pepper to taste. Bring to the boil and simmer for 3–4 minutes.

5 Cut each tomato segment in half. Add to the sauce and continue to cook for 2–3 minutes.

6 Serve the liver on a little of the sauce, with the remainder spooned over. Garnish with fresh sage leaves and serve with tiny new potatoes or sauté potatoes.

Chicken & Poultry

Poultry dishes provide some of Italy's finest food. Every part of the chicken is used, including the feet and innards for making soup. Spit-roasted chicken, flavoured strongly with aromatic rosemary, has become almost a national dish. Turkey, capon, duck, goose and guinea fowl are also popular. This chapter contains a superb collection of mouthwatering recipes. You will be astonished at how quickly and easily you can prepare some of these gourmet dishes.

Italian-Style Sunday Roast

A mixture of cheese, rosemary and sun-dried tomatoes is stuffed under the chicken skin, then roasted with garlic, potatoes and vegetables.

NUTRITIONAL INFORMATION

Calories ....488 Sugars 6g
Protein ....37g Fat 23g
Carbohydrate ...34g Saturates 11g

 35 MINS   1½ HOURS

SERVES 6

INGREDIENTS

2.5 kg/5 lb 8 oz chicken

sprigs of fresh rosemary

175 g/6 oz/¾ cup feta cheese,
  coarsely grated

2 tbsp sun-dried tomato paste

60 g/2 oz/4 tbsp butter, softened

1 bulb garlic

1 kg/2 lb 4 oz new potatoes, halved if large

1 each red, green and yellow (bell) pepper,
  cut into chunks

3 courgettes (zucchini), sliced thinly

2 tbsp olive oil

2 tbsp plain (all-purpose) flour

600 ml/1 pint/2½ cups chicken stock

salt and pepper

1 Rinse the chicken inside and out with cold water and drain well. Carefully cut between the skin and the top of the breast meat using a small pointed knife. Slide a finger into the slit and carefully enlarge it to form a pocket. Continue until the skin is completely lifted away from both breasts and the top of the legs.

2 Chop the leaves from 3 rosemary stems. Mix with the feta cheese, sun-dried tomato paste, butter and pepper to taste, then spoon under the skin. Put the chicken in a large roasting tin (pan), cover with foil and cook in a preheated oven, 190°C/375°F/Gas Mark 5, for 20 minutes per 500 g/1 lb 2 oz, plus 20 minutes.

3 Break the garlic bulb into cloves but do not peel. Add the vegetables to the chicken after 40 minutes.

4 Drizzle with oil, tuck in a few stems of rosemary and season with salt and pepper. Cook for the remaining calculated time, removing the foil for the last 40 minutes to brown the chicken.

5 Transfer the chicken to a serving platter. Place some of the vegetables around the chicken and transfer the remainder to a warmed serving dish. Pour the fat out of the roasting tin (pan) and stir the flour into the remaining pan juices. Cook for 2 minutes then gradually stir in the stock. Bring to the boil, stirring until thickened. Strain into a sauce boat and serve with the chicken.

Garlic & Herb Chicken

There is a delicious surprise of creamy herb and garlic soft cheese hidden inside these chicken parcels!

NUTRITIONAL INFORMATION

Calories . . . . . . .272 Sugars 4g
Protein . . . . .29g Fat 13g
Carbohydrate . . . .4g Saturates 6g

20 MINS   25 MINS

SERVES 4

I N G R E D I E N T S

4 chicken breasts, skin removed

100 g/3½ oz full fat soft cheese, flavoured
    with herbs and garlic

8 slices Parma ham (prosciutto)

150 ml/¼ pint/⅔ cup red wine

150 ml/¼ pint/⅔ cup chicken stock

1 tbsp brown sugar

1 Using a sharp knife, make a horizontal slit along the length of each chicken breast to form a pocket.

2 Beat the cheese with a wooden spoon to soften it. Spoon the cheese into the pocket of the chicken breasts.

3 Wrap 2 slices of Parma ham (prosciutto) around each chicken breast and secure firmly in place with a length of string.

4 Pour the wine and chicken stock into a large frying pan (skillet) and bring to the boil. When the mixture is just starting to boil, add the sugar and stir well to dissolve.

5 Add the chicken breasts to the mixture in the frying pan (skillet). Leave to simmer for 12–15 minutes or until the chicken is tender and the juices

run clear when a skewer is inserted into the thickest part of the meat.

6 Remove the chicken from the pan, set aside and keep warm.

7 Reheat the sauce and boil until reduced and thickened. Remove the string from the chicken and cut into slices. Pour the sauce over the chicken to serve.

VARIATION
Try adding 2 finely chopped sun-dried tomatoes to the soft cheese in step 2, if you prefer.

Chicken & Seafood Parcels

These mouth-watering mini-parcels of chicken and prawns (shrimp) on a bed of pasta will delight your guests.

NUTRITIONAL INFORMATION

Calories 799	Sugars 5g	
Protein 50g	Fat 45g	
Carbohydrate . . .51g	Saturates 13g	

45 MINS   25 MINS

SERVES 4

INGREDIENTS

60 g/2 oz/4 tbsp butter, plus extra
for greasing

4 x 200 g/7 oz chicken suprêmes, trimmed

115 g/4 oz large spinach leaves, trimmed
and blanched in hot salted water

4 slices of Parma ham (prosciutto)

12–16 raw tiger prawns (shrimp), shelled
and deveined

450 g/1 lb dried tagliatelle

1 tbsp olive oil

3 leeks, shredded

1 large carrot, grated

150 ml/¼ pint/⅔ cup thick mayonnaise

2 large cooked beetroot (beet)

salt

1 Grease 4 large pieces of foil and set aside. Place each suprême between 2 pieces of baking parchment and pound with a rolling pin to flatten.

2 Divide half of the spinach between the suprêmes, add a slice of ham to each and top with more spinach. Place 3–4 prawns (shrimp) on top of the spinach. Fold the pointed end of the suprême over the prawns (shrimp), then fold over again to form a parcel. Wrap in

foil, place on a baking tray (cookie sheet) and bake in a preheated oven at 200°C/400°F/Gas Mark 6 for 20 minutes.

3 Meanwhile, bring a saucepan of salted water to the boil. Add the pasta and oil and cook for 8–10 minutes or until tender. Drain and transfer to a serving dish.

4 Melt the butter in a frying pan (skillet). Fry the leeks and carrots for 3 minutes. Transfer the vegetables to the centre of the pasta.

5 Work the mayonnaise and 1 beetroot (beet) in a food processor or blender until smooth. Rub through a strainer and pour around the pasta and vegetables.

6 Cut the remaining beetroot (beet) into diamond shapes and place them neatly around the mayonnaise. Remove the foil from the chicken and, using a sharp knife, cut the suprêmes into thin slices. Arrange the chicken and prawn (shrimp) slices on top of the vegetables and pasta, and serve.

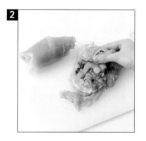

Chicken with Vegetables

This dish combines succulent chicken with tasty vegetables, flavoured with wine and olives.

NUTRITIONAL INFORMATION

Calories . . . . .470 Sugars 7g
Protein . . . . .29g Fat 34g
Carbohydrate . . . .7g Saturates 16g

20 MINS　　1½ HOURS

SERVES 4

INGREDIENTS

4 chicken breasts, part boned

25 g/1 oz/2 tbsp butter

2 tbsp olive oil

1 large onion, chopped finely

2 garlic cloves, crushed

2 (bell) peppers, red, yellow or green, cored, deseeded and cut into large pieces

225 g/8 oz large closed cup mushrooms, sliced or quartered

175 g/6 oz tomatoes, peeled and halved

150 ml/¼ pint/⅔ cup dry white wine

125–175 g/4–6 oz green olives, pitted

4–6 tbsp double (heavy) cream

salt and pepper

chopped flat-leaf parsley, to garnish

1 Season the chicken with salt and pepper to taste. Heat the oil and butter in a frying pan (skillet), add the chicken and fry until browned all over. Remove the chicken from the pan.

2 Add the onion and garlic to the frying pan (skillet) and fry gently until just beginning to soften. Add the (bell) peppers to the pan with the mushrooms and continue to cook for a few minutes longer, stirring occasionally.

3 Add the tomatoes and plenty of seasoning to the pan and then transfer the vegetable mixture to an ovenproof casserole. Place the chicken on the bed of vegetables.

4 Add the wine to the frying pan (skillet) and bring to the boil. Pour the wine over the chicken and cover the casserole tightly. Cook in a preheated oven, 180°C/350°F/Gas Mark 4, for 50 minutes.

5 Add the olives to the chicken, mix lightly then pour on the cream. Re-cover the casserole and return to the oven for 10–20 minutes or until the chicken is very tender.

6 Adjust the seasoning and serve the pieces of chicken, surrounded by the vegetables and sauce, with pasta or tiny new potatoes. Sprinkle with chopped parsley to garnish.

Rich Chicken Casserole

This casserole is packed with the sunshine flavours of Italy.
Sun-dried tomatoes add a wonderful richness.

NUTRITIONAL INFORMATION

Calories 320   Sugars 8g
Protein ....34g   Fat 17g
Carbohydrate ....8g   Saturates 4g

 15 MINS   1¼ HOURS

SERVES 4

INGREDIENTS

8 chicken thighs

2 tbsp olive oil

1 medium red onion, sliced

2 garlic cloves, crushed

1 large red (bell) pepper, sliced thickly

thinly pared rind and juice of 1 small orange

125 ml/4 fl oz/½ cup chicken stock

400 g/14 oz can chopped tomatoes

25 g/1 oz/½ cup sun-dried tomatoes,
   thinly sliced

1 tbsp chopped fresh thyme

50 g/1¾ oz/½ cup pitted black olives

salt and pepper

orange rind and thyme sprigs, to garnish

crusty fresh bread, to serve

1 In a heavy or non-stick large frying pan (skillet), fry the chicken without fat over a fairly high heat, turning occasionally until golden brown. Using a slotted spoon, drain off any excess fat from the chicken and transfer to a flameproof casserole.

2 Add the oil to the pan and fry the onion, garlic and (bell) pepper over a moderate heat for 3–4 minutes. Transfer the vegetables to the casserole.

3 Add the orange rind and juice, chicken stock, canned tomatoes and sun-dried tomatoes to the casserole and stir to combine.

4 Bring to the boil then cover the casserole with a lid and simmer very gently over a low heat for about 1 hour, stirring occasionally. Add the chopped fresh thyme and pitted black olives, then adjust the seasoning with salt and pepper to taste.

5 Scatter orange rind and thyme over the casserole to garnish, and serve with crusty bread.

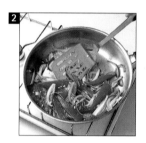

COOK'S TIP

Sun-dried tomatoes have a dense texture and concentrated taste, and add intense flavour to slow-cooking casseroles.

Chicken Tortellini

Tortellini were said to have been created in the image of the goddess Venus's navel. Whatever the story, they are a delicious blend of Italian flavours.

NUTRITIONAL INFORMATION

Calories ....635 Sugars 4g
Protein ....31g Fat 36g
Carbohydrate ...50g Saturates 16g

1 HOUR   35 MINS

SERVES 4

INGREDIENTS

115 g/4 oz boned chicken breast, skinned

60 g/2 oz Parma ham (prosciutto)

40 g/1½ oz cooked spinach, well drained

1 tbsp finely chopped onion

2 tbsp freshly grated Parmesan cheese

pinch of ground allspice

1 egg, beaten

450 g/1 lb basic pasta dough

salt and pepper

2 tbsp chopped fresh parsley, to garnish

SAUCE

300 ml/½ pint/1¼ cups single (light) cream

2 garlic cloves, crushed

115 g/4 oz button mushrooms, thinly sliced

4 tbsp freshly grated Parmesan cheese

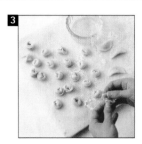

1 Bring a saucepan of seasoned water to the boil. Add the chicken and poach for about 10 minutes. Leave to cool slightly, then put in a food processor with the Parma ham (prosciutto), spinach and onion and process until finely chopped. Stir in the Parmesan cheese, allspice and egg and season with salt and pepper to taste.

2 Thinly roll out the pasta dough and cut into 4–5 cm/1½–2 inch rounds.

3 Place ½ tsp of the filling in the centre of each round. Fold the pieces in half and press the edges to seal. Then wrap each piece around your index finger, cross over the ends and curl the rest of the dough backwards to make a navel shape. Re-roll the trimmings and repeat until all of the dough is used up.

4 Bring a saucepan of salted water to the boil. Add the tortellini, in batches, bring back to the boil and cook for

5 minutes. Drain well and transfer to a serving dish.

5 To make the sauce, bring the cream and garlic to the boil in a small pan, then simmer for 3 minutes. Add the mushrooms and half of the cheese, season with salt and pepper to taste and simmer for 2–3 minutes. Pour the sauce over the chicken tortellini. Sprinkle over the remaining Parmesan cheese, garnish with the parsley and serve.

Pasta & Chicken Medley

Strips of cooked chicken are tossed with coloured pasta, grapes and carrot sticks in a pesto-flavoured dressing.

NUTRITIONAL INFORMATION

Calories 609   Sugars 11g
Protein . . . . .26g   Fat 38g
Carbohydrate . . .45g   Saturates 6g

30 MINS   10 MINS

SERVES 2

INGREDIENTS

125–150 g/4½–5½ oz dried pasta shapes, such as twists or bows

1 tbsp oil

2 tbsp mayonnaise

2 tsp bottled pesto sauce

1 tbsp soured cream or natural fromage frais

175 g/6 oz cooked skinless, boneless chicken meat

1–2 celery stalks

125 g/4½ oz/1 cup black grapes (preferably seedless)

1 large carrot, trimmed

salt and pepper

celery leaves, to garnish

FRENCH DRESSING

1 tbsp wine vinegar

3 tbsp extra-virgin olive oil

salt and pepper

1 To make the French dressing, whisk all the ingredients together until smooth.

2 Cook the pasta with the oil for 8–10 minutes in plenty of boiling salted water until just tender. Drain thoroughly, rinse and drain again. Transfer to a bowl and mix in 1 tablespoon of the French dressing while hot; set aside until cold.

3 Combine the mayonnaise, pesto sauce and soured cream or fromage frais in a bowl, and season to taste.

4 Cut the chicken into narrow strips. Cut the celery diagonally into narrow slices. Reserve a few grapes for garnish, halve the rest and remove any pips (seeds). Cut the carrot into narrow julienne strips.

5 Add the chicken, the celery, the halved grapes, the carrot and the mayonnaise mixture to the pasta, and toss thoroughly. Check the seasoning, adding more salt and pepper if necessary.

6 Arrange the pasta mixture on two plates and garnish with the reserved black grapes and the celery leaves.

Italian Chicken Parcels

This cooking method makes the chicken aromatic and succulent, and reduces the oil needed as the chicken and vegetables cook in their own juices.

NUTRITIONAL INFORMATION

Calories	234	Sugars	.........5g
Protein	........28g	Fat	..........12g
Carbohydrate	....5g	Saturates	.......5g

 25 MINS   30 MINS

SERVES 6

INGREDIENTS

1 tbsp olive oil

6 skinless chicken breast fillets

250 g/9 oz/2 cups Mozzarella cheese

500 g/1 lb 2 oz/3½ cups courgettes
(zucchini), sliced

6 large tomatoes, sliced

1 small bunch fresh basil or oregano

pepper

rice or pasta, to serve

1   Cut 6 pieces of foil, each measuring about 25 cm/10 inches square. Brush the foil squares lightly with oil and set aside until required.

2   With a sharp knife, slash each chicken breast at regular intervals. Slice the Mozzarella cheese and place between the cuts in the chicken.

COOK'S TIP

To aid cooking, place the vegetables and chicken on the shiny side of the foil so that once the parcel is wrapped up the dull surface of the foil is facing outwards. This ensures that the heat is absorbed into the parcel and not reflected away from it.

3   Divide the courgettes (zucchini) and tomatoes between the pieces of foil and sprinkle with pepper to taste. Tear or roughly chop the basil or oregano and scatter over the vegetables in each parcel.

4   Place the chicken on top of each pile of vegetables then wrap in the foil to enclose the chicken and vegetables, tucking in the ends.

5   Place on a baking tray (cookie sheet) and bake in a preheated oven, 200°C/400°C/Gas Mark 6, for about 30 minutes.

6   To serve, unwrap each foil parcel and serve with rice or pasta.

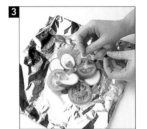

Pasta with Chicken Sauce

Spinach ribbon noodles, topped with a rich tomato sauce and creamy chicken, make a very appetizing dish.

NUTRITIONAL INFORMATION

Calories 995   Sugars 8g
Protein . . . . .36g   Fat 74g
Carbohydrate . . .50g   Saturates 34g

 15 MINS   45 MINS

SERVES 4

I N G R E D I E N T S

250 g/9 oz fresh green tagliatelle

1 tbsp olive oil

salt

fresh basil leaves, to garnish

T O M A T O   S A U C E

2 tbsp olive oil

1 small onion, chopped

1 garlic clove, chopped

400 g/14 oz can chopped tomatoes

2 tbsp chopped fresh parsley

1 tsp dried oregano

2 bay leaves

2 tbsp tomato purée (paste)

1 tsp sugar

salt and pepper

C H I C K E N   S A U C E

60 g/2 oz/4 tbsp unsalted butter

400 g/14 oz boned chicken breasts,
   skinned and cut into thin strips

90 g/3 oz/¾ cup blanched almonds

300 ml/½ pint/1¼ cups double
   (heavy) cream

salt and pepper

1 To make the tomato sauce, heat the oil in a pan over a medium heat. Add the onion and fry until translucent. Add the garlic and fry for 1 minute. Stir in the tomatoes, parsley, oregano, bay leaves, tomato purée (paste), sugar and salt and pepper to taste, bring to the boil and simmer, uncovered, for 15–20 minutes, until reduced by half. Remove the pan from the heat and discard the bay leaves.

2 To make the chicken sauce, melt the butter in a frying pan (skillet) over a medium heat. Add the chicken and almonds and stir-fry for 5–6 minutes, or until the chicken is cooked through.

3 Meanwhile, bring the cream to the boil in a small pan over a low heat and boil for about 10 minutes, until reduced by almost half. Pour the cream over the chicken and almonds, stir and season to taste with salt and pepper. Set aside and keep warm.

4 Bring a large pan of lightly salted water to the boil. Add the tagliatelle and olive oil and cook for 8–10 minutes until tender, but still firm to the bite. Drain and transfer to a warm serving dish. Spoon over the tomato sauce and arrange the chicken sauce down the centre. Garnish with the basil leaves and serve immediately.

Chicken & Lobster on Penne

While this is certainly a treat to get the taste buds tingling, it is not as extravagant as it sounds.

NUTRITIONAL INFORMATION

Calories 696   Sugars 4g
Protein . . . . .59g   Fat 32g
Carbohydrate . . .45g   Saturates 9g

20 MINS   30 MINS

SERVES 6

INGREDIENTS

butter, for greasing

6 chicken suprêmes

450 g/1 lb dried penne rigate

6 tbsp extra virgin olive oil

90 g/3 oz/1 cup freshly grated
   Parmesan cheese

salt

FILLING

115 g/4 oz lobster meat, chopped

2 shallots, very finely chopped

2 figs, chopped

1 tbsp Marsala

2 tbsp breadcrumbs

1 large egg, beaten

salt and pepper

  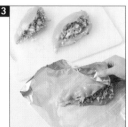

1 Grease 6 pieces of foil large enough to enclose each chicken suprême and lightly grease a baking tray (cookie sheet).

2 Place all of the filling ingredients into a mixing bowl and blend together thoroughly with a spoon.

3 Cut a pocket in each chicken suprême with a sharp knife and fill with the lobster mixture. Wrap each chicken suprême in foil, place the parcels on the greased baking tray (cookie sheet) and bake in a preheated oven at 200°C/400°F/Gas Mark 6 for 30 minutes.

4 Meanwhile, bring a large pan of lightly salted water to the boil. Add the pasta and 1 tablespoon of the olive oil and cook for about 10 minutes, or until tender but still firm to the bite. Drain the pasta thoroughly and transfer to a large serving plate. Sprinkle over the remaining olive oil and the grated Parmesan cheese, set aside and keep warm.

5 Carefully remove the foil from around the chicken suprêmes. Slice the suprêmes very thinly, arrange over the pasta and serve immediately.

COOK'S TIP

The cut of chicken known as suprême consists of the breast and wing. It is always skinned.

Roman Chicken

This classic Roman dish makes an ideal light meal. It is equally good cold and could be taken on a picnic – serve with bread to mop up the juices.

NUTRITIONAL INFORMATION

Calories 317   Sugars 8g
Protein . . . . .22g   Fat 22g
Carbohydrate . . . .9g   Saturates 4g

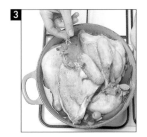

35 MINS   1 HOUR

SERVES 4

I N G R E D I E N T S

4 tbsp olive oil

6 chicken pieces

2 garlic cloves, crushed with 1 tsp salt

1 large red onion, sliced

4 large mixed red, green and yellow
  (bell) peppers, cored, deseeded and
  cut into strips

125 g/4½ oz/⅔ cup pitted green olives

½ quantity Tomato Sauce (see page 14)

300 ml/½ pint/1¼ cups hot chicken stock

2 sprigs fresh marjoram

salt and pepper

1 Heat half of the oil in a flameproof casserole and brown the chicken pieces on all sides. Remove the chicken and set aside.

2 Add the remaining oil to the casserole and fry the garlic and onion until softened. Stir in the (bell) peppers, olives and tomato sauce.

3 Return the chicken to the casserole with the stock and marjoram. Cover the casserole and simmer for about 45 minutes or until the chicken is tender. Season with salt and pepper to taste and serve with crusty bread.

Chicken Pepperonata

All the sunshine colours and flavours of Italy are combined in this easy dish.

NUTRITIONAL INFORMATION

Calories	328	Sugars	.........7g
Protein	........35g	Fat	..........15g
Carbohydrate	...13g	Saturates	.......4g

 15 MINS   40 MINS

SERVES 4

I N G R E D I E N T S

8 skinless chicken thighs

2 tbsp wholemeal (whole wheat) flour

2 tbsp olive oil

1 small onion, sliced thinly

1 garlic clove, crushed

1 each large red, yellow and green (bell)
   peppers, sliced thinly

400 g/14 oz can chopped tomatoes

1 tbsp chopped oregano

salt and pepper

fresh oregano, to garnish

crusty wholemeal (whole wheat) bread,
   to serve

1 Remove the skin from the chicken thighs and toss in the flour.

2 Heat the oil in a wide frying pan (skillet) and fry the chicken quickly until sealed and lightly browned, then remove from the pan.

3 Add the onion to the pan and gently fry until soft. Add the garlic, (bell) peppers, tomatoes and oregano, then bring to the boil, stirring.

4 Arrange the chicken over the vegetables, season well with salt and pepper, then cover the pan tightly and simmer for 20–25 minutes or until the chicken is completely cooked and tender.

5 Season with salt and pepper to taste, garnish with oregano and serve with crusty wholemeal (whole wheat) bread.

COOK'S TIP

For extra flavour, halve the (bell) peppers and grill (broil) under a preheated grill (broiler) until the skins are charred. Leave to cool then remove the skins and seeds. Slice the (bell) peppers thinly and use in the recipe.

Chicken with Orange Sauce

The refreshing combination of chicken and orange sauce makes this a perfect dish for a warm summer evening.

NUTRITIONAL INFORMATION

Calories 797   Sugars 28g
Protein . . . . .59g   Fat 25g
Carbohydrate . . .77g   Saturates 6g

 15 MINS   25 MINS

SERVES 4

I N G R E D I E N T S

30 ml/1 fl oz/⅛ cup rapeseed oil

3 tbsp olive oil

4 x 225 g/8 oz chicken suprêmes

150 ml/¼ pint/⅔ cup orange brandy

15 g/½ oz/2 tbsp plain (all-purpose) flour

150 ml/¼ pint/⅔ cup freshly squeezed
   orange juice

25 g/1 oz courgette (zucchini), cut into
   matchstick strips

25 g/1 oz red (bell) pepper, cut into
   matchstick strips

25 g/1 oz leek, finely shredded

400 g/14 oz dried wholemeal
   (whole-wheat) spaghetti

3 large oranges, peeled and cut into
   segments

rind of 1 orange, cut into very fine strips

2 tbsp chopped fresh tarragon

150 ml/¼ pint/⅔ cup fromage frais or
   ricotta cheese

salt and pepper

fresh tarragon leaves, to garnish

1 Heat the rapeseed oil and 1 tablespoon of the olive oil in a frying pan (skillet). Add the chicken and cook quickly until golden brown. Add the orange brandy and cook for 3 minutes. Sprinkle over the flour and cook for 2 minutes.

2 Lower the heat and add the orange juice, courgette (zucchini), (bell) pepper and leek and season. Simmer for 5 minutes until the sauce has thickened.

3 Meanwhile, bring a pan of salted water to the boil. Add the spaghetti and 1 tablespoon of the olive oil and cook for 10 minutes. Drain the spaghetti, transfer to a serving dish and drizzle over the remaining oil.

4 Add half of the orange segments, half of the orange rind, the tarragon and fromage frais or ricotta cheese to the sauce in the pan and cook for 3 minutes.

5 Place the chicken on top of the pasta, pour over a little sauce, garnish with orange segments, rind and tarragon. Serve immediately.

Skewered Chicken Spirals

These unusual chicken kebabs (kabobs) have a wonderful Italian flavour, and the bacon helps keep them moist during cooking.

NUTRITIONAL INFORMATION

Calories 231   Sugars 1g
Protein . . . . .29g   Fat 13g
Carbohydrate . . . .1g   Saturates 5g

 15 MINS   10 MINS

SERVES 4

INGREDIENTS

4 skinless, boneless chicken breasts

1 garlic clove, crushed

2 tbsp tomato purée (paste)

4 slices smoked back bacon

large handful of fresh basil leaves

oil for brushing

salt and pepper

1 Spread out a piece of chicken between two sheets of cling film (plastic wrap) and beat firmly with a rolling pin to flatten the chicken to an even thickness. Repeat with the remaining chicken breasts.

2 Mix the garlic and tomato purée (paste) and spread over the chicken. Lay a bacon slice over each, then scatter with the basil. Season with salt and pepper.

3 Roll up each piece of chicken firmly, then cut into thick slices.

4 Thread the slices on to 4 skewers, making sure the skewer holds the chicken in a spiral shape.

5 Brush lightly with oil and cook on a preheated hot barbecue (grill) or grill (broiler) for about 10 minutes, turning once. Serve hot with a green salad.

Parma-Wrapped Chicken

Stuffed with ricotta, nutmeg and spinach, then wrapped with wafer thin slices of Parma ham (prosciutto) and gently cooked in white wine.

NUTRITIONAL INFORMATION

Calories	426	Sugars	.........4g
Protein	........44g	Fat	..........21g
Carbohydrate	....9g	Saturates	.......8g

🍲 30 MINS   🕐 45 MINS

SERVES 4

INGREDIENTS

125 g/4½ oz/½ cup frozen spinach, defrosted

125 g/4½ oz/½ cup ricotta cheese

pinch of grated nutmeg

4 skinless, boneless chicken breasts, each weighing 175 g/6 oz

4 Parma ham (prosciutto) slices

25 g/1 oz/2 tbsp butter

1 tbsp olive oil

12 small onions or shallots

125 g/4½ oz/1½ cups button mushrooms, sliced

1 tbsp plain (all-purpose) flour

150 ml/¼ pint/⅔ cup dry white or red wine

300 ml/½ pint/1¼ cups chicken stock

salt and pepper

1 Put the spinach into a sieve (strainer) and press out the water with a spoon. Mix with the ricotta and nutmeg and season with salt and pepper to taste.

2 Using a sharp knife, slit each chicken breast through the side and enlarge each cut to form a pocket. Fill with the spinach mixture, reshape the chicken breasts, wrap each breast tightly in a slice of ham and secure with cocktail sticks. Cover and chill in the refrigerator.

3 Heat the butter and oil in a frying pan (skillet) and brown the chicken breasts for 2 minutes on each side. Transfer the chicken to a large, shallow ovenproof dish and keep warm until required.

4 Fry the onions and mushrooms for 2–3 minutes until lightly browned. Stir in the plain (all-purpose) flour, then gradually add the wine and stock. Bring to the boil, stirring constantly. Season with salt and pepper and spoon the mixture around the chicken.

5 Cook the chicken uncovered in a preheated oven, 200°C/400°F/Gas Mark 6, for 20 minutes. Turn the breasts over and cook for a further 10 minutes. Remove the cocktail sticks and serve with the sauce, together with carrot purée and green beans, if wished.

Chicken Scallops

Served in scallop shells, this makes a stylish presentation for a starter or a light lunch.

NUTRITIONAL INFORMATION

Calories ....532 Sugars 3g
Protein ....25g Fat 34g
Carbohydrate ...33g Saturates 14g

20 MINS   25 MINS

SERVES 4

INGREDIENTS

175 g/6 oz short-cut macaroni, or other
   short pasta shapes

3 tbsp vegetable oil, plus extra for brushing

1 onion, chopped finely

3 rashers unsmoked collar or back bacon,
   rind removed, chopped

125 g/4½ oz button mushrooms, sliced
   thinly or chopped

175 g/6 oz/¾ cup cooked chicken, diced

175 ml/6 fl oz/¾ cup crème fraîche

4 tbsp dry breadcrumbs

60 g/2 oz/½ cup mature (sharp) Cheddar,
   grated

salt and pepper

flat-leaf parsley sprigs, to garnish

1 Cook the pasta in a large pan of boiling salted water, to which you have added 1 tablespoon of the oil, for 8–10 minutes or until tender. Drain the pasta, return to the pan and cover.

2 Heat the grill (broiler) to medium. Heat the remaining oil in a pan over medium heat and fry the onion until it is translucent. Add the chopped bacon and mushrooms and cook for 3–4 minutes, stirring once or twice.

3 Stir in the pasta, chicken and crème fraîche and season to taste with salt and pepper.

4 Brush four large scallop shells with oil. Spoon in the chicken mixture and smooth to make neat mounds.

5 Mix together the breadcrumbs and cheese, and sprinkle over the top of the shells. Press the topping lightly into the chicken mixture, and grill (broil) for 4–5 minutes, until golden brown and bubbling. Garnish with sprigs of flat-leaf parsley, and serve hot.

Chicken & Balsamic Vinegar

A rich caramelized sauce, flavoured with balsamic vinegar and wine, adds a piquant flavour. The chicken needs to be marinated overnight.

NUTRITIONAL INFORMATION

Calories	148	Sugars	.......0.2g
Protein	........11g	Fat	...........8g
Carbohydrate	...0.2g	Saturates	.......3g

🥔 10 MINS 🕐 35 MINS

SERVES 4

I N G R E D I E N T S

4 chicken thighs, boned

2 garlic cloves, crushed

200 ml/7 fl oz/¾ cup red wine

3 tbsp white wine vinegar

1 tbsp oil

15 g/½ oz/1 tbsp butter

6 shallots

3 tbsp balsamic vinegar

2 tbsp fresh thyme

salt and pepper

cooked polenta or rice, to serve

1 Using a sharp knife, make a few slashes in the skin of the chicken. Brush the chicken with the crushed garlic and place in a non-metallic dish.

2 Pour the wine and white wine vinegar over the chicken and season with salt and pepper to taste. Cover and leave to marinate in the refrigerator overnight.

3 Remove the chicken pieces with a perforated spoon, draining well, and reserve the marinade.

4 Heat the oil and butter in a frying pan (skillet). Add the shallots and cook for 2–3 minutes or until they begin to soften.

5 Add the chicken pieces to the pan and cook for 3-4 minutes, turning, until browned all over. Reduce the heat and add half of the reserved marinade. Cover and cook for 15–20 minutes, adding more marinade when necessary.

6 Once the chicken is tender, add the balsamic vinegar and thyme and cook for a further 4 minutes.

7 Transfer the chicken and marinade to serving plates and serve with polenta or rice.

COOK'S TIP

To make the chicken pieces look a little neater, use wooden skewers to hold them together or secure them with a length of string.

Chicken with Green Olives

Olives are a popular flavouring for poultry and game in the Apulia region of Italy, where this recipe originates.

NUTRITIONAL INFORMATION

Calories 614   Sugars 6g
Protein . . . . .34g   Fat 30g
Carbohydrate . . .49g   Saturates 11g

15 MINS   1½ HOURS

SERVES 4

INGREDIENTS

3 tbsp olive oil

25 g/1 oz/2 tbsp butter

4 chicken breasts, part boned

1 large onion, finely chopped

2 garlic cloves, crushed

2 red, yellow or green (bell) peppers, cored, seeded and cut into large pieces

250 g/9 oz button mushrooms, sliced or quartered

175 g/6 oz tomatoes, skinned and halved

150 ml/¼ pint/⅔ cup dry white wine

175 g/6 oz/1½ cups stoned (pitted) green olives

4–6 tbsp double (heavy) cream

400 g/14 oz dried pasta

salt and pepper

chopped flat leaf parsley, to garnish

1 Heat 2 tbsp of the oil and the butter in a frying pan (skillet). Add the chicken breasts and fry until golden brown all over. Remove the chicken from the pan.

2 Add the onion and garlic to the pan and fry over a medium heat until beginning to soften. Add the (bell) peppers and mushrooms and cook for 2–3 minutes.

3 Add the tomatoes and season to taste with salt and pepper. Transfer the vegetables to a casserole and arrange the chicken on top.

4 Add the wine to the pan and bring to the boil. Pour the wine over the chicken. Cover and cook in a preheated oven at 180°C/350°F/Gas Mark 4 for 50 minutes.

5 Add the olives to the casserole and mix in. Pour in the cream, cover and return to the oven for 10–20 minutes.

6 Meanwhile, bring a large pan of lightly salted water to the boil. Add the pasta and the remaining oil and cook for 8–10 minutes or until tender, but still firm to the bite. Drain the pasta well and transfer to a serving dish.

7 Arrange the chicken on top of the pasta, spoon over the sauce, garnish with the parsley and serve immediately. Alternatively, place the pasta in a large serving bowl and serve separately.

Chicken Lasagne

You can use your favourite mushrooms, such as chanterelles or oyster mushrooms, for this delicately flavoured dish.

NUTRITIONAL INFORMATION

Calories 708   Sugars 17g
Protein . . . . .35g   Fat 35g
Carbohydrate . . .57g   Saturates 14g

 40 MINS   1¾ HOURS

SERVES 4

INGREDIENTS

butter, for greasing

14 sheets pre-cooked lasagne

850 ml/1½ pints/3¾ cups Béchamel Sauce
   (see page 14)

75 g/3 oz/1 cup grated Parmesan cheese

WILD MUSHROOM SAUCE

2 tbsp olive oil

2 garlic cloves, crushed

1 large onion, finely chopped

225 g/8 oz wild mushrooms, sliced

300 g/10½ oz/2½ cups minced
   (ground) chicken

80 g/3 oz chicken livers, finely chopped

115 g/4 oz Parma ham (prosciutto), diced

150 ml/¼ pint/⅔ cup Marsala

285g/10 oz can chopped tomatoes

1 tbsp chopped fresh basil leaves

2 tbsp tomato purée (paste)

salt and pepper

1 To make the chicken and wild mushroom sauce, heat the olive oil in a large saucepan. Add the garlic, onion and mushrooms and cook, stirring frequently, for 6 minutes.

2 Add the minced (ground) chicken, chicken livers and Parma ham (prosciutto) and cook over a low heat for 12 minutes, or until the meat has browned.

3 Stir the Marsala, tomatoes, basil and tomato purée (paste) into the mixture in the pan and cook for 4 minutes. Season with salt and pepper to taste, cover and leave to simmer for 30 minutes. Uncover the pan, stir and leave to simmer for a further 15 minutes.

4 Lightly grease an ovenproof dish with butter. Arrange sheets of lasagne over the base of the dish, spoon over a layer of wild mushroom sauce, then spoon over a layer of Béchamel Sauce. Place another layer of lasagne on top and repeat the process twice, finishing with a layer of Béchamel Sauce. Sprinkle over the grated cheese and bake in a preheated oven at 190°C/375°F/Gas Mark 5 for 35 minutes until golden brown and bubbling. Serve immediately.

Grilled (Broiled) Chicken

This Italian-style dish is richly flavoured with pesto, which is a mixture of basil, olive oil, pine nuts and Parmesan cheese.

NUTRITIONAL INFORMATION

Calories	787	Sugars	.........6g
Protein	........45g	Fat	..........38g
Carbohydrate	...70g	Saturates	.......9g

🍲 10 MINS   🕐 25 MINS

SERVES 4

INGREDIENTS

8 part-boned chicken thighs

olive oil, for brushing

400 ml/14 fl oz/1⅔ cups passata
  (sieved tomatoes)

125 ml/4 fl oz/½ cup green or
  red pesto sauce

12 slices French bread

90 g/3 oz/1 cup freshly grated
  Parmesan cheese

60 g/2 oz/½ cup pine nuts or flaked
  (slivered) almonds

salad leaves, to serve

1 Arrange the chicken in a single layer in a wide flameproof dish and brush lightly with oil. Place under a preheated grill (broiler) for about 15 minutes, turning occasionally, until golden brown.

COOK'S TIP

Although leaving the skin on the chicken means that it will have a higher fat content, many people like the rich taste and crispy skin especially when it is blackened by the barbecue (grill). The skin also keeps in the cooking juices.

2 Pierce the chicken with a skewer to test if it is cooked through – the juices will run clear, not pink, when it is ready.

3 Pour off any excess fat. Warm the passata (sieved tomatoes) and half the pesto sauce in a small pan and pour over the chicken. Grill (broil) for a few more minutes, turning until coated.

4 Meanwhile, spread the remaining pesto on to the slices of bread. Arrange the bread over the chicken and sprinkle with the Parmesan cheese. Scatter the pine nuts over the cheese. Grill (broil) for 2–3 minutes, or until browned and bubbling. Serve with salad leaves.

Barbecued (Grilled) Chicken

You need a bit of brute force to prepare the chicken, but once marinated it's an easy and tasty candidate for the barbecue (grill).

NUTRITIONAL INFORMATION

Calories . . . . . . .129 Sugars 0g

Protein . . . . .22g Fat 5g

Carbohydrate . . . .0g Saturates 1g

2½ HOURS 30 MINS

SERVES 4

INGREDIENTS

1.5 kg/3 lb 5 oz chicken

grated rind of 1 lemon

4 tbsp lemon juice

2 sprigs rosemary

1 small red chilli, chopped finely

150 ml/¼ pint/⅔ cup olive oil

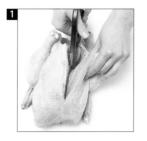
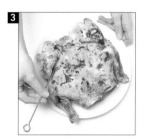

1 Split the chicken down the breast bone and open it out. Trim off excess fat, and remove the parson's nose, wing and leg tips. Break the leg and wing joints to enable you to pound it flat. This ensures that it cooks evenly. Cover the split chicken with clingfilm (plastic wrap) and pound it as flat as possible with a rolling pin.

2 Mix the lemon rind and juice, rosemary sprigs, chilli and olive oil together in a small bowl. Place the chicken in a large dish and pour over the marinade, turning the chicken to coat it evenly. Cover the dish and leave the chicken to marinate for at least 2 hours.

3 Cook the chicken over a hot barbecue (the coals should be white, and red when fanned) for about 30 minutes, turning it regularly until the skin is golden and crisp. To test if it is cooked, pierce one of the chicken thighs; the juices will run clear, not pink, when it is ready. Serve.

Chicken Cacciatora

This is a popular Italian classic in which browned chicken quarters are cooked in a tomato and (bell) pepper sauce.

NUTRITIONAL INFORMATION

Calories ....397 Sugars 4g
Protein ....37g Fat 17g
Carbohydrate ...22g Saturates 4g

20 MINS   1 HOUR

SERVES 4

I N G R E D I E N T S

1 roasting chicken, about 1.5 kg/ 3 lb 5 oz,
  cut into 6 or 8 serving pieces

125 g/4½ oz/1 cup plain (all-purpose) flour

3 tbsp olive oil

150 ml/¼ pint/⅔ cup dry white wine

1 green (bell) pepper, deseeded and sliced

1 red (bell) pepper, deseeded and sliced

1 carrot, chopped finely

1 celery stalk, chopped finely

1 garlic clove, crushed

200 g/7 oz can of chopped tomatoes

salt and pepper

1 Rinse and pat dry the chicken pieces with paper towels. Lightly dust them with seasoned flour.

2 Heat the oil in a large frying pan (skillet). Add the chicken and fry over a medium heat until browned all over. Remove from the pan and set aside.

3 Drain off all but 2 tablespoons of the fat in the pan. Add the wine and stir for a few minutes. Then add the (bell) peppers, carrots, celery and garlic, season with salt and pepper to taste and simmer together for about 15 minutes.

4 Add the chopped tomatoes to the pan. Cover and simmer for 30 minutes, stirring often, until the chicken is completely cooked through.

5 Check the seasoning before serving piping hot.

Boned Chicken & Parmesan

It's really very easy to bone a whole chicken, but if you prefer, you can ask your butcher to do this for you.

🍲 35 MINS   🕐 1½ HOURS

SERVES 6

I N G R E D I E N T S

1 chicken, weighing about 2.25 kg/5 lb

8 slices Mortadella or salami

125 g/4½ oz/2 cups fresh white or
  brown breadcrumbs

125 g/4½ oz/1 cup freshly grated
  Parmesan cheese

2 garlic cloves, crushed

6 tbsp chopped fresh basil or parsley

1 egg, beaten

pepper

fresh spring vegetables, to serve

1 Bone the chicken, keeping the skin intact. Dislocate each leg by breaking it at the thigh joint. Cut down each side of the backbone, taking care not to pierce the breast skin.

2 Pull the backbone clear of the flesh and discard. Remove the ribs, severing any attached flesh with a sharp knife.

3 Scrape the flesh from each leg and cut away the bone at the joint with a knife or shears.

4 Use the bones for stock. Lay out the boned chicken on a board, skin side down. Arrange the Mortadella slices over the chicken, overlapping slightly.

5 Put the breadcrumbs, Parmesan, garlic and basil or parsley in a bowl. Season with pepper to taste and mix together well. Stir in the beaten egg to bind the mixture together. Spoon the mixture down the middle of the boned chicken, roll the meat around it and then tie securely with string.

6 Place in a roasting dish and brush lightly with olive oil. Roast in a preheated oven, 200°C/400°F/Gas Mark 6, for 1½ hours or until the juices run clear when pierced.

7 Serve hot or cold, in slices, with fresh spring vegetables.

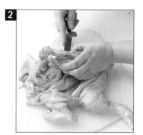

VARIATION

Replace the Mortadella with rashers of streaky bacon, if preferred.

Pan-Cooked Chicken

Artichokes are a familiar ingredient in Italian cookery. In this dish, they are used to delicately flavour chicken.

NUTRITIONAL INFORMATION

Calories	296	Sugars	.........2g
Protein	........27g	Fat	..........15g
Carbohydrate	....7g	Saturates	.......6g

15 MINS   55 MINS

SERVES 4

I N G R E D I E N T S

4 chicken breasts, part boned

25 g/1 oz/2 tbsp butter

2 tbsp olive oil

2 red onions, cut into wedges

2 tbsp lemon juice

150 ml/¼ pt/⅔ cup dry white wine

150 ml/¼ pt/⅔ cup chicken stock

2 tsp plain (all-purpose) flour

400 g/14 oz can artichoke halves,
    drained and halved

salt and pepper

chopped fresh parsley, to garnish

1 Season the chicken with salt and pepper to taste. Heat the oil and 15 g/ ½ oz/1 tablespoon of the butter in a large frying pan (skillet). Add the chicken and fry for 4–5 minutes on each side until lightly golden. Remove from the pan using a slotted spoon.

2 Toss the onion in the lemon juice, and add to the frying pan (skillet). Gently fry, stirring, for 3–4 minutes until just beginning to soften.

3 Return the chicken to the pan. Pour in the wine and stock, bring to the boil, cover and simmer gently for 30 minutes.

4 Remove the chicken from the pan, reserving the cooking juices, and keep warm. Bring the juices to the boil, and boil rapidly for 5 minutes.

5 Blend the remaining butter with the flour to form a paste. Reduce the juices to a simmer and spoon the paste into the frying pan (skillet), stirring until thickened.

6 Adjust the seasoning according to taste, stir in the artichoke hearts and cook for a further 2 minutes. Pour the mixture over the chicken and garnish with chopped parsley.

Mustard-Baked Chicken

Chicken pieces are cooked in a succulent, mild mustard sauce, then coated in poppy seeds and served on a bed of fresh pasta shells.

NUTRITIONAL INFORMATION

Calories	652	Sugars	.........5g
Protein	........51g	Fat	..........31g
Carbohydrate	...46g	Saturates	......12g

10 MINS 35 MINS

SERVES 4

INGREDIENTS

8 chicken pieces (about 115 g/4 oz each)

60g/2 oz/4 tbsp butter, melted

4 tbsp mild mustard (see Cook's Tip)

2 tbsp lemon juice

1 tbsp brown sugar

1 tsp paprika

3 tbsp poppy seeds

400 g/14 oz fresh pasta shells

1 tbsp olive oil

salt and pepper

1 Arrange the chicken pieces in a single layer in a large ovenproof dish.

2 Mix together the butter, mustard, lemon juice, sugar and paprika in a bowl and season with salt and pepper to taste. Brush the mixture over the upper

COOK'S TIP

Dijon is the type of mustard most often used in cooking, as it has a clean and only mildly spicy flavour. German mustard has a sweet-sour taste, with Bavarian mustard being slightly sweeter. American mustard is mild and sweet.

surfaces of the chicken pieces and bake in a preheated oven at 200°C/400°F/Gas Mark 6 for 15 minutes.

3 Remove the dish from the oven and carefully turn over the chicken pieces. Coat the upper surfaces of the chicken with the remaining mustard mixture, sprinkle the chicken pieces with poppy seeds and return to the oven for a further 15 minutes.

4 Meanwhile, bring a large saucepan of lightly salted water to the boil. Add the pasta shells and olive oil and cook for 8-10 minutes or until tender, but still firm to the bite.

5 Drain the pasta thoroughly and arrange on a warmed serving dish. Top the pasta with the chicken, pour over the sauce and serve immediately.

Chicken Marengo

Napoleon's chef was ordered to cook a sumptuous meal on the eve of the battle of Marengo – this feast of flavours was the result.

NUTRITIONAL INFORMATION

Calories 521   Sugars 6g
Protein . . . . .47g   Fat 19g
Carbohydrate . . .34g   Saturates 8g

20 MINS   50 MINS

SERVES 4

INGREDIENTS

8 chicken pieces

2 tbsp olive oil

300 g/10½ oz passata (sieved tomatoes)

200 ml/7 fl oz/¾ cup white wine

2 tsp dried mixed herbs

40 g/1½ oz butter, melted

2 garlic cloves, crushed

8 slices white bread

100 g/3½ oz mixed mushrooms
   (such as button, oyster and ceps)

40 g/1½ oz black olives, chopped

1 tsp sugar

fresh basil, to garnish

1 Using a sharp knife, remove the bone from each of the chicken pieces.

2 Heat 1 tbsp of oil in a large frying pan (skillet). Add the chicken pieces and cook for about 4–5 minutes, turning occassionally, or until browned all over.

3 Add the passata (sieved tomatoes), wine and mixed herbs to the frying pan (skillet). Bring to the boil and then leave to simmer for 30 minutes or until the chicken is tender and the juices run clear when a skewer is inserted into the thickest part of the meat.

4 Mix the melted butter and crushed garlic together. Lightly toast the slices of bread and brush with the garlic butter.

5 Add the remaining oil to a separate frying pan (skillet) and cook the mushrooms for 2–3 minutes or until just browned.

6 Add the olives and sugar to the chicken mixture and warm through.

7 Transfer the chicken and sauce to serving plates. Serve with the bruschetta (fried bread) and fried mushrooms.

Italian Chicken Spirals

These little foil parcels retain all the natural juices of the chicken while cooking conveniently over the pasta while it boils.

NUTRITIONAL INFORMATION

Calories 367   Sugars 1g
Protein . . . . .33g   Fat 12g
Carbohydrate . . .35g   Saturates 2g

20 MINS   20 MINS

SERVES 4

INGREDIENTS

4 skinless, boneless chicken breasts

25 g/1 oz/1 cup fresh basil leaves

15 g/½ oz/2 tbsp hazelnuts

1 garlic clove, crushed

250 g/9 oz/2 cups wholemeal (whole
   wheat) pasta spirals

2 sun-dried tomatoes or fresh tomatoes

1 tbsp lemon juice

1 tbsp olive oil

1 tbsp capers

60 g/2 oz/½ cup black olives

1 Beat the chicken breasts with a rolling pin to flatten evenly.

2 Place the basil and hazelnuts in a food processor and process until finely chopped. Mix with the garlic and salt and pepper to taste.

3 Spread the basil mixture over the chicken breasts and roll up from one short end to enclose the filling. Wrap the chicken roll tightly in foil so that they hold their shape, then seal the ends well.

4 Bring a pan of lightly salted water to the boil and cook the pasta for 8–10 minutes or until tender, but still firm to the bite. Meanwhile, place the chicken parcels in a steamer or colander set over the pan, cover tightly, and steam for 10 minutes.

5 Using a sharp knife, dice the tomatoes.

6 Drain the pasta and return to the pan with the lemon juice, olive oil, tomatoes, capers and olives. Heat through.

7 Pierce the chicken with a skewer to make sure that the juices run clear and not pink (this shows that the chicken is cooked through),. Slice the chicken, arrange over the pasta and serve.

COOK'S TIP

Sun-dried tomatoes have a wonderful, rich flavour but if they're unavailable, use fresh tomatoes instead.

Slices of Duckling with Pasta

A raspberry and honey sauce superbly counterbalances the richness of the duckling.

NUTRITIONAL INFORMATION

Calories 686   Sugars 15g
Protein . . . . .62g   Fat 20g
Carbohydrate . . .70g   Saturates 7g

🕐 15 MINS   🕐 25 MINS

SERVES 4

INGREDIENTS

4 x 275 g/9 oz boned breasts of duckling

25 g/1 oz/2 tbsp butter

50 g/1¾ oz/⅜ cup finely chopped carrots

50 g/1¾ oz/4 tbsp finely chopped shallots

1 tbsp lemon juice

150 ml/¼ pint/⅔ cup meat stock

4 tbsp clear honey

115 g/4 oz/¾ cup fresh or thawed frozen
    raspberries

25 g/1 oz/¼ cup plain (all-purpose) flour

1 tbsp Worcestershire sauce

400 g/14 oz fresh linguine

1 tbsp olive oil

salt and pepper

TO GARNISH

fresh raspberries

fresh sprig of flat-leaf parsley

1 Trim and score the duck breasts with a sharp knife and season well all over. Melt the butter in a frying pan (skillet), add the duck breasts and fry all over until lightly coloured.

2 Add the carrots, shallots, lemon juice and half the meat stock and simmer over a low heat for 1 minute. Stir in half of the honey and half of the raspberries.

Sprinkle over half of the flour and cook, stirring constantly for 3 minutes. Season with pepper to taste and add the Worcestershire sauce.

3 Stir in the remaining stock and cook for 1 minute. Stir in the remaining honey and remaining raspberries and sprinkle over the remaining flour. Cook for a further 3 minutes.

4 Remove the duck breasts from the pan, but leave the sauce to continue simmering over a very low heat.

5 Meanwhile, bring a large saucepan of lightly salted water to the boil. Add the linguine and olive oil and cook for 8–10 minutes or until tender, but still firm to the bite. Drain and divide between 4 individual plates.

6 Slice the duck breast lengthways into 5 mm/¼ inch thick pieces. Pour a little sauce over the pasta and arrange the sliced duck in a fan shape on top of it. Garnish with raspberries and flat-leaf parsley and serve immediately.

Pheasant Lasagne

This scrumptious and unusual baked lasagne is virtually a meal in itself.
It is served with baby onions and green peas.

NUTRITIONAL INFORMATION

Calories 1038	Sugars 13g	
Protein 65g	Fat 64g	
Carbohydrate . . .54g	Saturates 27g	

🍲 40 MINS   🕒 1¼ HOURS

SERVES 4

INGREDIENTS

butter, for greasing

14 sheets pre-cooked lasagne

850 ml/1½ pints/3¾ cups Béchamel Sauce
(see page 14)

75 g/2¾ oz/ ¾ cup grated Mozzarella
cheese

FILLING

225 g/8 oz pork fat, diced

60 g/2 oz/2 tbsp butter

16 small onions

8 large pheasant breasts, thinly sliced

25 g/1 oz/ ¼ cup plain (all-purpose) flour

600 ml/1 pint/2½ cups chicken stock

bouquet garni

450 g/1 lb fresh peas, shelled

salt and pepper

1 To make the filling, put the pork fat into a saucepan of boiling, salted water and simmer for 3 minutes, then drain and pat dry.

2 Melt the butter in a large frying pan (skillet). Add the pork fat and onions to the pan and cook for about 3 minutes, or until lightly browned.

3 Remove the pork fat and onions from the pan and set aside. Add the slices of pheasant and cook over a low heat for 12 minutes, until browned all over. Transfer to an ovenproof dish.

4 Stir the flour into the pan and cook until just brown, then blend in the stock. Pour the mixture over the pheasant, add the bouquet garni and cook in a preheated oven, at 200°C/400°F/Gas Mark 6, for 5 minutes. Remove the bouquet garni. Add the onions, pork fat and peas and return to the oven for 10 minutes.

5 Put the pheasant and pork fat in a food processor and mince (grind) finely.

6 Lower the oven temperature to 190°C/ 375°F/Gas Mark 5. Grease an ovenproof dish with butter. Make layers of lasagne, pheasant sauce and Béchamel Sauce in the dish, ending with Béchamel Sauce. Sprinkle over the cheese and bake for 30 minutes.

Pesto Baked Partridge

Partridge has a more delicate flavour than many game birds and this subtle sauce complements it perfectly.

NUTRITIONAL INFORMATION

Calories ....895 Sugars 5g
Protein ....79g Fat 45g
Carbohydrate ...45g Saturates 18g

15 MINS   40 MINS

SERVES 4

INGREDIENTS

8 partridge pieces (about 115 g/4 oz each)

60 g/2 oz/4 tbsp butter, melted

4 tbsp Dijon mustard

2 tbsp lime juice

1 tbsp brown sugar

6 tbsp Pesto Sauce (shop bought)

450 g/1 lb dried rigatoni

1 tbsp olive oil

115 g/4 oz/1⅓ cups freshly grated
    Parmesan cheese

salt and pepper

1 Arrange the partridge pieces, smooth side down, in a single layer in a large, ovenproof dish.

2 Mix together the butter, Dijon mustard, lime juice and brown sugar in a bowl. Season to taste. Brush this mixture over the partridge pieces and bake in a preheated oven at 200°C/400°F/Gas Mark 6 for 15 minutes.

3 Remove the dish from the oven and coat the partridge pieces with 3 tbsp of the Pesto Sauce. Return to the oven and bake for a further 12 minutes.

4 Remove the dish from the oven and carefully turn over the partridge pieces. Coat the top of the partridges with the remaining mustard mixture and return to the oven for a further 10 minutes.

5 Meanwhile, bring a large pan of lightly salted water to the boil. Add the rigatoni and olive oil and cook for 8–10 minutes until tender, but still firm to the bite. Drain and transfer to a serving dish. Toss the pasta with the remaining Pesto Sauce and the Parmesan cheese.

6 Serve the partridge with the pasta, pouring over the cooking juices.

VARIATION

You could also prepare young pheasant in the same way.

Pasta

The simplicity and satisfying nature of pasta in all its varieties makes it a universal favourite. Easy to cook and economical, pasta is wonderfully versatile. It can be served with sauces made from meat, fish or vegetables, or baked in the oven. The classic Spaghetti Bolognese needs no introduction, and yet it is said that there are almost as

many versions of this delicious regional dish as there are lovers of Italian food! Fish and seafood are irresistible combined with pasta and need only the briefest of cooking times. Pasta combined with vegetables provides inspiration for countless dishes which will please vegetarians and meat-eaters alike. The delicious pasta dishes in this chapter range from easy, economic mid-week suppers to sophisticated and elegant meals for special occasions.

Spaghetti Bolognese

The original recipe takes about 4 hours to cook and should be left over night to allow the flavours to mingle. This version is much quicker.

NUTRITIONAL INFORMATION

Calories	.591	Sugars	.7g
Protein	.29g	Fat	.24g
Carbohydrate	.64g	Saturates	.9g

20 MINS   1 HR 5 MINS

SERVES 4

I N G R E D I E N T S

1 tbsp olive oil

1 onion, finely chopped

2 garlic cloves, chopped

1 carrot, scraped and chopped

1 stick celery, chopped

50 g/1¾ oz pancetta or streaky bacon, diced

350 g/12 oz lean minced beef

400 g/14 oz can chopped tomatoes

2 tsp dried oregano

125 ml/4 fl oz/scant ½ cup red wine

2 tbsp tomato purée (paste)

salt and pepper

675 g/1½ lb fresh spaghetti or 350 g/12 oz dried spaghetti

1 Heat the oil in a large frying pan (skillet). Add the onions and cook for 3 minutes.

2 Add the garlic, carrot, celery and pancetta or bacon and sauté for 3–4 minutes or until just beginning to brown.

3 Add the beef and cook over a high heat for another 3 minutes or until all of the meat is brown.

4 Stir in the tomatoes, oregano and red wine and bring to the boil. Reduce the heat and leave to simmer for about 45 minutes.

5 Stir in the tomato purée (paste) and season with salt and pepper.

6 Cook the spaghetti in a pan of boiling water for 8–10 minutes until tender, but still has 'bite'. Drain thoroughly.

7 Transfer the spaghetti to a serving plate and pour over the bolognese sauce. Toss to mix well and serve hot.

VARIATION

Try adding 25 g/1 oz dried porcini, soaked for 10 minutes in 2 tablespoons of warm water, to the bolognese sauce in step 4, if you wish.

Pasta Carbonara

Lightly cooked eggs and pancetta are combined with cheese to make this rich, classic sauce.

NUTRITIONAL INFORMATION

Calories	547	Sugars	.........1g
Protein	........21g	Fat	..........31g
Carbohydrate	...49g	Saturates	......14g

 15 MINS   20 MINS

SERVES 4

I N G R E D I E N T S

1 tbsp olive oil

40 g/1½ oz/3 tbsp butter

100 g/3½ oz pancetta or
    unsmoked bacon, diced

3 eggs, beaten

2 tbsp milk

1 tbsp thyme, stalks removed

675 g/1½ lb fresh or 350 g/12 oz dried
    conchigoni rigati

50 g/1¾ oz Parmesan cheese, grated

salt and pepper

1 Heat the oil and butter in a frying pan (skillet) until the mixture is just beginning to froth.

2 Add the pancetta or bacon to the pan and cook for 5 minutes or until browned all over.

3 Mix together the eggs and milk in a small bowl. Stir in the thyme and season to taste with salt and pepper.

4 Cook the pasta in a saucepan of boiling water for 8–10 minutes until tender, but still has 'bite'. Drain thoroughly.

5 Add the cooked, drained pasta to the frying pan (skillet) with the eggs and cook over a high heat for about 30 seconds or until the eggs just begin to cook and set. Do not overcook the eggs or they will become rubbery.

6 Add half of the grated Parmesan cheese, stirring to combine.

7 Transfer the pasta to a serving plate, pour over the sauce and toss to mix well.

8 Sprinkle the rest of the grated Parmesan over the top and serve immediately.

VARIATION

For an extra rich Carbonara sauce, stir in 4 tablespoons of double (heavy) cream with the eggs and milk in step 3. Follow exactly the same cooking method.

Three-Cheese Macaroni

Based on a traditional family favourite, this pasta bake has plenty of flavour. Serve with a crisp salad for a quick, tasty supper.

NUTRITIONAL INFORMATION

Calories 672	Sugars 10g
Protein 31g	Fat 44g
Carbohydrate ...40g	Saturates 23g

30 MINS   45 MINS

SERVES 4

I N G R E D I E N T S

600 ml/1 pint/2½ cups Béchamel Sauce
(see page 14)

225 g/8 oz/2 cups macaroni

1 egg, beaten

125 g/4½ oz/1 cup grated mature
(sharp) Cheddar

1 tbsp wholegrain mustard

2 tbsp chopped fresh chives

4 tomatoes, sliced

125 g/4½ oz/1 cup grated Red Leicester
(brick) cheese

60 g/2 oz/½ cup grated blue cheese

2 tbsp sunflower seeds

salt and pepper

snipped fresh chives, to garnish

1 Make the Béchamel Sauce, put into a bowl and cover with cling film (plastic wrap) to prevent a skin forming. Set aside.

2 Bring a saucepan of salted water to the boil and cook the macaroni for 8–10 minutes or until just tender. Drain well and place in an ovenproof dish.

3 Stir the beaten egg, Cheddar, mustard, chives and seasoning into the Béchamel Sauce and spoon over the macaroni, making sure it is well covered. Top with a layer of sliced tomatoes.

4 Sprinkle over the Red Leicester (brick) and blue cheeses, and sunflower seeds. Put on a baking tray (cookie sheet) and bake in a preheated oven, 190°C/375°F/Gas Mark 5, for 25–30 minutes or until bubbling and golden. Garnish with chives and serve immediately.

Italian Tomato Sauce & Pasta

Fresh tomatoes make a delicious Italian-style sauce which goes particularly well with pasta.

NUTRITIONAL INFORMATION

Calories	304	Sugars	.........8g
Protein	........15g	Fat	..........14g
Carbohydrate	...31g	Saturates	.......5g

 10 MINS   25 MINS

SERVES 2

I N G R E D I E N T S

1 tbsp olive oil

1 small onion, chopped finely

1–2 cloves garlic, crushed

350 g/12 oz tomatoes, peeled and chopped

2 tsp tomato purée (paste)

2 tbsp water

300–350 g/10½–12 oz dried pasta shapes

90 g/3 oz/¾ cup lean bacon,
    derinded and diced

40 g/1½ oz/½ cup mushrooms, sliced

1 tbsp chopped fresh parsley or 1 tsp
    chopped fresh coriander (cilantro)

2 tbsp soured cream or natural fromage
    frais (optional)

salt and pepper

COOK'S TIP

Sour cream contains
18–20% fat, so if you are
following a low fat diet you can leave
it out of this recipe or substitute a
low-fat alternative.

1 To make the tomato sauce, heat the oil in a saucepan and fry the onion and garlic gently until soft.

2 Add the tomatoes, tomato purée (paste), water and salt and pepper to taste to the mixture in the pan and bring to the boil. Cover and simmer gently for 10 minutes.

3 Meanwhile, cook the pasta in a saucepan of boiling salted water for 8–10 minutes, or until just tender. Drain the pasta thoroughly and transfer to warm serving dishes.

4 Heat the bacon gently in a frying pan (skillet) until the fat runs, then add the mushrooms and continue cooking for 3–4 minutes. Drain off any excess oil.

5 Add the bacon and mushrooms to the tomato mixture, together with the parsley or coriander (cilantro) and the soured cream or fromage frais, if using. Reheat and serve with the pasta.

Pasta with Green Vegetables

The different shapes and textures of the vegetables make a mouthwatering presentation in this light and summery dish.

NUTRITIONAL INFORMATION

Calories	517	Sugars	.........5g
Protein	........17g	Fat	..........32g
Carbohydrate	...42g	Saturates	......18g

  10 MINS 25 MINS

SERVES 4

I N G R E D I E N T S

225 g/8 oz gemelli or other pasta shapes

1 tbsp olive oil

2 tbsp chopped fresh parsley

2 tbsp freshly grated Parmesan

salt and pepper

S A U C E

1 head of green broccoli, cut into florets

2 courgettes (zucchini), sliced

225 g/8 oz asparagus spears, trimmed

125 g/4½ oz mangetout (snow peas), trimmed

125 g/4½ oz frozen peas

25 g/1 oz/2 tbsp butter

3 tbsp vegetable stock

5 tbsp double (heavy) cream

large pinch of freshly grated nutmeg

1 Cook the pasta in a large pan of salted boiling water, adding the olive oil, for 8–10 minutes or until tender. Drain the pasta in a colander, return to the pan, cover and keep warm.

2 Steam the broccoli, courgettes (zucchini), asparagus spears and mangetout (snow peas) over a pan of boiling, salted water until just beginning to soften. Remove from the heat and plunge into cold water to prevent further cooking. Drain and set aside.

3 Cook the peas in boiling, salted water for 3 minutes, then drain. Refresh in cold water and drain again.

4 Put the butter and vegetable stock in a pan over a medium heat. Add all of the vegetables except for the asparagus spears and toss carefully with a wooden spoon to heat through, taking care not to break them up. Stir in the cream, allow the sauce to heat through and season with salt, pepper and nutmeg.

5 Transfer the pasta to a warmed serving dish and stir in the chopped parsley. Spoon the sauce over, and sprinkle on the freshly grated Parmesan. Arrange the asparagus spears in a pattern on top. Serve hot.

Pasta & Vegetable Sauce

A Mediterranean mixture of red (bell) peppers, garlic and courgettes (zucchini) cooked in olive oil and tossed with pasta.

NUTRITIONAL INFORMATION

Calories 341   Sugars 8g
Protein . . . . .13g   Fat 20g
Carbohydrate . . .30g   Saturates 8g

15 MINS   20 MINS

SERVES 4

INGREDIENTS

3 tbsp olive oil

1 onion, sliced

2 garlic cloves, chopped

3 red (bell) peppers, deseeded and cut
  into strips

3 courgettes (zucchini), sliced

400 g/14 oz can chopped tomatoes

3 tbsp sun-dried tomato paste

2 tbsp chopped fresh basil

225 g/8 oz fresh pasta spirals

125 g/4½ oz/1 cup grated Gruyère
  (Swiss) cheese

salt and pepper

fresh basil sprigs, to garnish

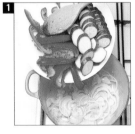

1 Heat the oil in a heavy-based saucepan or flameproof casserole. Add the onion and garlic and cook, stirring occasionally, until softened. Add the (bell) peppers and courgettes (zucchini) and fry for 5 minutes, stirring occasionally.

2 Add the tomatoes, sun-dried tomato paste, basil and seasoning, cover and cook for 5 minutes.

3 Meanwhile, bring a large saucepan of salted water to the boil and add the pasta. Stir and bring back to the boil.

Reduce the heat slightly and cook, uncovered, for 3 minutes, or until just tender. Drain thoroughly and add to the vegetables. Toss gently to mix well.

4 Put the mixture into a shallow ovenproof dish and sprinkle over the cheese.

5 Cook under a preheated grill (broiler) for 5 minutes until the cheese is golden. Garnish with basil sprigs and serve.

COOK'S TIP

Be careful not to overcook fresh pasta – it should be 'al dente' (retaining some 'bite'). It takes only a few minutes to cook as it is still full of moisture.

Basil & Pine Nut Pesto

Delicious stirred into pasta, soups and salad dressings, pesto is available in most supermarkets, but making your own gives a concentrated flavour.

NUTRITIONAL INFORMATION

Calories . . . . .321 Sugars 1g
Protein . . . . .11g Fat 17g
Carbohydrate . . .32g Saturates 4g

15 MINS   10 MINS

SERVES 4

I N G R E D I E N T S

about 40 fresh basil leaves,
    washed and dried

3 garlic cloves, crushed

25 g/1 oz pine nuts

50 g/1¾ oz Parmesan cheese, finely grated

2–3 tbsp extra virgin olive oil

salt and pepper

675 g/1½ lb fresh pasta or
    350 g/12 oz dried pasta

 Rinse the basil leaves and pat them dry with paper towels.

2 Put the basil leaves, garlic, pine nuts and grated Parmesan into a food processor and blend for about 30 seconds or until smooth. Alternatively, pound all of the ingredients by hand, using a mortar and pestle.

3 If you are using a food processor, keep the motor running and slowly add the olive oil. Alternatively, add the oil drop by drop while stirring briskly. Season with salt and pepper to taste.

4 Cook the pasta in a saucepan of boiling water allowing 3–4 minutes for fresh pasta or 8–10 minutes for dried, or until it is cooked through, but still has

'bite'. Drain the pasta thoroughly in a colander.

5 Transfer the pasta to a serving plate and serve with the pesto. Toss to mix well and serve hot.

COOK'S TIP

You can store pesto in the refrigerator for about 4 weeks. Cover the surface of the pesto with olive oil before sealing the container or bottle, to prevent the basil from oxidising and turning black.

Tagliatelle with Pumpkin

This unusual pasta dish comes from the Emilia Romagna region of Italy.

NUTRITIONAL INFORMATION

Calories ....454 Sugars 4g
Protein ....9g Fat 33g
Carbohydrate ...33g Saturates 12g

15 MINS

35 MINS

SERVES 4

INGREDIENTS

500 g/1 lb 2 oz pumpkin or butternut
squash

2 tbsp olive oil

1 onion, chopped finely

2 garlic cloves, crushed

4–6 tbsp chopped fresh parsley

good pinch of ground or freshly grated
nutmeg

about 250 ml/9 fl oz/1 cup chicken or
vegetable stock

125 g/4½ oz Parma ham (prosciutto), cut
into narrow strips

275 g/9 oz tagliatelle, green or white (fresh
or dried)

150 ml/¼ pint/⅔ cup double (heavy) cream

salt and pepper

freshly grated Parmesan, to serve

1 Peel the pumpkin or squash and scoop out the seeds and membrane. Cut the flesh into 1 cm/½ inch dice.

2 Heat the olive oil in a pan and gently fry the onion and garlic until softened. Add half of the parsley and fry for 1–2 minutes.

3 Add the pumpkin or squash and continue to cook for 2–3 minutes. Season well with salt, pepper and nutmeg.

4 Add half of the stock, bring to the boil, cover and simmer for about 10 minutes or until the pumpkin is tender, adding more stock as necessary. Add the Parma ham (prosciutto) and continue to cook for 2 minutes, stirring frequently.

5 Meanwhile, cook the tagliatelle in a large saucepan of boiling salted water, allowing 3–4 minutes for fresh pasta or 8–10 minutes for dried. Drain thoroughly and turn into a warmed dish.

6 Add the cream to the ham mixture and heat gently. Season and spoon over the pasta. Sprinkle with the remaining parsley and grated Parmesan separately.

Pasta with Cheese & Broccoli

Some of the simplest and most satisfying dishes are made with pasta, such as this delicious combination of tagliatelle with two-cheese sauce.

NUTRITIONAL INFORMATION

Calories 624   Sugars 2g
Protein . . . . .22g   Fat 45g
Carbohydrate . . .34g   Saturates 28g

 5 MINS   15 MINS

SERVES 4

INGREDIENTS

300 g/10½ oz dried tagliatelle tricolore
(plain, spinach- and tomato-flavoured
noodles)

225 g/8 oz/2½ cups broccoli, broken into
small florets

350g/12 oz/1½ cups Mascarpone cheese

125 g/4½ oz/1 cup blue cheese, chopped

1 tbsp chopped fresh oregano

25 g/1 oz/2 tbsp butter

salt and pepper

sprigs of fresh oregano, to garnish

freshly grated Parmesan, to serve

1 Cook the tagliatelle in plenty of boiling salted water for 8–10 minutes or until just tender.

2 Meanwhile, cook the broccoli florets in a small amount of lightly salted, boiling water. Avoid overcooking the broccoli, so that it retains much of its colour and texture.

3 Heat the Mascarpone and blue cheeses together gently in a large saucepan until they are melted. Stir in the oregano and season with salt and pepper to taste.

4 Drain the pasta thoroughly. Return it to the saucepan and add the butter, tossing the tagliatelle to coat it. Drain the broccoli well and add to the pasta with the sauce, tossing gently to mix.

5 Divide the pasta between 4 warmed serving plates. Garnish with sprigs of fresh oregano and serve with freshly grated Parmesan.

Spicy Tomato Tagliatelle

A deliciously fresh and slightly spicy tomato sauce which is excellent for lunch or a light supper.

NUTRITIONAL INFORMATION

Calories	306	Sugars	.........7g
Protein	.........8g	Fat	..........12g
Carbohydrate	...45g	Saturates	.......7g

15 MINS   35 MINS

SERVES 4

INGREDIENTS

50 g/1¾ oz/3 tbsp butter

1 onion, finely chopped

1 garlic clove, crushed

2 small red chillies,
   deseeded and diced

450 g/1 lb fresh tomatoes, skinned,
   deseeded and diced

200 ml/7 fl oz/¾ cup vegetable stock

2 tbsp tomato purée (paste)

1 tsp sugar

salt and pepper

675 g/1½ lb fresh green and white
   tagliatelle, or 350 g/12 oz dried

1 Melt the butter in a large saucepan. Add the onion and garlic and cook for 3–4 minutes or until softened.

2 Add the chillies to the pan and continue cooking for about 2 minutes.

3 Add the tomatoes and stock, reduce the heat and leave to simmer for 10 minutes, stirring.

4 Pour the sauce into a food processor and blend for 1 minute until smooth.

Alternatively, push the sauce through a sieve.

5 Return the sauce to the pan and add the tomato purée (paste) sugar, and salt and pepper to taste. Gently reheat over a low heat, until piping hot.

6 Cook the tagliatelle in a pan of boiling water for 8–10 minutes or until it is tender, but still has 'bite'. Drain the tagliatelle, transfer to serving plates and serve with the tomato sauce.

VARIATION

Try topping your pasta dish with 50 g/1¾ oz pancetta or unsmoked bacon, diced and dry-fried for 5 minutes until crispy.

Pasta & Bean Casserole

A satisfying winter dish, this is a slow-cooked, one-pot meal. The haricot (navy) beans need to be soaked overnight, so prepare well in advance.

NUTRITIONAL INFORMATION

Calories 323	Sugars 5g
Protein 13g	Fat 12g
Carbohydrate ...41g	Saturates 2g

25 MINS   3½ HOURS

SERVES 6

INGREDIENTS

225 g/8 oz/generous 1 cup dried haricot
   (navy) beans, soaked overnight and
   drained

225 g/8 oz penne,
   or other short pasta shapes

6 tbsp olive oil

850 ml/1½ pints/3½ cups vegetable stock

2 large onions, sliced

2 cloves garlic, chopped

2 bay leaves

1 tsp dried oregano

1 tsp dried thyme

5 tbsp red wine

2 tbsp tomato purée (paste)

2 celery stalks, sliced

1 fennel bulb, sliced

125 g/4½ oz mushrooms, sliced

225 g/8 oz tomatoes, sliced

1 tsp dark muscovado sugar

4 tbsp dry white breadcrumbs

salt and pepper

TO SERVE

salad leaves

crusty bread

1 Put the beans in a large pan, cover them with water and bring to the boil. Boil the beans rapidly for 20 minutes, then drain them.

2 Cook the pasta for only 3 minutes in a large pan of boiling salted water, adding 1 tablespoon of the oil. Drain in a colander and set aside.

3 Put the beans in a large flameproof casserole, pour on the vegetable stock and stir in the remaining olive oil, the onions, garlic, bay leaves, herbs, wine and tomato purée (paste).

4 Bring to the boil, cover the casserole and cook in a preheated oven, 180°C/350°F/Gas Mark 4, for 2 hours.

5 Add the reserved pasta, the celery, fennel, mushrooms and tomatoes, and season with salt and pepper.

6 Stir in the sugar and sprinkle on the breadcrumbs. Cover the casserole and continue cooking for 1 hour. Serve hot, with salad leaves and crusty bread.

Pasta & Cheese Puddings

These delicious pasta puddings are served with a tasty tomato and bay leaf sauce.

NUTRITIONAL INFORMATION

Calories 517   Sugars 8g
Protein . . . . .19g   Fat 27g
Carbohydrate . . .47g   Saturates 13g

45 MINS   50 MINS

SERVES 4

INGREDIENTS

15 g/½ oz/1 tbsp butter or margarine, softened

60 g/2 oz/½ cup dried white breadcrumbs

175 g/6 oz tricolour spaghetti

300 ml/½ pint/1¼ cups Béchamel Sauce (see page 14)

1 egg yolk

125 g/4½ oz/1 cup Gruyère (Swiss) cheese, grated

salt and pepper

fresh flat-leaf parsley, to garnish

TOMATO SAUCE

2 tsp olive oil

1 onion, chopped finely

1 bay leaf

150 ml/¼ pint/⅔ cup dry white wine

150 ml/¼ pint/⅔ cup passatta (sieved tomatoes)

1 tbsp tomato purée (paste)

1 Grease four 180 ml/6 fl oz/¾ cup moulds (molds) or ramekins with the butter or margarine. Evenly coat the insides with half of the breadcrumbs.

2 Break the spaghetti into 5 cm/2 inch lengths. Bring a saucepan of lightly salted water to the boil and cook the spaghetti for 5–6 minutes or until just tender. Drain well and put in a bowl.

3 Mix the Béchamel Sauce, egg yolk, cheese and seasoning into the cooked pasta and pack into the moulds (molds).

4 Sprinkle with the remaining breadcrumbs and place the moulds (molds) on a baking tray (cookie sheet). Bake in a preheated oven, 220°C/425°F/Gas Mark 7, for 20 minutes until golden. Leave to stand for 10 minutes.

5 Meanwhile, make the sauce. Heat the oil in a pan and fry the onion and bay leaf for 2–3 minutes or until just softened.

6 Stir in the wine, passata (sieved tomatoes), tomato purée (paste) and seasoning. Bring to the boil and simmer for 20 minutes or until thickened. Discard the bay leaf.

7 Run a palette knife (spatula) around the inside of the moulds (molds). Turn on to serving plates, garnish and serve with the tomato sauce.

Tagliatelle with Garlic Butter

Pasta is not difficult to make yourself, just a little time consuming. The resulting pasta only takes a couple of minutes to cook and tastes wonderful.

NUTRITIONAL INFORMATION

Calories 642	Sugars 2g
Protein 16g	Fat 29g
Carbohydrate ...84g	Saturates 13g

45 MINS   5 MINS

SERVES 4

I N G R E D I E N T S

450 g/1 lb strong white flour,
    plus extra for dredging

2 tsp salt

4 eggs, beaten

3 tbsp olive oil

75 g/2¾ oz/5 tbsp butter, melted

3 garlic cloves, finely chopped

2 tbsp chopped, fresh parsley

pepper

1 Sift the flour into a large bowl and stir in the salt.

2 Make a well in the middle of the dry ingredients and add the eggs and 2 tablespoons of oil. Using a wooden spoon, stir in the eggs, gradually drawing in the flour. After a few minutes the dough will be too stiff to use a spoon and you will need to use your fingers.

3 Once all of the flour has been incorporated, turn the dough out on to a floured surface and knead for about 5 minutes, or until smooth and elastic. If you find the dough is too wet, add a little more flour and continue kneading. Cover with cling film (plastic wrap) and leave to rest for at least 15 minutes.

4 The basic dough is now ready; roll out the pasta thinly and create the pasta shapes required. This can be done by hand or using a pasta machine. Results from a machine are usually neater and thinner, but not necessarily better.

5 To make the tagliatelle by hand, fold the thinly rolled pasta sheets into 3 and cut out long, thin stips, about 1 cm/ ½ inch wide.

6 To cook, bring a pan of water to the boil, add 1 tbsp of oil and the pasta. It will take 2–3 minutes to cook, and the texture should have a slight bite to it. Drain.

7 Mix together the butter, garlic and parsley. Stir into the pasta, season with a little pepper to taste and serve immediately.

COOK'S TIP

Generally allow about 150 g/5½ oz fresh pasta or about 100 g/3½ oz dried pasta per person.

Spaghetti with Ricotta Sauce

This makes a quick and easy starter, and is particularly ideal for the summer.

NUTRITIONAL INFORMATION

Calories 688   Sugars 5g
Protein . . . . .17g   Fat 51g
Carbohydrate . . .43g   Saturates 16g

15 MINS   20 MINS

SERVES 4

INGREDIENTS

350 g/12 oz spaghetti

3 tbsp olive oil

45 g/1½ oz/3 tbsp butter, cut into small
    pieces

2 tbsp chopped parsley

SAUCE

125 g/4½ oz/1 cup freshly ground almonds

125 g/4½ oz/½ cup Ricotta

large pinch of grated nutmeg

large pinch of ground cinnamon

150 ml/¼ pint/⅔ cup crème fraîche

125 ml/4 fl oz/½ cup hot chicken stock

1 tbsp pine kernels

pepper

coriander (cilantro) leaves, to garnish

COOK'S TIP

To toss spaghetti and coat
it with a sauce or dressing, use
the 2 largest forks you can find.
Holding one fork in each hand,
ease the prongs under the spaghetti
from each side and lift them
towards the centre. Repeat evenly
until the pasta is well coated.

1 Cook the spaghetti in a large pan of boiling salted water, to which you have added 1 tablespoon of the oil, for 8–10 minutes or until tender. Drain the pasta in a colander, return to the pan and toss with the butter and parsley. Cover the pan and keep warm.

2 To make the sauce, mix together the ground almonds, Ricotta, nutmeg, cinnamon and crème fraîche to make a thick paste. Gradually pour on the remaining oil, stirring constantly until it is well blended. Gradually pour on the hot stock, stirring all the time, until the sauce is smooth.

3 Transfer the spaghetti to warmed serving dishes, pour on the sauce and toss well. Sprinkle each serving with pine kernels (nuts) and garnish with coriander (cilantro) leaves. Serve warm.

Artichoke & Olive Spaghetti

The tasty flavours of artichoke hearts and black olives are a winning combination.

NUTRITIONAL INFORMATION

Calories 393   Sugars 11g
Protein . . . . .14g   Fat 11g
Carbohydrate . . .63g   Saturates 2g

20 MINS   35 MINS

SERVES 4

INGREDIENTS

2 tbsp olive oil

1 large red onion, chopped

2 garlic cloves, crushed

1 tbsp lemon juice

4 baby aubergines (eggplant), quartered

600 ml/1 pint/2½ cups passata (sieved
   tomatoes)

2 tsp caster (superfine) sugar

2 tbsp tomato purée (paste)

400 g/14 oz can artichoke hearts, drained
   and halved

125 g/4½ oz/¾ cup pitted black olives

350 g/12 oz wholewheat dried spaghetti

salt and pepper

sprigs of fresh basil, to garnish

olive bread, to serve

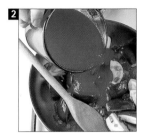
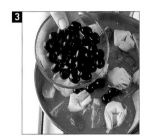

1 Heat 1 tablespoon of the oil in a large frying pan (skillet) and gently fry the onion, garlic, lemon juice and aubergines (eggplant) for 4–5 minutes or until lightly browned.

2 Pour in the passata (sieved tomatoes), season with salt and pepper to taste and add the sugar and tomato purée (paste). Bring to the boil, reduce the heat and simmer for 20 minutes.

3 Gently stir in the artichoke halves and olives and cook for 5 minutes.

4 Meanwhile, bring a large saucepan of lightly salted water to the boil, and cook the spaghetti for 8–10 minutes or until just tender. Drain well, toss in the

remaining olive oil and season with salt and pepper to taste.

5 Transfer the spaghetti to a warmed serving bowl and top with the vegetable sauce. Garnish with basil sprigs and serve with olive bread.

Chilli & (Bell) Pepper Pasta

This roasted (bell) pepper and chilli sauce is sweet and spicy – the perfect combination!

NUTRITIONAL INFORMATION

Calories	423	Sugars	.........5g
Protein	.........9g	Fat	..........27g
Carbohydrate	...38g	Saturates	.......4g

25 MINS   30 MINS

SERVES 4

INGREDIENTS

2 red (bell) peppers, halved and deseeded

1 small red chilli

4 tomatoes, halved

2 garlic cloves

50 g/1¾ oz ground almonds

7 tbsp olive oil

675 g/1½ lb fresh pasta or 350 g/12 oz
   dried pasta

fresh oregano leaves, to garnish

  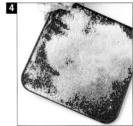

1 Place the (bell) peppers, skin-side up, on a baking tray (cookie sheet) with the chilli and tomatoes. Cook under a preheated grill (broiler) for 15 minutes or until charred. After 10 minutes turn the tomatoes skin-side up. Place the (bell) peppers and chillies in a polythene bag and leave to sweat for 10 minutes.

2 Remove the skin from the (bell) peppers and chillies and slice the flesh into strips, using a sharp knife.

3 Peel the garlic, and peel and deseed the tomatoes.

4 Place the almonds on a baking tray (cookie sheet) and place under the grill (broiler) for 2–3 minutes until golden.

5 Using a food processor, blend the (bell) pepper, chilli, garlic and tomatoes to make a purée. Keep the motor running and slowly add the olive oil to form a thick sauce. Alternatively, mash the mixture with a fork and beat in the olive oil, drop by drop.

6 Stir the toasted ground almonds into the mixture.

7 Warm the sauce in a saucepan until it is heated through.

8 Cook the pasta in a saucepan of boiling water for 8–10 minutes if using dried, or 3–5 minutes if using fresh. Drain the pasta thoroughly and transfer to a serving dish. Pour over the sauce and toss to mix. Garnish with the fresh oregano leaves.

VARIATION

Add 2 tablespoons of red wine vinegar to the sauce and use as a dressing for a cold pasta salad, if you wish.

Tagliatelle & Garlic Sauce

This pasta dish can be prepared in a moment – the intense flavours are sure to make this a popular recipe.

NUTRITIONAL INFORMATION

Calories 501   Sugars 3g
Protein . . . . .15g   Fat 31g
Carbohydrate . . .43g   Saturates 11g

 15 MINS   20 MINS

SERVES 4

I N G R E D I E N T S

2 tbsp walnut oil

1 bunch spring onions (scallions), sliced

2 garlic cloves, sliced thinly

225 g/8 oz mushrooms, sliced

500 g/1 lb 2 oz fresh green and white
    tagliatelle

225 g/8 oz frozen chopped leaf spinach,
    thawed and drained

125 g/4½ oz/½ cup full-fat soft cheese with
    garlic and herbs

4 tbsp single (light) cream

60 g/2 oz/½ cup chopped, unsalted
    pistachio nuts

2 tbsp shredded fresh basil

salt and pepper

sprigs of fresh basil, to garnish

Italian bread, to serve

1 Gently heat the oil in a wok or frying pan (skillet) and fry the spring onions (scallions) and garlic for 1 minute or until just softened. Add the mushrooms, stir well, cover and cook gently for 5 minutes or until softened.

2 Meanwhile, bring a large saucepan of lightly salted water to the boil and cook the pasta for 3–5 minutes or until just tender. Drain the pasta thoroughly and return to the saucepan.

3 Add the spinach to the mushrooms and heat through for 1–2 minutes. Add the cheese and allow to melt slightly. Stir in the cream and continue to heat without allowing to boil.

4 Pour the mixture over the pasta, season to taste and mix well. Heat gently, stirring, for 2–3 minutes.

5 Pile into a warmed serving bowl and sprinkle over the pistachio nuts and shredded basil. Garnish with basil sprigs and serve with Italian bread.

Pasta with Nuts & Cheese

Simple and inexpensive, this tasty pasta dish can be prepared fairly quickly.

NUTRITIONAL INFORMATION

Calories 531   Sugars 4g
Protein . . . . .20g   Fat 35g
Carbohydrate . . .35g   Saturates 16g

  10 MINS   30 MINS

SERVES 4

I N G R E D I E N T S

60 g/2 oz/1 cup pine kernels (nuts)

350 g/12 oz dried pasta shapes

2 courgettes (zucchini), sliced

125 g/4½ oz/1¼ cups broccoli,
   broken into florets

200 g/7 oz/1 cup full-fat soft cheese

150 ml/¼ pint/⅔ cup milk

1 tbsp chopped fresh basil

125 g/4½ oz button mushrooms, sliced

90 g/3 oz blue cheese, crumbled

salt and pepper

sprigs of fresh basil, to garnish

green salad, to serve

1 Scatter the pine kernels (nuts) on to a baking tray (cookie sheet) and grill (broil), turning occasionally, until lightly browned all over. Set aside.

2 Cook the pasta in plenty of boiling salted water for 8–10 minutes or until just tender.

3 Meanwhile, cook the courgettes (zucchini) and broccoli in a small amount of boiling, lightly salted water for about 5 minutes or until just tender.

4 Put the soft cheese into a pan and heat gently, stirring constantly. Add the milk and stir to mix. Add the basil and mushrooms and cook for 2–3 minutes. Stir in the blue cheese and season.

5 Drain the pasta and the vegetables and mix together. Pour over the cheese and mushroom sauce and add the pine kernels (nuts). Toss to mix. Garnish with basil sprigs and serve with a green salad.

Macaroni & Tuna Fish Layer

A layer of tuna fish with garlic, mushroom and red (bell) pepper is sandwiched between two layers of macaroni with a crunchy topping.

NUTRITIONAL INFORMATION

Calories	691	Sugars	........10g
Protein	........41g	Fat	..........33g
Carbohydrate	...62g	Saturates	......15g

20 MINS   50 MINS

SERVES 2

INGREDIENTS

125–150 g/4½–5½ oz/1¼ cup dried
 macaroni

2 tbsp oil

1 garlic clove, crushed

60 g/2 oz/¾ cup button mushrooms, sliced

½ red (bell) pepper, thinly sliced

200 g/7 oz can of tuna fish in brine,
 drained and flaked

½ tsp dried oregano

salt and pepper

SAUCE

25 g/1 oz/2 tbsp butter or margarine

1 tbsp plain (all-purpose) flour

250 ml/9 fl oz/1 cup milk

2 tomatoes, sliced

2 tbsp dried breadcrumbs

25 g/1 oz/¼ cup mature (sharp) Cheddar or
 Parmesan cheese, grated

VARIATION

Replace the tuna fish with chopped cooked chicken, beef, pork or ham or with 3–4 sliced hard-boiled (hard-cooked) eggs.

1 Cook the macaroni in boiling salted water, with 1 tablespoon of the oil added, for 10–12 minutes or until tender. Drain, rinse and drain thoroughly.

2 Heat the remaining oil in a saucepan or frying pan (skillet) and fry the garlic, mushrooms and (bell) pepper until soft. Add the tuna fish, oregano and seasoning, and heat through.

3 Grease an ovenproof dish (about 1 litre/1¾ pint/4 cup capacity), and add half of the cooked macaroni. Cover with the tuna mixture and then add the remaining macaroni.

4 To make the sauce, melt the butter or margarine in a saucepan, stir in the flour and cook for 1 minute. Add the milk gradually and bring to the boil. Simmer for 1–2 minutes, stirring continuously, until thickened. Season to taste. Pour the sauce over the macaroni.

5 Lay the sliced tomatoes over the sauce and sprinkle with the breadcrumbs and cheese.

6 Place in a preheated oven, at 200°C/400°F/Gas Mark 6, for about 25 minutes, or until piping hot and the top is well browned.

Fish & Vegetable Lasagne

Layers of cheese sauce, smoked cod and wholewheat lasagne can be assembled overnight and left ready to cook on the following day.

NUTRITIONAL INFORMATION

Calories	456	Sugars	.........8g
Protein	........33g	Fat	..........24g
Carbohydrate	...24g	Saturates	......15g

🥔 25 MINS   🕐 50 MINS

SERVES 6

INGREDIENTS

8 sheets wholewheat lasagne

500 g/1 lb 2 oz smoked cod

600 ml/1 pint/2½ cups milk

1 tbsp lemon juice

8 peppercorns

2 bay leaves

a few parsley stalks

60 g/2 oz/½ cup mature (sharp)
   Cheddar, grated

25 g/1 oz/¼ cup Parmesan, grated

salt and pepper

a few whole prawns (shrimp), to garnish

SAUCE

60 g/2 oz/¼ cup butter, plus extra for
   greasing

1 large onion, sliced

1 green (bell) pepper, cored, deseeded and
   chopped

1 small courgette (zucchini), sliced

60 g/2 oz/½ cup plain (all-purpose) flour

150 ml/¼ pint/⅔ cup white wine

150 ml/¼ pint/⅔ cup single (light) cream

125 g/4½ oz shelled prawns (shrimp)

60 g/2 oz/½ cup mature (sharp)
   Cheddar, grated

1 Cook the lasagne in a pan of boiling, salted water until almost tender, as described on page 344. Drain and reserve.

2 Place the smoked cod, milk, lemon juice, peppercorns, bay leaves and parsley stalks in a frying pan (skillet). Bring to the boil, cover and simmer for 10 minutes.

3 Lift the fish from the pan with a slotted spoon. Remove the skin and any bones. Flake the fish. Strain and reserve the liquor.

4 To make the sauce, melt the butter in a pan and fry the onion, (bell) pepper and courgette (zucchini) for 2–3 minutes. Stir in the flour and cook for 1 minute. Gradually add the fish liquor, then stir in the wine, cream and prawns (shrimp). Simmer for 2 minutes. Remove from the heat, add the cheese, and season.

5 Grease a shallow baking dish. Pour in a quarter of the sauce and spread evenly over the base. Cover the sauce with three sheets of lasagne, then with another quarter of the sauce.

6 Arrange the fish on top, then cover with half of the remaining sauce. Finish with the remaining lasagne, then the rest of the sauce. Sprinkle the Cheddar and Parmesan over the sauce.

7 Bake in a preheated oven, 190°C/ 375°F/Gas Mark 5, for 25 minutes, or until the top is golden brown and bubbling. Garnish and serve.

Pasta & Chilli Tomatoes

The pappardelle and vegetables are tossed in a delicious chilli and tomato sauce for a quick and economical meal.

NUTRITIONAL INFORMATION

Calories 353   Sugars 7g
Protein ....10g   Fat 24g
Carbohydrate ...26g   Saturates 4g

 15 MINS   20 MINS

SERVES 4

INGREDIENTS

275 g/9½ oz pappardelle

3 tbsp groundnut oil

2 cloves garlic, crushed

2 shallots, sliced

225 g/8 oz green beans, sliced

100 g/3½ oz cherry tomatoes, halved

1 tsp chilli flakes

4 tbsp crunchy peanut butter

150 ml/¼ pint/⅔ cup coconut milk

1 tbsp tomato purée (paste)

sliced spring onions (scallions), to garnish

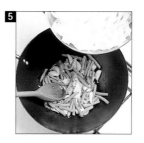

1 Cook the pappardelle in a large saucepan of boiling, lightly salted water for 5-6 minutes.

2 Heat the groundnut oil in a large pan or preheated wok.

3 Add the garlic and shallots and stir-fry for 1 minute.

4 Drain the pappardelle thoroughly and set aside.

5 Add the green beans and drained pasta to the wok and stir-fry for 5 minutes.

6 Add the cherry tomatoes to the wok and mix well.

7 Mix together the chilli flakes, peanut butter, coconut milk and tomato purée (paste).

8 Pour the chilli mixture over the noodles, toss well to combine and heat through.

9 Transfer to warm serving dishes and garnish. Serve immediately.

VARIATION

Add slices of chicken or beef to the recipe and stir-fry with the beans and pasta in step 5 for a more substantial main meal.

Vermicelli & Clam Sauce

This recipe is quick to prepare and cook – it's so delicious that it will be devoured even faster!

NUTRITIONAL INFORMATION

Calories	502	Sugars	.........2g
Protein	........27g	Fat	..........17g
Carbohydrate	...58g	Saturates	.......7g

 15 MINS   25 MINS

SERVES 4

I N G R E D I E N T S

400 g/14 oz vermicelli, spaghetti, or other
  long pasta

1 tbsp olive oil

25 g/1 oz/2 tbsp butter

2 tbsp Parmesan shavings, to garnish

sprig of basil, to garnish

S A U C E

1 tbsp olive oil

2 onions, chopped

2 garlic cloves, chopped

2 x 200 g/7 oz jars clams in brine

125 ml/4 fl oz/½ cup white wine

4 tbsp chopped fresh parsley

½ tsp dried oregano

pinch of freshly grated nutmeg

salt and pepper

1 Cook the pasta in a large pan of boiling salted water, adding the olive oil, for 8–10 minutes or until tender. Drain the pasta in a colander and return to the pan. Add the butter, cover and shake the pan. Keep warm until required.

2 To make the clam sauce, heat the oil in a pan over a medium heat and fry the onion until it is translucent. Stir in the garlic and cook for 1 minute.

3 Strain the liquid from one jar of clams, pour into the pan and add the wine. Stir well, bring to simmering point and simmer for 3 minutes. Drain the brine from the second jar of clams and discard.

4 Add the shellfish and herbs to the pan, and season with pepper to taste

and the nutmeg. Lower the heat and cook until the sauce is heated through.

5 Transfer the pasta to a warmed serving dish and pour on the sauce.

6 Sprinkle with the Parmesan and garnish with the basil sprig. Serve hot.

Macaroni & Squid Casserole

This pasta dish is easy to make and is a very hearty meal for a large number of guests.

NUTRITIONAL INFORMATION

Calories	237	Sugars	.........4g
Protein	........12g	Fat	...........11g
Carbohydrate	...19g	Saturates	.......2g

 15 MINS   35 MINS

SERVES 6

INGREDIENTS

225 g/8 oz short-cut macaroni, or other
  short pasta shapes

1 tbsp olive oil

2 tbsp chopped fresh parsley

salt and pepper

SAUCE

350 g/12 oz cleaned squid,
  cut into 4 cm/½ in strips

6 tbsp olive oil

2 onions, sliced

250 ml/9 fl oz/1 cup fish stock

150 ml/¼ pint/⅔ cup red wine

350 g/12 oz tomatoes, peeled
  and thinly sliced

2 tbsp tomato purée (paste)

1 tsp dried oregano

2 bay leaves

1 Cook the pasta for only 3 minutes in a large pan of boiling salted water, adding the oil. Drain in a colander, return to the pan, cover and keep warm.

2 To make the sauce, heat the oil in a pan over medium heat and fry the onion until translucent. Add the squid and stock and simmer for 5 minutes. Pour on the wine and add the tomatoes, tomato purée (paste), oregano and bay leaves. Bring the sauce to the boil, season with salt and pepper to taste and cook, uncovered, for 5 minutes.

3 Add the pasta, stir well, cover the pan and continue simmering for 10 minutes, or until the macaroni and squid are almost tender. By this time the sauce should be thick and syrupy. If it is too liquid, uncover the pan and continue cooking for a few minutes. Taste the sauce and adjust the seasoning if necessary.

4 Remove the bay leaves and stir in most of the parsley, reserving a little to garnish. Transfer to a warmed serving dish. Sprinkle on the remaining parsley and serve hot. Serve with warm, crusty bread, such as ciabatta.

Spaghetti & Salmon Sauce

The smoked salmon ideally complements the spaghetti to give a very luxurious dish.

NUTRITIONAL INFORMATION

Calories	782	Sugars	.........3g
Protein	........20g	Fat	..........48g
Carbohydrate	...48g	Saturates	......27g

 10 MINS   15 MINS

SERVES 4

I N G R E D I E N T S

500 g/1 lb 2 oz buckwheat spaghetti

2 tbsp olive oil

90 g/3 oz/½ cup feta cheese, crumbled

coriander (cilantro) or parsley, to garnish

S A U C E

300 ml/½ pint/1¼ cups double (heavy) cream

150 ml/¼ pint/⅔ cup whisky or brandy

125 g/4½ oz smoked salmon

large pinch of cayenne pepper

2 tbsp chopped coriander (cilantro) or parsley

salt and pepper

1 Cook the spaghetti in a large saucepan of salted boiling water, adding 1 tablespoon of the olive oil, for 8–10 minutes or until tender. Drain the pasta in a colander. Return the pasta to the pan, sprinkle over the remaining oil, cover and shake the pan. Set aside and keep warm until required.

2 In separate small saucepans, heat the cream and the whisky or brandy to simmering point. Do not let them boil.

3 Combine the cream with the whisky or brandy.

4 Cut the smoked salmon into thin strips and add to the cream mixture. Season with a little black pepper and cayenne pepper to taste, and then stir in the chopped coriander (cilantro) or parsley.

5 Transfer the spaghetti to a warmed serving dish, pour on the sauce and toss thoroughly using two large forks. Scatter the crumbled cheese over the pasta and garnish with the coriander (cilantro) or parsley. Serve at once.

Pasta & Mussel Sauce

Serve this aromatic seafood dish with plenty of fresh, crusty bread to soak up the delicious sauce.

NUTRITIONAL INFORMATION

Calories	735	Sugars	.........3g
Protein	........37g	Fat	..........46g
Carbohydrate	...41g	Saturates	......26g

25 MINS   25 MINS

SERVES 6

I N G R E D I E N T S

400 g/14 oz pasta shells

1 tbsp olive oil

S A U C E

3.5 litres/6 pints mussels, scrubbed

250 ml/9 fl oz/1 cup dry white wine

2 large onions, chopped

125 g/4½ oz/½ cup unsalted butter

6 large garlic cloves, chopped finely

5 tbsp chopped fresh parsley

300 ml/½ pint/1¼ cups double
   (heavy) cream

salt and pepper

crusty bread, to serve

1 Pull off the 'beards' from the mussels and rinse well in several changes of water. Discard any mussels that refuse to close when tapped. Put the mussels in a large pan with the white wine and half of the onions. Cover the pan, shake and cook over a medium heat for 2–3 minutes until the mussels open.

2 Remove the pan from the heat, lift out the mussels with a slotted spoon, reserving the liquor, and set aside until they are cool enough to handle. Discard any mussels that have not opened.

3 Melt the butter in a pan over medium heat and fry the remaining onion for 3–4 minutes or until translucent. Stir in the garlic and cook for 1 minute. Gradually pour on the reserved cooking liquor, stirring to blend thoroughly. Stir in the parsley and cream. Season to taste and bring to simmering point. Taste and adjust the seasoning if necessary.

4 Cook the pasta in a large pan of salted boiling water, adding the oil, for 8–10 minutes or until tender. Drain the pasta in a colander, return to the pan, cover and keep warm.

5 Remove the mussels from their shells, reserving a few shells for garnish. Stir the mussels into the cream sauce. Tip the pasta into a warmed serving dish, pour on the sauce and, using 2 large spoons, toss it together well. Garnish with a few of the reserved mussel shells. Serve hot, with warm, crusty bread.

Pasta & Sicilian Sauce

This Sicilian recipe of anchovies mixed with pine nuts and sultanas in a tomato sauce is delicious with all types of pasta.

NUTRITIONAL INFORMATION

Calories 286   Sugars 14g
Protein . . . . .11g   Fat 8g
Carbohydrate . . .46g   Saturates 1g

25 MINS   30 MINS

SERVES 4

I N G R E D I E N T S

450 g/1 lb tomatoes, halved

25 g/1 oz pine nuts

50 g/1¾ oz sultanas

50 g/1¾ oz can anchovies, drained and
  halved lengthways

2 tbsp concentrated tomato purée (paste)

675 g/1½ lb fresh or
  350 g/12 oz dried penne

1 Cook the tomatoes under a preheated grill (broiler) for about 10 minutes. Leave to cool slightly, then once cool enough to handle, peel off the skin and dice the flesh.

2 Place the pine nuts on a baking tray (cookie sheet) and lightly toast under the grill (broiler) for 2–3 minutes or until golden brown.

VARIATION

Add 100 g/3½ oz bacon, grilled (broiled) for 5 minutes until crispy, then chopped, instead of the anchovies, if you prefer.

3 Soak the sultanas in a bowl of warm water for about 20 minutes. Drain the sultanas thoroughly.

4 Place the tomatoes, pine nuts and sultanas in a small saucepan and gently heat.

5 Add the anchovies and tomato purée, heating the sauce for a further 2–3 minutes or until hot.

6 Cook the pasta in a saucepan of boiling water for 8–10 minutes or until it is cooked through, but still has 'bite'. Drain thoroughly.

7 Transfer the pasta to a serving plate and serve with the hot Sicilian sauce.

Pasta Pudding

A tasty mixture of creamy fish and pasta cooked in a bowl, unmoulded and drizzled with tomato sauce presents macaroni in a new guise.

NUTRITIONAL INFORMATION

Calories 536   Sugars 4g
Protein . . . . .35g   Fat 35g
Carbohydrate . . .21g   Saturates 17g

    35 MINS   2 HOURS

SERVES 4

I N G R E D I E N T S

125 g/4½ oz short-cut macaroni, or other
    short pasta shapes

1 tbsp olive oil

15 g/½ oz/1 tbsp butter, plus extra for
    greasing

500 g/1 lb 2 oz white fish fillets, such as
    cod, haddock or coley

a few parsley stalks

6 black peppercorns

125 ml/4 fl oz/½ cup double (heavy) cream

2 eggs, separated

2 tbsp chopped dill, or parsley

pinch of grated nutmeg

60 g/2 oz/½ cup Parmesan, grated

Basic Tomato Sauce (see page 14), to serve

pepper

dill or parsley sprigs, to garnish

1 Cook the pasta in a pan of salted boiling water, adding the oil, for 8–10 minutes. Drain, return to the pan, add the butter and cover. Keep warm.

2 Place the fish in a frying pan (skillet) with the parsley stalks and peppercorns and pour on just enough water to cover. Bring to the boil, cover, and simmer for 10 minutes. Lift out the fish with a fish slice,

reserving the liquor. When the fish is cool enough to handle, skin and remove any bones. Cut into bite-sized pieces.

3 Transfer the pasta to a large bowl and stir in the cream, egg yolks and dill. Stir in the fish, taking care not to break it up, and enough liquor to make a moist but firm mixture. It should fall easily from a spoon, but not be too runny. Whisk the egg whites until stiff but not dry, then fold into the mixture.

4 Grease a heatproof bowl or pudding basin and spoon in the mixture to within 4 cm/1½ inch of the rim. Cover the

top with greased greaseproof paper and a cloth, or with foil, and tie firmly around the rim. Do not use foil if you cook the pudding in a microwave.

5 Stand the pudding on a trivet in a large pan of boiling water to come halfway up the sides. Cover and steam for 1½ hours, topping up the boiling water as needed, or cook in a microwave on maximum power for 7 minutes.

6 Run a knife around the inside of the bowl and invert on to a warm serving dish. Pour some tomato sauce over the top; serve the rest separately. Garnish and serve.

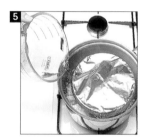

Spaghetti & Shellfish

Frozen shelled prawns (shrimp) from the freezer can become the star ingredient in this colourful and tasty dish.

35 MINS   30 MINS

SERVES 4

I N G R E D I E N T S

225 g/8 oz short-cut spaghetti, or long
   spaghetti broken into 15 cm/6 inch
   lengths

2 tbsp olive oil

300 ml/½ pint/1¼ cups chicken stock

1 tsp lemon juice

1 small cauliflower, cut into florets

2 carrots, sliced thinly

125 g/4½ oz mangetout (snow peas),
   trimmed

60 g/2 oz/¼ cup butter

1 onion, sliced

225 g/8 oz courgettes (zucchini),
   sliced thinly

1 garlic clove, chopped

350 g/12 oz frozen shelled prawns
   (shrimp), defrosted

2 tbsp chopped fresh parsley

25 g/1 oz/¼ cup Parmesan, grated

salt and pepper

½ tsp paprika, to sprinkle

4 unshelled prawns (shrimp),
   to garnish (optional)

1 Cook the spaghetti in a large pan of boiling salted water, adding 1 tbsp of the oil, for 8–10 minutes or until tender. Drain, then return to the pan and stir in the remaining oil. Cover and keep warm.

2 Bring the chicken stock and lemon juice to the boil. Add the cauliflower and carrots and cook for 3–4 minutes until they are barely tender. Remove with a slotted spoon and set aside. Add the mangetout (snow peas) and cook for 1–2 minutes, until they begin to soften. Remove with a slotted spoon and add to the other vegetables. Reserve the stock for future use.

3 Melt half of the butter in a frying pan (skillet) over a medium heat and fry the onion and courgettes (zucchini) for about 3 minutes. Add the garlic and prawns (shrimp) and cook for a further 2–3 minutes until thoroughly heated through.

4 Stir in the reserved vegetables and heat through. Season with salt and pepper, then stir in the remaining butter.

5 Transfer the spaghetti to a warmed serving dish. Pour on the sauce and parsley. Toss well using 2 forks, until thoroughly coated. Sprinkle on the grated cheese and paprika, and garnish with unshelled prawns (shrimp), if using. Serve immediately.

Pasta Vongole

Fresh clams are available from most good fishmongers. If you prefer, used canned clams, which are less messy to eat but not as attractive.

NUTRITIONAL INFORMATION

Calories 410	Sugars 1g
Protein 39g	Fat 9g
Carbohydrate . . .39g	Saturates 1g

🍲 20 MINS   🕐 20 MINS

SERVES 4

I N G R E D I E N T S

675 g/1½ lb fresh clams or 1 x 290 g/10 oz
    can clams, drained

400 g/14 oz mixed seafood, such as
    prawns (shrimps), squid and mussels,
    defrosted if frozen

2 tbsp olive oil

2 cloves garlic, finely chopped

150 ml/¼ pint/⅔ cup white wine

150 ml/¼ pint/⅔ cup fish stock

2 tbsp chopped tarragon

salt and pepper

675 g/1½ lb fresh pasta or
    350 g/12 oz dried pasta

1 If you are using fresh clams, scrub them clean and discard any that are already open.

2 Heat the oil in a large frying pan (skillet). Add the garlic and the clams to the pan and cook for 2 minutes, shaking the pan to ensure that all of the clams are coated in the oil.

3 Add the remaining seafood mixture to the pan and cook for a further 2 minutes.

4 Pour the wine and stock over the mixed seafood and garlic and bring to the boil. Cover the pan, reduce the heat and leave to simmer for 8–10 minutes or until the shells open. Discard any clams or mussels that do not open.

5 Meanwhile, cook the pasta in a saucepan of boiling water for 8–10 minutes or until it is cooked through, but still has 'bite'. Drain the pasta thoroughly.

6 Stir the tarragon into the sauce and season with salt and pepper to taste.

7 Transfer the pasta to a serving plate and pour over the sauce. Serve immediately.

VARIATION

Red clam sauce can be made by adding 8 tablespoons of passata (sieved tomatoes) to the sauce along with the stock in step 4. Follow the same cooking method.

Spaghetti, Tuna & Parsley

This is a recipe to look forward to when parsley is at its most prolific, in the growing season.

NUTRITIONAL INFORMATION

Calories	970	Sugars	.........2g
Protein	........23g	Fat	..........80g
Carbohydrate	...42g	Saturates	......18g

 10 MINS   15 MINS

SERVES 4

INGREDIENTS

500 g/1 lb 2 oz spaghetti

1 tbsp olive oil

25 g/1 oz/2 tbsp butter

black olives, to serve (optional)

SAUCE

200 g/7 oz can tuna, drained

60 g/2 oz can anchovies, drained

250 ml/9 fl oz/1 cup olive oil

250 ml/9 fl oz/1 cup roughly chopped fresh, flat-leaf parsley

150 ml/¼ pint/⅔ cup crème fraîche

salt and pepper

1 Cook the spaghetti in a large saucepan of salted boiling water, adding the olive oil, for 8–10 minutes or until tender. Drain the spaghetti in a colander and return to the pan. Add the butter, toss thoroughly to coat and keep warm until required.

2 Remove any bones from the tuna and flake into smaller pieces, using 2 forks. Put the tuna in a blender or food processor with the anchovies, olive oil and parsley and process until the sauce is smooth. Pour in the crème fraîche and process for a few seconds to blend. Taste the sauce and season with salt and pepper.

3 Warm 4 plates. Shake the saucepan of spaghetti over a medium heat for a few minutes or until it is thoroughly warmed through.

4 Pour the sauce over the spaghetti and toss quickly, using 2 forks. Serve immediately with a small dish of black olives, if liked.

Penne & Butternut Squash

The creamy, nutty flavour of squash complements the 'al dente' texture of the pasta perfectly. This recipe has been adapted for the microwave.

NUTRITIONAL INFORMATION

Calories	499	Sugars	.........4g
Protein	........20g	Fat	..........26g
Carbohydrate	...49g	Saturates	......13g

15 MINS   30 MINS

SERVES 4

INGREDIENTS

2 tbsp olive oil

1 garlic clove, crushed

60 g/2 oz/1 cup fresh white breadcrumbs

500 g/1 lb 2 oz peeled and deseeded
    butternut squash

8 tbsp water

500 g/1 lb 2 oz fresh penne,
    or other pasta shape

15 g/½ oz/1 tbsp butter

1 onion, sliced

125 g/4½ oz/½ cup ham, cut into strips

200 ml/7 fl oz/scant cup single (light) cream

60 g/2 oz/½ cup Cheddar cheese, grated

2 tbsp chopped fresh parsley

salt and pepper

COOK'S TIP

If the squash weighs
more than is needed for this
recipe, blanch the excess for
3–4 minutes on HIGH power in a
covered bowl with a little water.
Drain, cool and place in a freezer
bag. Store in the freezer for
up to 3 months.

1 Mix together the oil, garlic and breadcrumbs and spread out on a large plate. Cook on HIGH power for 4–5 minutes, stirring every minute, until crisp and beginning to brown. Set aside.

2 Dice the squash. Place in a large bowl with half of the water. Cover and cook on HIGH power for 8–9 minutes, stirring occasionally. Leave to stand for 2 minutes.

3 Place the pasta in a large bowl, add a little salt and pour over boiling water to cover by 2.5 cm/1 inch. Cover and cook on HIGH power for 5 minutes, stirring once, until the pasta is just tender but still firm to the bite. Leave to stand, covered, for 1 minute before draining.

4 Place the butter and onion in a large bowl. Cover and cook on HIGH power for 3 minutes.

5 Coarsely mash the squash, using a fork. Add to the onion with the pasta, ham, cream, cheese, parsley and remaining water. Season generously and mix well. Cover and cook on HIGH power for 4 minutes until heated through.

6 Serve the pasta sprinkled with the crisp garlic crumbs.

Sicilian Spaghetti Cake

Any variety of long pasta could be used for this very tasty dish from Sicily.

NUTRITIONAL INFORMATION

Calories 876   Sugars 10g
Protein ....37g   Fat 65g
Carbohydrate ...39g   Saturates 18g

30 MINS   50 MINS

SERVES 4

INGREDIENTS

2 aubergines (eggplant), about 650 g/
  1 lb 7 oz

150 ml/¼ pint/⅔ cup olive oil

350 g/12 oz finely minced (ground)
  lean beef

1 onion, chopped

2 garlic cloves, crushed

2 tbsp tomato purée (paste)

400 g/14 oz can chopped tomatoes

1 tsp Worcestershire sauce

1 tsp chopped fresh oregano or marjoram
  or ½ tsp dried oregano or marjoram

45 g/1½ oz stoned black olives, sliced

1 green, red or yellow (bell) pepper, cored,
  deseeded and chopped

175 g/6 oz spaghetti

125 g/4½ oz/1 cup Parmesan, grated

1 Brush a 20 cm/8 inch loose-based round cake tin (pan) with olive oil, place a disc of baking parchment in the base and brush with oil. Trim the aubergines (eggplants) and cut into slanting slices, 5 mm/¼ inch thick. Heat some of the oil in a frying pan (skillet). Fry a few slices of aubergine (eggplant) at a time until lightly browned, turning once, and adding more oil as necessary. Drain on kitchen paper.

2 Put the minced (ground) beef, onion and garlic into a saucepan and cook, stirring frequently, until browned all over. Add the tomato purée (paste), tomatoes, Worcestershire sauce, herbs and seasoning. Simmer for 10 minutes, stirring occasionally, then add the olives and (bell) pepper and cook for 10 minutes.

3 Bring a large saucepan of salted water to the boil. Cook the spaghetti for 8–10 minutes or until just tender. Drain the spaghetti thoroughly. Turn the spaghetti into a bowl and mix in the meat mixture and Parmesan, tossing together with 2 forks.

4 Lay overlapping slices of aubergine (eggplant) over the base of the cake tin (pan) and up the sides. Add the meat mixture, pressing it down, and cover with the remaining aubergine (eggplant) slices.

5 Stand the cake tin (pan) in a baking tin (pan) and cook in a preheated oven, 200°C/400°F/Gas Mark 6, for 40 minutes. Leave to stand for 5 minutes then loosen around the edges and invert on to a warmed serving dish, releasing the tin (pan) clip. Remove the baking parchment. Serve immediately.

Vegetable Pasta Nests

These large pasta nests look impressive when presented filled with grilled (broiled) mixed vegetables, and taste delicious.

NUTRITIONAL INFORMATION

Calories 392   Sugars 1g
Protein ....6g   Fat 28g
Carbohydrate ...32g   Saturates 9g

 25 MINS   40 MINS

SERVES 4

INGREDIENTS

175 g/6 oz spaghetti

1 aubergine (eggplant), halved and sliced

1 courgette (zucchini), diced

1 red (bell) pepper, seeded and chopped
   diagonally

6 tbsp olive oil

2 garlic cloves, crushed

50 g/1¾ oz/4 tbsp butter or margarine,
   melted

15 g/½ oz/1 tbsp dry white breadcrumbs

salt and pepper

fresh parsley sprigs, to garnish

1 Bring a large saucepan of water to the boil and cook the spaghetti for 8–10 minutes or until 'al dente'. Drain the spaghetti in a colander and set aside until required.

2 Place the aubergine (eggplant), courgette (zucchini) and (bell) pepper on a baking tray (cookie sheet).

3 Mix the oil and garlic together and pour over the vegetables, tossing to coat all over.

4 Cook under a preheated hot grill (broiler) for about 10 minutes,

turning, until tender and lightly charred. Set aside and keep warm.

5 Divide the spaghetti among 4 lightly greased Yorkshire pudding tins (pans). Using 2 forks, curl the spaghetti to form nests.

6 Brush the pasta nests with melted butter or margarine and sprinkle with the breadcrumbs. Bake in a preheated oven, at 200°C/400°F/ Gas Mark 6, for 15 minutes or until lightly golden. Remove the pasta nests from the tins (pans) and

transfer to serving plates. Divide the grilled (broiled) vegetables between the pasta nests, season and garnish.

COOK'S TIP

'Al dente' means 'to the bite' and describes cooked pasta that is not too soft, but still has a 'bite' to it.

Lasagne Verde

The sauce in this delicious baked pasta dish can be used as an alternative sauce for Spaghetti Bolognese (see page 184).

NUTRITIONAL INFORMATION

Calories 619   Sugars 7g
Protein . . . . .29g   Fat 45g
Carbohydrate . . .21g   Saturates 19g

1¾ HOURS   55 MINS

SERVES 6

I N G R E D I E N T S

Ragù Sauce (see page 12)

1 tbsp olive oil

225 g/8 oz lasagne verde

Béchamel Sauce (see page 14)

60 g/2 oz/½ cup Parmesan, grated

salt and pepper

green salad, tomato salad or black olives,
   to serve

1 Begin by making the Ragù Sauce as described on page 12, but cook for 10–12 minutes longer than the time given, in an uncovered pan, to allow the excess liquid to evaporate. To layer the sauce with lasagne, it needs to be reduced to the consistency of a thick paste.

2 Have ready a large saucepan of boiling, salted water and add the olive oil. Drop the pasta sheets into the boiling water a few at a time, and return the water to the boil before adding further pasta sheets. If you are using fresh lasagne, cook the sheets for a total of 8 minutes. If you are using dried or partly precooked pasta, cook it according to the directions given on the packet.

3 Remove the pasta sheets from the saucepan with a slotted spoon. Spread them in a single layer on damp tea towels (dish cloths).

4 Grease a rectangular ovenproof dish, about 25–28 cm/10–11 inches long. To assemble the dish, spoon a little of the meat sauce into the prepared dish, cover with a layer of lasagne, then spoon over a little Béchamel Sauce and sprinkle with some of the cheese. Continue making layers in this way, covering the final layer of lasagne with the remaining Béchamel Sauce.

5 Sprinkle on the remaining cheese and bake in a preheated oven, 190°C/375°F/Gas Mark 5, for 40 minutes or until the sauce is golden brown and bubbling. Serve with a green salad, a tomato salad, or a bowl of black olives.

Pasticcio

A recipe that has both Italian and Greek origins, this dish may be served hot or cold, cut into thick, satisfying squares.

NUTRITIONAL INFORMATION

Calories	590	Sugars	.........8g
Protein	........34g	Fat	..........39g
Carbohydrate	...23g	Saturates	......16g

 35 MINS   1¼ HOURS

SERVES 6

INGREDIENTS

225 g/8 oz fusilli, or other short
    pasta shapes

1 tbsp olive oil

4 tbsp double (heavy) cream

salt

rosemary sprigs, to garnish

SAUCE

2 tbsp olive oil, plus extra for brushing

1 onion, sliced thinly

1 red (bell) pepper, cored, deseeded
    and chopped

2 cloves garlic, chopped

625 g/1 lb 6 oz minced (ground) lean beef

400 g/14 oz can chopped tomatoes

125 ml/4 fl oz/½ cup dry white wine

2 tbsp chopped fresh parsley

50 g/1¾ oz can anchovies, drained
    and chopped

salt and pepper

TOPPING

300 ml/½ pint/1¼ cups natural
(unsweetened) yogurt

3 eggs

pinch of freshly grated nutmeg

40 g/1½ oz/⅓ cup Parmesan, grated

1 To make the sauce, heat the oil in a large frying pan (skillet) and fry the onion and red (bell) pepper for 3 minutes. Stir in the garlic and cook for 1 minute more. Stir in the beef and cook, stirring frequently, until no longer pink.

2 Add the tomatoes and wine, stir well and bring to the boil. Simmer, uncovered, for 20 minutes, or until the sauce is fairly thick. Stir in the parsley and anchovies, and season to taste.

3 Cook the pasta in a large pan of boiling salted water, adding the oil, for 8–10 minutes or until tender. Drain the pasta in a colander, then transfer to a bowl. Stir in the cream and set aside.

4 To make the topping, beat together the yogurt and eggs and season with nutmeg, and salt and pepper to taste.

5 Brush a shallow baking dish with oil. Spoon in half of the pasta and cover with half of the meat sauce. Repeat these layers, then spread the topping evenly over the final layer. Sprinkle the cheese on top.

6 Bake in a preheated oven, 190°C/375°F/Gas Mark 5, for 25 minutes, or until the topping is golden brown and bubbling. Garnish with sprigs of rosemary and serve with a selection of raw vegetable crudités.

Chicken & Tomato Lasagne

This variation of the traditional beef dish has layers of pasta and chicken or turkey baked in red wine, tomatoes and a delicious cheese sauce.

NUTRITIONAL INFORMATION

Calories 550   Sugars 11g
Protein . . . . .35g   Fat 29g
Carbohydrate . . .34g   Saturates 12g

20 MINS   1¼ HOURS

SERVES 4

INGREDIENTS

350 g/12 oz fresh lasagne (about 9 sheets)
   or 150 g/5½ oz dried lasagne
   (about 9 sheets)
1 tbsp olive oil
1 red onion, finely chopped
1 garlic clove, crushed
100 g/3½ oz mushrooms, wiped and sliced
350 g/12 oz chicken or turkey breast, cut
   into chunks
150 ml/¼ pint/⅔ cup red wine, diluted with
   100 ml/3½ fl oz/scant ⅓ cup water
250 g/9 oz passata (sieved tomatoes)
1 tsp sugar

BÉCHAMEL SAUCE

75 g/2¾ oz/5 tbsp butter
50 g/1¾ oz plain (all-purpose) flour
600 ml/1 pint/2½ cups milk
1 egg, beaten
75 g/2¾ oz Parmesan cheese, grated
salt and pepper

1 Cook the lasagne in a pan of boiling water according to the instructions on the packet. Lightly grease a deep ovenproof dish.

2 Heat the oil in a pan. Add the onion and garlic and cook for 3–4 minutes. Add the mushrooms and chicken and stir-fry for 4 minutes or until the meat browns.

3 Add the wine, bring to the boil, then simmer for 5 minutes. Stir in the passata (sieved tomatoes) and sugar and cook for 3–5 minutes until the meat is tender and cooked through. The sauce should have thickened, but still be quite runny.

4 To make the Béchamel Sauce, melt the butter in a pan, stir in the flour and cook for 2 minutes. Remove the pan from the heat and gradually add the milk, mixing to form a smooth sauce. Return the pan to the heat and bring to the boil, stirring until thickened. Leave to cool slightly, then beat in the egg and half of the cheese. Season to taste.

5 Place 3 sheets of lasagne in the base of the dish and spread with half of the chicken mixture. Repeat the layers. Top with the last 3 sheets of lasagne, pour over the Béchamel Sauce and sprinkle with the Parmesan. Bake in a preheated oven, at 190°C/375°F/Gas Mark 5, for 30 minutes until golden and the pasta is cooked.

Tagliatelle with Meatballs

There is an appetizing contrast of textures and flavours in this satisfying family dish.

NUTRITIONAL INFORMATION

Calories	910	Sugars	........13g
Protein	........40g	Fat	..........54g
Carbohydrate	...65g	Saturates	......19g

45 MINS   1 HR 5 MINS

SERVES 4

INGREDIENTS

500 g/1 lb 2 oz minced (ground) lean beef

60 g/2 oz/1 cup soft white breadcrumbs

1 garlic clove, crushed

2 tbsp chopped fresh parsley

1 tsp dried oregano

large pinch of freshly grated nutmeg

¼ tsp ground coriander

60 g/2 oz/½ cup Parmesan, grated

2–3 tbsp milk

flour, for dusting

4 tbsp olive oil

400 g/14 oz tagliatelle

25 g/1 oz/2 tbsp butter, diced

salt and pepper

SAUCE

3 tbsp olive oil

2 large onions, sliced

2 celery sticks, sliced thinly

2 garlic cloves, chopped

400 g/14 oz can chopped tomatoes

125 g/4½ oz bottled sun-dried tomatoes, drained and chopped

2 tbsp tomato purée (paste)

1 tbsp dark muscovado sugar

150 ml/¼ pint/⅔ cup white wine, or water

1 To make the sauce, heat the oil in a frying pan (skillet) and fry the onions and celery until translucent. Add the garlic and cook for 1 minute. Stir in the tomatoes, tomato purée (paste), sugar and wine, and season. Bring to the boil and simmer for 10 minutes.

2 Meanwhile, break up the meat in a bowl with a wooden spoon until it becomes a sticky paste. Stir in the breadcrumbs, garlic, herbs and spices. Stir in the cheese and enough milk to make a firm paste. Flour your hands, take large spoonfuls of the mixture and shape it into 12 balls. Heat 3 tbsp of the oil in a frying pan (skillet) and fry the meatballs for 5–6 minutes until browned.

3 Pour the tomato sauce over the meatballs. Lower the heat, cover the pan and simmer for 30 minutes, turning once or twice. Add a little extra water if the sauce begins to dry.

4 Cook the pasta in a large saucepan of boiling salted water, adding the remaining oil, for 8–10 minutes or until tender. Drain the pasta, then turn into a warmed serving dish, dot with the butter and toss with two forks. Spoon the meatballs and sauce over the pasta and serve.

Tortelloni

These tasty little squares of pasta stuffed with mushrooms and cheese are surprisingly filling. This recipe makes 36 tortelloni.

NUTRITIONAL INFORMATION

Calories 360	Sugars 1g
Protein 9g	Fat 21g
Carbohydrate ...36g	Saturates 12g

  1¼ HOURS   25 MINS

SERVES 4

I N G R E D I E N T S

about 300 g/10½ oz fresh pasta, rolled out
  to thin sheets

75 g/2¾ oz/5 tbsp butter

50 g/1¾ oz shallots, finely chopped

3 garlic clove, crushed

50 g/1¾ oz mushrooms, wiped and
  finely chopped

½ stick celery, finely chopped

25 g/1 oz Pecorino cheese, finely grated,
  plus extra to garnish

1 tbsp oil

salt and pepper

1 Using a serrated pasta cutter, cut 5 cm/2 inch squares from the sheets of fresh pasta. To make 36 tortelloni you will need 72 squares. Once the pasta is cut, cover the squares with cling film (plastic wrap) to stop them drying out.

2 Heat 25 g/1 oz/3 tbsp of the butter in a frying pan (skillet). Add the shallots, 1 crushed garlic clove, the mushrooms and celery and cook for 4–5 minutes.

3 Remove the pan from the heat, stir in the cheese and season with salt and pepper to taste.

4 Spoon ½ teaspoon of the mixture on to the middle of 36 pasta squares. Brush the edges of the squares with water and top with the remaining 36 squares. Press the edges together to seal. Leave to rest for 5 minutes.

5 Bring a large pan of water to the boil, add the oil and cook the tortelloni, in batches, for 2–3 minutes. The tortelloni will rise to the surface when cooked and the pasta should be tender with a slight 'bite'. Remove from the pan with a perforated spoon and drain thoroughly.

6 Meanwhile, melt the remaining butter in a pan. Add the remaining garlic and plenty of pepper and cook for 1–2 minutes. Transfer the tortelloni to serving plates and pour over the garlic butter. Garnish with grated pecorino cheese and serve immediately.

Meat & Pasta Loaf

The cheesy pasta layer comes as a pleasant surprise inside this lightly spiced meat loaf.

NUTRITIONAL INFORMATION

Calories .... .497	Sugars 4g	
Protein .... .26g	Fat .... .37g	
Carbohydrate ...16g	Saturates ..... .16g	

45 MINS

1¼ HOURS

SERVES 6

I N G R E D I E N T S

25 g/1 oz/2 tbsp butter, plus extra
  for greasing

1 onion, chopped finely

1 small red (bell) pepper, cored, deseeded
  and chopped

1 garlic clove, chopped

500 g/1 lb 2 oz minced (ground) lean beef

25 g/1 oz/½ cup soft white breadcrumbs

½ tsp cayenne pepper

1 tbsp lemon juice

½ tsp grated lemon rind

2 tbsp chopped fresh parsley

90 g/3 oz short pasta, such as fusilli

4 bay leaves

1 tbsp olive oil

Cheese Sauce (see page 15)

175 g/6 oz streaky bacon rashers, rind
  removed

salt and pepper

salad leaves, to garnish

1 Melt the butter in a pan over a medium heat and fry the onion and pepper for about 3 minutes, until the onion is translucent. Stir in the garlic and cook for 1 minute.

2 Put the meat into a large bowl and mash it with a wooden spoon until it becomes a sticky paste. Tip in the fried vegetables and stir in the breadcrumbs, cayenne, lemon juice, lemon rind and parsley. Season the mixture with salt and pepper and set aside.

3 Cook the pasta in a large pan of boiling water, to which you have added salt and the olive oil, for 8–10 minutes or until tender. Drain the pasta, then stir it into the cheese sauce.

4 Grease a 1 kg/2 lb 4 oz loaf tin (pan) and arrange the bay leaves in the base. Stretch the bacon rashers with the back of a knife blade and arrange them to line the base and the sides of the tin (pan).

5 Spoon in half of the meat mixture, level the surface and cover it with the pasta. Spoon in the remaining meat mixture, level the top and cover the tin (pan) with foil.

6 Cook the meat loaf in the preheated oven, 180°C/350°F/Gas Mark 4, for 1 hour, or until the juices run clear and the loaf has shrunk away from the sides of the tin (pan). Pour off any excess fat from the tin (pan) and turn the loaf out on a warmed serving dish. Garnish with the salad leaves and serve hot.

Tagliatelle & Chicken Sauce

Spinach ribbon noodles covered with a rich tomato sauce and topped with creamy chicken makes a very appetizing dish.

NUTRITIONAL INFORMATION

Calories	853	Sugars	.........6g
Protein	........32g	Fat	...........71g
Carbohydrate	...23g	Saturates	......34g

🍳 30 MINS   🕐 25 MINS

SERVES 4

I N G R E D I E N T S

Basic Tomato Sauce (see page 14)

225 g/8 oz fresh green ribbon noodles

1 tbsp olive oil

salt

basil leaves, to garnish

C H I C K E N   S A U C E

60 g/2 oz/¼ cup unsalted butter

400 g/14 oz boned, skinned chicken
   breast, thinly sliced

90 g/3 oz/¾ cup blanched almonds

300 ml/½ pint/1¼ cups double
   (heavy) cream

salt and pepper

basil leaves, to garnish

1 Make the tomato sauce, and keep warm.

2 To make the chicken sauce, melt the butter in a pan over a medium heat and fry the chicken strips and almonds for 5–6 minutes, stirring frequently, until the chicken is cooked through.

3 Meanwhile, pour the cream into a small pan over a low heat, bring it to the boil and boil for about 10 minutes, until reduced by almost half. Pour the cream over the chicken and almonds, stir well, and season with salt and pepper to taste. Set aside and keep warm.

4 Cook the pasta in a pan of boiling salted water, to which you have added the oil, for 8–10 minutes or until tender. Drain, then return to the pan, cover and keep warm.

5 Turn the pasta into a warmed serving dish and spoon the tomato sauce over it. Spoon the chicken and cream over the centre, scatter over the basil leaves and serve at once.

Pizzas & Breads

There is little to beat the irresistible aroma and taste of a freshly-made pizza cooked in a wood-fired oven. The recipes for the homemade dough base and freshly made

tomato sauce in this chapter will give you the closest thing possible to an authentic Italian pizza. You can add any type of topping, from salamis and cooked meats, to vegetables and fragrant herbs – the choice is yours! The Italians make delicious bread, combining all of the flavours of the Mediterranean. You can use the breads in this chapter to mop up the juices from a range of Italian dishes, or you can eat them on their own as a tasty snack.

Bread Dough Base

Traditionally, pizza bases are made from bread dough; this recipe will give you a base similar to an Italian pizza.

NUTRITIONAL INFORMATION

Calories	182	Sugars	.........2g
Protein	.........5g	Fat	...........3g
Carbohydrate	...36g	Saturates	.....0.5g

  1½ HOURS   0 MINS

SERVES 4

INGREDIENTS

15 g/½ oz fresh yeast or 1 tsp dried or
   easy-blend yeast

90 ml/3½ fl oz/6 tbsp tepid water

½ tsp sugar

1 tbsp olive oil

175 g/6 oz plain (all-purpose) flour

1 tsp salt

1 Combine the fresh yeast with the water and sugar in a bowl. If using dried yeast, sprinkle it over the surface of the water and whisk in until dissolved.

2 Leave the mixture to rest in a warm place for 10–15 minutes until frothy on the surface. Stir in the olive oil.

3 Sift the flour and salt into a large bowl. If using easy-blend yeast, stir it in at this point. Make a well in the centre and pour in the yeast liquid, or water and oil (without the sugar for easy-blend yeast).

4 Using either floured hands or a wooden spoon, mix together to form a dough. Turn out on to a floured work surface and knead for about 5 minutes or until smooth and elastic.

5 Place the dough in a large greased plastic bag and leave in a warm place for about 1 hour or until doubled in size. Airing cupboards are often the best places for this process, as the temperature remains constant.

6 Turn out on to a lightly floured work surface and 'knock back' by punching the dough. This releases any air bubbles which would make the pizza uneven. Knead 4 or 5 times. The dough is now ready to use.

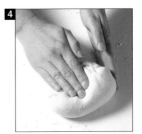

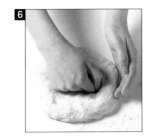

Scone (Biscuit) Base

This is a quicker alternative to the bread dough base. If you do not have time to wait for bread dough to rise, a scone (biscuit) base is ideal.

NUTRITIONAL INFORMATION

Calories 215   Sugars 3g
Protein . . . . .5g   Fat 7g
Carbohydrate . . .35g   Saturates 4g

20 MINS   0 MINS

SERVES 4

I N G R E D I E N T S

175 g/6 oz self-raising flour

½ tsp salt

25 g/1 oz butter

125 ml/4 fl oz/½ cup milk

1 Sift the flour and salt into a large mixing bowl.

2 Rub in the butter with your fingertips until it resembles fine breadcrumbs.

3 Make a well in the centre of the flour and butter mixture and pour in nearly all of the milk at once. Mix in quickly with a knife. Add the remaining milk only if necessary to mix to a soft dough.

4 Turn the dough out on to a floured work surface and knead by turning and pressing with the heel of your hand 3 or 4 times.

5 Either roll out or press the dough into a 25 cm/10 inch circle on a lightly greased baking tray (cookie sheet) or pizza pan. Push up the edge slightly all round to form a ridge and use immediately.

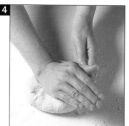

Potato Base

This is an unusual pizza base made from mashed potatoes and flour and is a great way to use up any leftover boiled potatoes.

NUTRITIONAL INFORMATION

Calories 170   Sugars 1g
Protein . . . . .4g   Fat 3g
Carbohydrate . . .34g   Saturates 1g

2¼ HOURS   0 MINS

SERVES 4

INGREDIENTS

225 g/8 oz boiled potatoes

60 g/2 oz/¼ cup butter or margarine

125 g/4½ oz/1 cup self-raising flour

½ tsp salt

1 If the potatoes are hot, mash them, then stir in the butter until it has melted and is distributed evenly throughout the potatoes. Leave to cool.

2 Sift the flour and salt together and stir into the mashed potato to form a soft dough.

3 If the potatoes are cold, mash them without adding the butter. Sift the flour and salt into a bowl.

4 Rub in the butter with your fingertips until the mixture resembles fine breadcrumbs, then stir the flour and butter mixture into the mashed potatoes to form a soft dough.

5 Either roll out or press the dough into a 25 cm/10 inch circle on a lightly greased baking tray (cookie sheet) or pizza pan, pushing up the edge slightly all round to form a ridge before adding the topping of your choice. This potato base is rather tricky to lift before it is cooked, so you will find it much easier to handle if you roll it out directly on to the baking tray (cookie sheet).

6 If the base is not required for cooking immediately, cover it with cling film (plastic wrap) and chill it for up to 2 hours.

Tomato Sauce

This is a basic topping sauce for pizzas. Using canned chopped tomatoes for this dish saves time.

NUTRITIONAL INFORMATION

Calories 41	Sugars 3g
Protein 1g	Fat 3g
Carbohydrate 3g	Saturates 0.4g

 5 MINS   25 MINS

SERVES 4

I N G R E D I E N T S

1 small onion, chopped

1 garlic clove, crushed

1 tbsp olive oil

200 g/7 oz can chopped tomatoes

2 tsp tomato purée (paste)

½ tsp sugar

½ tsp dried oregano

1 bay leaf

salt and pepper

1 Fry the onion and garlic gently in the oil for 5 minutes or until softened but not browned.

2 Add the tomatoes, tomato purée (paste), sugar, oregano, bay leaf and salt and pepper to taste. Stir well.

3 Bring the sauce to the boil, cover and leave to simmer gently for 20 minutes, stirring occasionally, until you have a thickish sauce.

4 Remove the bay leaf and season to taste. Leave to cool completely before using. This sauce keeps well in a screw-top jar in the refrigerator for up to 1 week.

Special Tomato Sauce

This sauce is made with fresh tomatoes. Use the plum variety whenever available and always choose the reddest ones for the best flavour.

NUTRITIONAL INFORMATION

Calories 81   Sugars 6g
Protein . . . . .1g   Fat 6g
Carbohydrate . . . .6g   Saturates 1g

🥄 10 MINS   🕐 35 MINS

SERVES 4

I N G R E D I E N T S

1 small onion, chopped

1 small red (bell) pepper, chopped

1 garlic clove, crushed

2 tbsp olive oil

225 g/8 oz tomatoes

1 tbsp tomato purée (paste)

1 tsp soft brown sugar

2 tsp chopped fresh basil

½ tsp dried oregano

1 bay leaf

salt and pepper

1 Fry the onion, (bell) pepper and garlic gently in the oil for 5 minutes until softened but not browned.

2 Cut a cross in the base of each tomato and place them in a bowl. Pour on boiling water and leave for about 45 seconds. Drain, and then plunge in cold water. The skins will slide off easily.

3 Chop the tomatoes, discarding any hard cores.

4 Add the tomatoes to the onion mixture with the tomato purée (paste), sugar, herbs and seasoning. Stir well. Bring to the boil, cover and leave to simmer gently for about 30 minutes, stirring occasionally, or until you have a thickish sauce.

5 Remove the bay leaf and adjust the seasoning to taste. Leave to cool completely before using.

6 This sauce will keep well in a screw-top jar in the refrigerator for up to 1 week.

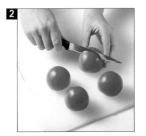

Pizza Margherita

Pizza means 'pie' in Italian. The fresh bread dough is not difficult to make but it does take a little time.

NUTRITIONAL INFORMATION

Calories 456   Sugars 7g
Protein . . . . .16g   Fat 13g
Carbohydrate . . .74g   Saturates 5g

 1 HOUR   45 MINS

SERVES 4

I N G R E D I E N T S

BASIC PIZZA DOUGH

7 g/½ oz dried yeast

1 tsp sugar

250 ml/9 fl oz/1 cup hand-hot water

350 g/12 oz strong flour

1 tsp salt

1 tbsp olive oil

TOPPING

400 g/14 oz can tomatoes, chopped

2 garlic cloves, crushed

2 tsp dried basil

1 tbsp olive oil

2 tbsp tomato purée

100 g/3½ oz Mozzarella cheese, chopped

2 tbsp freshly grated Parmesan cheese

salt and pepper

1 Place the yeast and sugar in a measuring jug and mix with 50 ml/2 fl oz/4 tbsp of the water. Leave the yeast mixture in a warm place for 15 minutes or until frothy.

2 Mix the flour with the salt and make a well in the centre. Add the oil, the yeast mixture and the remaining water. Using a wooden spoon, mix to form a smooth dough.

3 Turn the dough out on to a floured surface and knead for 4–5 minutes or until smooth.

4 Return the dough to the bowl, cover with an oiled sheet of cling film (plastic wrap) and leave to rise for 30 minutes or until doubled in size.

5 Knead the dough for 2 minutes. Stretch the dough with your hands, then place it on an oiled baking tray (cookie sheet), pushing out the edges until even. The dough should be no more than 6 mm/¼ inch thick because it will rise during cooking.

6 To make the topping, place the tomatoes, garlic, dried basil, olive oil and salt and pepper to taste in a large frying pan (skillet) and leave to simmer for 20 minutes or until the sauce has thickened. Stir in the tomato purée and leave to cool slightly.

7 Spread the topping evenly over the pizza base. Top with the Mozzarella and Parmesan cheeses and bake in a preheated oven, at 200°C/400°F/Gas Mark 6, for 20–25 minutes. Serve hot.

Vegetable & Goat's Cheese

Wonderfully colourful vegetables are roasted in olive oil with thyme and garlic. The goat's cheese adds a nutty, piquant flavour.

NUTRITIONAL INFORMATION

Calories 387	Sugars 9g	
Protein 10g	Fat 21g	
Carbohydrate ...42g	Saturates 5g	

 2½ HOURS   40 MINS

SERVES 4

INGREDIENTS

2 baby courgettes (zucchini), halved
   lengthways

2 baby aubergines (eggplant), quartered
   lengthways

½ red (bell) pepper, cut into 4 strips

½ yellow (bell) pepper, cut into 4 strips

1 small red onion, cut into wedges

2 garlic cloves, unpeeled

4 tbsp olive oil

1 tbsp red wine vinegar

1 tbsp chopped fresh thyme

Bread Dough Base (see page 226)

Tomato Sauce (see page 14)

90 g/3 oz goat's cheese

salt and pepper

fresh basil leaves, to garnish

1 Place all of the prepared vegetables in a large roasting tin (pan). Mix together the olive oil, vinegar, thyme and plenty of seasoning and pour over, coating well.

2 Roast the vegetables in a preheated oven, at 200°C/400°F/Gas Mark 6, for 15–20 minutes or until the skins have started to blacken in places, turning half-way through. Leave to rest for 5 minutes after roasting.

3 Carefully peel off the skins from the roast (bell) peppers and the garlic cloves. Slice the garlic.

4 Roll out or press the dough, using a rolling pin or your hands, into a 25 cm/ 10 inch circle on a lightly floured work surface. Place on a large greased baking tray (cookie sheet) or pizza pan and raise the edge a little. Cover and leave for 10 minutes to rise slightly in a warm place. Spread with the tomato sauce almost to the edge.

5 Arrange the roasted vegetables on top and dot with the cheese. Drizzle the oil and juices from the roasting tin (pan) over the pizza and season.

6 Bake in a preheated oven, at 200°C/ 400°F/Gas Mark 6, for 18–20 minutes, or until the edge is crisp and golden. Serve immediately, garnished with basil leaves.

Tomato Sauce & (Bell) Pepper

This pizza is made with a pastry base flavoured with cheese and topped with a delicious tomato sauce and roasted (bell) peppers.

NUTRITIONAL INFORMATION

Calories 611	Sugars 8g
Protein 14g	Fat 38g
Carbohydrate . . .56g	Saturates 21g

1½ HOURS   55 MINS

SERVES 4

INGREDIENTS

225 g/8 oz plain (all-purpose) flour

125 g/4½ oz butter, diced

½ tsp salt

2 tbsp dried Parmesan cheese

1 egg, beaten

2 tbsp cold water

2 tbsp olive oil

1 large onion, finely chopped

1 garlic clove, chopped

400 g/14 oz can chopped tomatoes

4 tbsp concentrated tomato purée (paste)

1 red (bell) pepper, halved

5 sprigs of thyme, stalks removed

6 black olives, pitted and halved

25 g/1 oz Parmesan cheese, grated

1 Sift the flour and rub in the butter to make breadcrumbs. Stir in the salt and dried Parmesan. Add the egg and 1 tablespoon of the water and mix with a round-bladed knife. Add more water if necessary to make a soft dough. Cover with cling film (plastic wrap) and chill for 30 minutes.

2 Meanwhile, heat the oil in a frying pan (skillet) and cook the onions and garlic for about 5 minutes or until golden.

Add the tomatoes and cook for 8–10 minutes. Stir in the tomato purée (paste).

3 Place the (bell) peppers, skin-side up, on a baking tray (cookie sheet) and cook under a preheated grill (broiler) for 15 minutes until charred. Place in a plastic bag and leave to sweat for 10 minutes. Peel off the skin and slice the flesh into thin strips.

4 Roll out the dough to fit a 23 cm/ 9 inch loose base fluted flan tin (pan).

Line with foil and bake in a preheated oven, at 200°C/400°F/Gas Mark 6, for 10 minutes or until just set. Remove the foil and bake for a further 5 minutes until lightly golden. Leave to cool slightly.

5 Spoon the tomato sauce over the pastry base and top with the (bell) peppers, thyme, olives and fresh Parmesan. Return to the oven for 15 minutes or until the pastry is crisp. Serve warm or cold.

Mushroom Pizza

Juicy mushrooms and stringy Mozzarella top this tomato-based pizza.
Use wild mushrooms or a combination of wild and cultivated mushrooms.

NUTRITIONAL INFORMATION

Calories	302	Sugars	.........7g
Protein	........10g	Fat	..........12g
Carbohydrate	...41g	Saturates	.......4g

  1¼ HOURS   45 MINS

SERVES 4

INGREDIENTS

1 portion Basic Pizza Dough (see page 231)

TOPPING

400g/14 oz can chopped tomatoes

2 garlic cloves, crushed

1 tsp dried basil

1 tbsp olive oil

2 tbsp tomato purée (paste)

200 g/7 oz mushrooms

150 g/5½ oz Mozzarella cheese, grated

salt and pepper

basil leaves, to garnish

1 Place the yeast and sugar in a measuring jug and mix with 50 ml/2 fl oz/4 tbsp of the water. Leave the yeast mixture in a warm place for 15 minutes or until frothy.

2 Mix the flour with the salt and make a well in the centre. Add the oil, the yeast mixture and the remaining water. Using a wooden spoon, mix to form a smooth dough.

3 Turn the dough out on to a floured surface and knead for 4–5 minutes or until smooth. Return the dough to the bowl, cover with an oiled sheet of cling film (plastic wrap) and leave to rise for 30 minutes or until doubled in size.

4 Remove the dough from the bowl. Knead the dough for 2 minutes. Using a rolling pin, roll out the dough to form an oval or a circular shape, then place it on an oiled baking tray (cookie sheet), pushing out the edges until even. The dough should be no more than 6 mm/¼ inch thick because it will rise during cooking.

5 Using a sharp knife, chop the mushrooms into slices.

6 To make the topping, place the tomatoes, garlic, dried basil, olive oil and salt and pepper in a large pan and simmer for 20 minutes or until the sauce has thickened. Stir in the tomato purée (paste) and leave to cool slightly.

7 Spread the sauce over the base of the pizza, top with the mushrooms and scatter over the Mozzarella. Bake in a preheated oven, at 200°C/400°F/Gas Mark 6, for 25 minutes. Garnish with basil leaves.

(Bell) Peppers & Red Onion

The vibrant colours of the (bell) peppers and onion make this a delightful pizza. Served cut into fingers, it is ideal for a party or buffet.

NUTRITIONAL INFORMATION

Calories . . . . . . .380 Sugars 19g
Protein . . . . .7g Fat 17g
Carbohydrate . . .53g Saturates 2g

2½ HOURS   25 MINS

SERVES 8

I N G R E D I E N T S

Bread Dough Base (see page 226)

2 tbsp olive oil

½ each red, green and yellow (bell) pepper, sliced thinly

1 small red onion, sliced thinly

1 garlic clove, crushed

Tomato Sauce (see page 14)

3 tbsp raisins

25 g/1 oz pine kernels (nuts)

1 tbsp chopped fresh thyme

olive oil, for drizzling

salt and pepper

1 Roll out or press the dough, using a rolling pin or your hands, on a lightly floured work surface to fit a 30 x 18 cm/12 x 7 inch greased Swiss roll tin (pan). Place in the tin (pan) and push up the edges slightly.

2 Cover and leave the dough to rise slightly in a warm place for about 10 minutes.

3 Heat the oil in a large frying pan (skillet). Add the (bell) peppers, onion and garlic, and fry gently for 5 minutes until they have softened but not browned. Leave to cool.

4 Spread the tomato sauce over the base of the pizza almost to the edge.

5 Sprinkle over the raisins and top with the cooled (bell) pepper mixture. Add the pine kernels (nuts) and thyme. Drizzle with a little olive oil and season well.

6 Bake in a preheated oven, at 200°C/400°F/Gas Mark 6, for 18–20 minutes, or until the edges are crisp and golden. Cut into fingers and serve immediately.

Gorgonzola & Pumpkin Pizza

A combination of blue Gorgonzola cheese and pears combine to give a colourful pizza. The wholemeal base adds a nutty flavour and texture.

NUTRITIONAL INFORMATION

Calories 470	Sugars 5g	
Protein 17g	Fat 15g	
Carbohydrate . . .72g	Saturates 6g	

  1¼ HOURS   35 MINS

SERVES 4

I N G R E D I E N T S

PIZZA DOUGH

7 g/¼ oz dried yeast

1 tsp sugar

250 ml/9 fl oz/1 cup hand-hot water

175 g/6 oz wholemeal flour

175 g/6 oz strong white flour

1 tsp salt

1 tbsp olive oil

TOPPING

400 g/14 oz pumpkin or squash,
    peeled and cubed

1 tbsp olive oil

1 pear, cored, peeled and sliced

100 g 3½ oz Gorgonzola cheese

1 sprig fresh rosemary, to garnish

1 Place the yeast and sugar in a measuring jug and mix with 50 ml/2 fl oz/4 tbsp of the water. Leave the yeast mixture in a warm place for 15 minutes or until frothy.

2 Mix both of the flours with the salt and make a well in the centre. Add the oil, the yeast mixture and the remaining water. Using a wooden spoon, mix to form a dough.

3 Turn the dough out on to a floured surface and knead for 4–5 minutes or until smooth.

4 Return the dough to the bowl, cover with an oiled sheet of cling film (plastic wrap) and leave to rise for 30 minutes or until doubled in size.

5 Remove the dough from the bowl. Knead the dough for 2 minutes. Using a rolling pin, roll out the dough to form a long oval shape, then place it on an oiled baking tray (cookie sheet), pushing out the edges until even. The dough should be no more than 6 mm/¼ inch thick because it will rise during cooking.

6 To make the topping, place the pumpkin in a shallow roasting tin (pan). Drizzle with the olive oil and cook under a preheated grill (broiler) for 20 minutes or until soft and lightly golden.

7 Top the dough with the pear and the pumpkin, brushing with the oil from the tin (pan). Sprinkle over the Gorgonzola. Bake in a preheated oven, at 200°C/400°F/Gas Mark 6 for 15 minutes or until the base is golden. Garnish with rosemary.

Giardiniera Pizza

As the name implies, this colourful pizza should be topped with fresh vegetables from the garden, especially in the summer months.

NUTRITIONAL INFORMATION

Calories	362	Sugars	.......10g
Protein	........13g	Fat	..........15g
Carbohydrate	...48g	Saturates	.......5g

🍎 🍎 🍎

3½ HOURS   🕐 20 MINS

SERVES 4

INGREDIENTS

6 spinach leaves

Potato Base (see page 228)

Special Tomato Sauce (see page 14)

1 tomato, sliced

1 celery stalk, sliced thinly

½ green (bell) pepper, sliced thinly

1 baby courgette (zucchini), sliced

25 g/1 oz asparagus tips

25 g/1 oz sweetcorn, defrosted if frozen

25 g/1 oz peas, defrosted if frozen

4 spring onions (scallions), trimmed and chopped

1 tbsp chopped fresh mixed herbs

60 g/2 oz Mozzarella, grated

2 tbsp freshly grated Parmesan

1 artichoke heart

olive oil, for drizzling

salt and pepper

1 Remove any tough stalks from the spinach and wash the leaves in cold water. Pat dry with paper towels.

2 Roll out or press the potato base, using a rolling pin or your hands, into a large 25 cm/10 inch circle on a lightly floured work surface. Place the round on a large greased baking tray (cookie sheet) or pizza pan and push up the edge a little. Spread with the tomato sauce.

3 Arrange the spinach leaves on the sauce, followed by the tomato slices. Top with the remaining vegetables and the herbs.

4 Mix together the cheeses and sprinkle over. Place the artichoke heart in the centre. Drizzle the pizza with a little olive oil and season.

5 Bake in a preheated oven, at 200°C/400°F/Gas Mark 6, for 18–20 minutes, or until the edges are crisp and golden brown. Serve immediately.

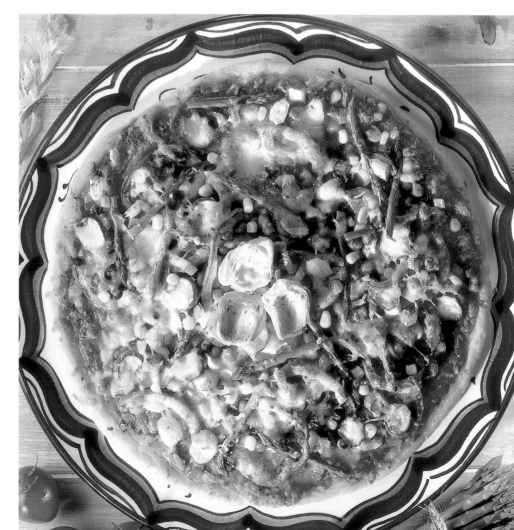

Tomato & Ricotta Pizza

This is a traditional dish from the Calabrian Mountains in southern Italy, where it is made with naturally sun-dried tomatoes and ricotta cheese.

NUTRITIONAL INFORMATION

Calories 274   Sugars 4g
Protein ....8g   Fat 11g
Carbohydrate ...38g   Saturates 4g

1¼ HOURS   30 MINS

SERVES 4

INGREDIENTS

1 portion Basic Pizza Dough (see page 231)

TOPPING

4 tbsp sun-dried tomato paste

150g/5½ oz ricotta cheese

10 sun-dried tomatoes

1 tbsp fresh thyme

salt and pepper

1 Place the yeast and sugar in a measuring jug and mix with 50 ml/2 fl oz/4 tbsp of the water. Leave the yeast mixture in a warm place for 15 minutes or until frothy.

2 Mix the flour with the salt and make a well in the centre. Add the oil, the yeast mixture and the remaining water. Using a wooden spoon, mix to form a dough.

3 Turn the dough out on to a floured surface and knead for 4–5 minutes or until smooth.

4 Return the dough to the bowl, cover with an oiled sheet of cling film (plastic wrap) and leave to rise for 30 minutes or until doubled in size.

5 Remove the dough from the bowl. Knead the dough for 2 minutes.

6 Using a rolling pin, roll out the dough to form a circle, then place it on an oiled baking tray (cookie sheet), pushing out the edges until even. The dough should be no more than 6 mm/¼ inch thick because it will rise during cooking.

7 Spread the sun-dried tomato paste over the dough, then add spoonfuls of ricotta cheese.

8 Cut the sun-dried tomatoes into strips and arrange these on top of the pizza.

9 Sprinkle the thyme, and salt and pepper to taste over the top of the pizza. Bake in a preheated oven, at 200°C/400°F/Gas Mark 6, for 30 minutes or until the crust is golden. Serve hot.

Florentine Pizza

A pizza adaptation of Eggs Florentine – sliced hard-boiled (hard-cooked) eggs on freshly cooked spinach, with a crunchy almond topping.

NUTRITIONAL INFORMATION

Calories 462   Sugars 6g
Protein ....18g   Fat 26g
Carbohydrate ...41g   Saturates 8g

3 HOURS   20 MINS

SERVES 4

INGREDIENTS

2 tbsp freshly grated Parmesan

Potato Base (see page 228)

Tomato Sauce (see page 14)

175 g/6 oz spinach

1 small red onion, sliced thinly

2 tbsp olive oil

¼ tsp freshly grated nutmeg

2 hard-boiled (hard-cooked) eggs

15 g/½ oz fresh white breadcrumbs

60 g/2 oz Jarlsberg, grated (or Cheddar or
   Gruyère, if not available)

2 tbsp flaked (slivered) almonds

olive oil, for drizzling

salt and pepper

1 Mix the Parmesan with the potato base. Roll out or press the dough, using a rolling pin or your hands, into a 25 cm/10 inch circle on a lightly floured work surface. Place on a large greased baking tray (cookie sheet) or pizza pan and push up the edge slightly. Spread the tomato sauce almost to the edge.

2 Remove the stalks from the spinach and wash the leaves thoroughly in plenty of cold water. Drain well and pat off the excess water with paper towels.

3 Fry the onion gently in the oil for 5 minutes or until softened. Add the spinach and continue to fry until just wilted. Drain off any excess liquid. Arrange on the pizza and sprinkle over the nutmeg.

4 Remove the shells from the eggs and slice. Arrange the slices of egg on top of the spinach.

5 Mix together the breadcrumbs, cheese and almonds, and sprinkle over. Drizzle with a little olive oil and season with salt and pepper to taste.

6 Bake in a preheated oven, at 200°C/400°F/Gas Mark 6, for 18–20 minutes, or until the edge is crisp and golden. Serve immediately.

Cheese & Artichoke Pizza

Sliced artichokes combined with mature (sharp) Cheddar, Parmesan and blue cheese give a really delicious topping to this pizza.

NUTRITIONAL INFORMATION

Calories	424	Sugars	.........9g
Protein	........16g	Fat	..........20g
Carbohydrate	...47g	Saturates	.......8g

 1¾ HOURS   20 MINS

SERVES 4

INGREDIENTS

Bread Dough Base (see page 226)

Special Tomato Sauce (see page 14)

60 g/2 oz blue cheese, sliced

125 g/4½ oz artichoke hearts in oil, sliced

½ small red onion, chopped

45 g/1½ oz mature (sharp) cheese, grated

2 tbsp freshly grated Parmesan

1 tbsp chopped fresh thyme

oil from artichokes for drizzling

salt and pepper

TO SERVE

salad leaves

cherry tomatoes, halved

1 Roll out or press the dough, using a rolling pin or your hands, to form a 25 cm/10 inch circle on a lightly floured work surface.

2 Place the pizza base on a large greased baking tray (cookie sheet) or pizza pan and push up the edge slightly. Cover and leave to rise for 10 minutes in a warm place.

3 Spread the tomato sauce almost to the edge of the base. Arrange the blue cheese on top of the tomato sauce, followed by the artichoke hearts and red onion.

4 Mix the Cheddar and Parmesan cheeses together with the thyme and sprinkle the mixture over the pizza. Drizzle a little of the oil from the jar of artichokes over the pizza and season to taste.

5 Bake in a preheated oven, at 200°C/400°F/Gas Mark 6, for 18–20 minutes, or until the edge is crisp and golden and the cheese is bubbling.

6 Mix the fresh salad leaves and cherry tomato halves together and serve with the pizza, cut into slices.

Cheese & Garlic Mushroom

This pizza dough is flavoured with garlic and herbs and topped with mixed mushrooms and melted cheese for a really delicious pizza.

NUTRITIONAL INFORMATION

Calories 541   Sugars 5g
Protein . . . . .16g   Fat 15g
Carbohydrate . . .91g   Saturates 6g

  45 MINS   30 MINS

SERVES 4

I N G R E D I E N T S

D O U G H

450 g/1 lb/3½ cups strong white flour

2 tsp easy-blend yeast

2 garlic cloves, crushed

2 tbsp chopped thyme

2 tbsp olive oil

300 ml/½ pint/1¼ cups tepid water

T O P P I N G

25 g/1 oz/2 tbsp butter or margarine

350 g/12 oz mixed mushrooms, sliced

2 garlic cloves, crushed

2 tbsp chopped parsley

2 tbsp tomato purée (paste)

6 tbsp passata (sieved tomatoes)

75 g/2¾ oz Mozzarella cheese, grated

salt and pepper

chopped parsley, to garnish

1 Put the flour, yeast, garlic and thyme in a bowl. Make a well in the centre and gradually stir in the oil and water. Bring together to form a soft dough.

2 Turn the dough on to a floured surface and knead for 5 minutes or until smooth. Roll into a 35 cm/14 inch round and place on a greased baking tray (cookie sheet). Leave in a warm place for 20 minutes or until the dough puffs up.

3 Meanwhile, make the topping. Melt the margarine or butter in a frying pan (skillet) and sauté the mushrooms, garlic and parsley for 5 minutes.

4 Mix the tomato purée (paste) and passata (sieved tomatoes) and spoon on to the pizza base, leaving a 1 cm/½ inch edge of dough. Spoon the mushroom mixture on top. Season well and sprinkle the cheese on top.

5 Cook the pizza in a preheated oven, at 190°C/375°F/Gas Mark 5, for 20–25 minutes or until the base is crisp and the cheese has melted. Garnish with chopped parsley and serve.

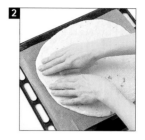

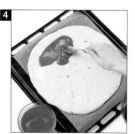

Wild Mushroom & Walnut

Wild mushrooms make a delicious pizza topping when mixed with walnuts and Roquefort cheese.

NUTRITIONAL INFORMATION

Calories 499   Sugars 9g
Protein . . . . .13g   Fat 32g
Carbohydrate . . .42g   Saturates 11g

  1¼ HOURS   25 MINS

SERVES 4

INGREDIENTS

Scone (Biscuit) Base (see page 227)

Special Tomato Sauce (see page 14)

125 g/4½ oz soft cheese

1 tbsp chopped fresh mixed herbs, such as parsley, oregano and basil

225 g/8 oz wild mushrooms, such as oyster, shiitake or ceps, or 125 g/4½ oz each wild and button mushrooms

2 tbsp olive oil

¼ tsp fennel seeds

25 g/1 oz walnuts, chopped roughly

45 g/1½ oz blue cheese

olive oil, for drizzling

salt and pepper

sprig of flat-leaf parsley, to garnish

1 Roll out or press the scone (biscuit) base, using a rolling pin or your hands, into a 25 cm/10 inch circle on a lightly floured work surface. Place on a large greased baking tray (cookie sheet) or pizza pan and push up the edge a little with your fingers to form a rim.

2 Carefully spread the tomato sauce almost to the edge of the pizza base. Dot with the soft cheese and chopped fresh herbs.

3 Wipe and slice the mushrooms. Heat the oil in a large frying pan (skillet) or wok and stir-fry the mushrooms and fennel seeds for 2–3 minutes. Spread over the pizza with the walnuts.

4 Crumble the cheese over the pizza, drizzle with a little olive oil and season with salt and pepper to taste.

5 Bake in a preheated oven, at 200°C/ 400°F/Gas Mark 6, for 18–20 minutes, or until the edge is crisp and golden. Serve immediately, garnished with a sprig of flat-leaf parsley.

Tomato & Olive Pizzas

Halved ciabatta bread or baguettes are a ready-made pizza base. The colours of the tomatoes and cheese contrast beautifully on top.

NUTRITIONAL INFORMATION

Calories	181	Sugars	.........4g
Protein	.........7g	Fat	..........10g
Carbohydrate	...18g	Saturates	.......4g

45 MINS   25 MINS

SERVES 4

I N G R E D I E N T S

2 loaves of ciabatta or 2 baguettes

Tomato Sauce (see page 14)

4 plum tomatoes, sliced thinly lengthways

150 g/5½ oz Mozzarella, sliced thinly

10 black olives, cut into rings

8 fresh basil leaves, shredded

olive oil, for drizzling

salt and pepper

1 Cut the bread in half lengthways and toast the cut side of the bread lightly. Carefully spread the toasted bread with the tomato sauce.

2 Arrange the tomato and Mozzarella slices alternately along the length.

3 Top with the olive rings and half of the basil. Drizzle over a little olive oil and season with salt and pepper.

4 Either place under a preheated medium grill (broiler) and cook until the cheese is melted and bubbling or bake in a preheated oven, 200°C/400°F/Gas Mark 6, for 15–20 minutes.

5 Sprinkle over the remaining basil and serve immediately.

Four Seasons Pizza

This is a traditional pizza on which the toppings are divided into four sections, each of which is supposed to depict a season of the year.

NUTRITIONAL INFORMATION

Calories 313   Sugars 8g
Protein . . . . .8g   Fat 13g
Carbohydrate . . .44g   Saturates 3g

2¾ HOURS   20 MINS

SERVES 4

INGREDIENTS

Bread Dough Base (see page 226)

Special Tomato Sauce (see page 14)

25 g/1 oz chorizo sausage, sliced thinly

25 g/1 oz button mushrooms, wiped and
  sliced thinly

45 g/1½ oz artichoke hearts, sliced thinly

25 g/1 oz Mozzarella, sliced thinly

3 anchovies, halved lengthways

2 tsp capers

4 pitted black olives, sliced

4 fresh basil leaves, shredded

olive oil, for drizzling

salt and pepper

1 Roll out or press the dough, using a rolling pin or your hands, into a 25 cm/10 inch circle on a lightly floured surface. Place on a large greased baking tray (cookie sheet) or pizza pan and push up the edge a little.

2 Cover and leave to rise slightly for 10 minutes in a warm place. Spread the tomato sauce over the pizza base, almost to the edge.

3 Put the sliced chorizo on to one quarter of the pizza, the sliced mushrooms on another, the artichoke hearts on a third, and the Mozzarella and anchovies on the fourth.

4 Dot with the capers, olives and basil leaves. Drizzle with a little olive oil and season. Do not put any salt on the anchovy section as the fish are very salty.

5 Bake in a preheated oven, at 200°C/ 400°F/Gas Mark 6, for 18–20 minutes, or until the crust is golden and crisp. Serve immediately.

Onion & Anchovy Pizza

This tasty onion pizza is topped with a lattice pattern of anchovies and black olives. Cut the pizza into squares to serve.

NUTRITIONAL INFORMATION

Calories 373	Sugars 5g
Protein 12g	Fat 20g
Carbohydrate . . .39g	Saturates 4g

1¾ HOURS   30 MINS

MAKES 6

INGREDIENTS

4 tbsp olive oil

3 onions, sliced thinly

1 garlic clove, crushed

1 tsp soft brown sugar

½ tsp crushed fresh rosemary

200 g/7 oz can chopped tomatoes

Bread Dough Base (see page 226)

2 tbsp freshly grated Parmesan

50 g/1¾ oz can anchovies

12–14 black olives

salt and pepper

1 Heat 3 tablespoons of the oil in a large saucepan and add the onions, garlic, sugar and rosemary. Cover and fry gently, stirring occasionally, for 10 minutes or until the onions are soft but not brown.

2 Add the tomatoes to the pan, stir and season with salt and pepper to taste. Leave to cool slightly.

3 Roll out or press the dough, using a rolling pin or your hands, on a lightly floured work surface to fit a 30 x 18 cm/ 12 x 7 inch greased Swiss roll tin (pan). Place in the tin (pan) and push up the edges slightly to form a rim.

4 Brush the remaining oil over the dough and sprinkle with the cheese. Cover and leave to rise slightly in a warm place for about 10 minutes.

5 Spread the onion and tomato topping over the base. Drain the anchovies, reserving the oil. Split each anchovy in half lengthways and arrange on the pizza in a lattice pattern. Place olives in between the anchovies and drizzle over a little of the reserved oil. Season to taste.

6 Bake in a preheated oven, at 200°C/ 400°F/Gas Mark 6, for 18–20 minutes, or until the edges are crisp and golden. Cut the pizza into 6 squares and serve immediately.

Aubergine (Eggplant) & Lamb

An unusual fragrant, spiced pizza topped with minced (ground) lamb and aubergine (eggplant) on a bread base.

NUTRITIONAL INFORMATION

Calories 430   Sugars 10g
Protein ....18g   Fat 22g
Carbohydrate ...44g   Saturates 7g

3 HOURS   30 MINS

SERVES 4

INGREDIENTS

1 small aubergine (eggplant), diced

Bread Dough Base (see page 416)

1 small onion, sliced thinly

1 garlic clove, crushed

1 tsp cumin seeds

1 tbsp olive oil

175 g/6 oz minced (ground) lamb

25 g/1 oz canned pimiento, thinly sliced

2 tbsp chopped fresh coriander (cilantro)

Special Tomato Sauce (see page 14)

90 g/3 oz Mozzarella, sliced thinly

olive oil, for drizzling

salt and pepper

1 Place the diced aubergine (eggplant) in a colander, sprinkle with the salt and let the bitter juices drain for about 20 minutes. Rinse thoroughly, then pat dry with paper towels.

2 Roll out or press the dough, using a rolling pin or your hands, into a 25 cm/10 inch circle on a lightly floured work surface. Place on a large greased baking tray (cookie sheet) or pizza pan and push up the edge to form a rim.

3 Cover and leave to rise slightly for 10 minutes in a warm place.

4 Fry the onion, garlic and cumin seeds gently in the oil for 3 minutes. Increase the heat slightly and add the lamb, aubergine (eggplant) and pimiento. Fry for 5 minutes, stirring occasionally. Add the coriander (cilantro) and season with salt and pepper to taste.

5 Spread the tomato sauce over the dough base, almost to the edge. Top with the lamb mixture.

6 Arrange the Mozzarella slices on top. Drizzle over a little olive oil and season with salt and pepper.

7 Bake in a preheated oven, at 200°C/400°F/Gas Mark 6, for 18–20 minutes, or until the crust is crisp and golden. Serve immediately.

Onion, Ham & Cheese Pizza

This pizza was a favourite of the Romans. It is slightly unusual because the topping is made without a tomato sauce base.

NUTRITIONAL INFORMATION

Calories ....333 Sugars 8g
Protein ....12g Fat 14g
Carbohydrate ...43g Saturates 4g

1 HOUR   40 MINS

SERVES 4

INGREDIENTS

1 portion of Basic Pizza Dough (see page 231)

TOPPING

2 tbsp olive oil

250 g/9 oz onions, sliced into rings

2 garlic cloves, crushed

1 red (bell) pepper, diced

100 g/3½ oz raw ham (prosciutto), cut into strips

100 g/3½ oz Mozzarella cheese, sliced

2 tbsp rosemary, stalks removed and roughly chopped

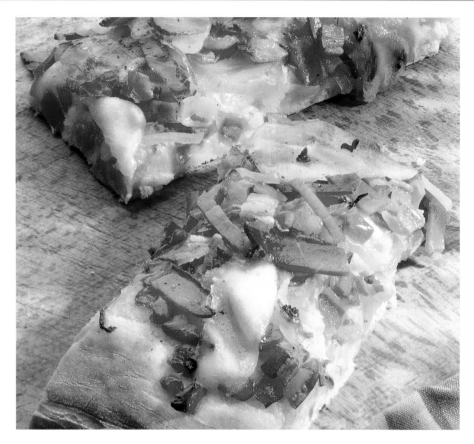

1 Place the yeast and sugar in a measuring jug and mix with 50 ml/2 fl oz/4 tbsp of the water. Leave the mixture in a warm place for 15 minutes or until frothy.

2 Mix the flour with the salt and make a well in the centre. Add the oil, the yeast mixture and the remaining water. Using a wooden spoon, mix to form a smooth dough.

3 Turn the dough out on to a floured surface and knead for 4–5 minutes or until smooth. Return the dough to the bowl, cover with an oiled sheet of cling film (plastic wrap) and leave to rise for 30 minutes or until doubled in size.

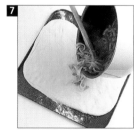

4 Remove the dough from the bowl. Knead the dough for 2 minutes. Using a rolling pin, roll out the dough to form a square shape, then place it on an oiled baking tray (cookie sheet), pushing out the edges until even. The dough should be no more than 6 mm/¼ inch thick because it will rise during cooking.

5 To make the topping, heat the oil in a pan. Add the onions and garlic and cook for 3 minutes. Add the (bell) pepper and fry for 2 minutes.

6 Cover the pan and cook the vegetables over a low heat for 10 minutes, stirring occasionally, until the onions are slightly caramelized. Leave to cool slightly.

7 Spread the topping evenly over the pizza base. Arrange the ham (prosciutto), Mozzarella and rosemary over the top.

8 Bake in a preheated oven, at 200°C/400°F/Gas Mark 6, for 20–25 minutes. Serve hot.

Smoky Bacon & Pepperoni

This more traditional kind of pizza is topped with peperoni, smoked bacon and (bell) peppers covered in a smoked cheese.

NUTRITIONAL INFORMATION

Calories 450   Sugars 6g
Protein ....19g   Fat 24g
Carbohydrate ...41g   Saturates 6g

 1½ HOURS   20 MINS

SERVES 4

I N G R E D I E N T S

Bread Dough Base (see page 226)

1 tbsp olive oil

1 tbsp freshly grated Parmesan

Tomato Sauce (see page 14)

125 g/4½ oz lightly smoked bacon, diced

½ green (bell) pepper, sliced thinly

½ yellow (bell) pepper, sliced thinly

60 g/2 oz pepperoni-style sliced spicy
    sausage

60 g/2 oz smoked Bavarian cheese, grated

½ tsp dried oregano

olive oil, for drizzling

salt and pepper

1 Roll out or press the dough, using a rolling pin or your hands, into a 25 cm/10 inch circle on a lightly floured work surface.

2 Place the dough base on a large greased baking tray (cookie sheet) or pizza pan and push up the edge a little with your fingers, to form a rim.

3 Brush the base with the olive oil and sprinkle with the Parmesan. Cover and leave to rise slightly in a warm place for about 10 minutes.

4 Spread the tomato sauce over the base almost to the edge. Top with the bacon and (bell) peppers. Arrange the pepperoni on top and sprinkle with the smoked cheese.

5 Sprinkle over the oregano and drizzle with a little olive oil. Season well.

6 Bake in a preheated oven, at 200°C/ 400°F/Gas Mark 6, for 18–20 minutes, or until the crust is golden and crisp around the edge. Cut the pizza into wedges and serve immediately.

Marinara Pizza

This pizza is topped with a cocktail of mixed seafood, such as prawns (shrimp), mussels, cockles and squid rings.

NUTRITIONAL INFORMATION

Calories ......359 Sugars 9g
Protein ....19g Fat 14g
Carbohydrate ...42g Saturates 4g

3¼ HOURS   20 MINS

SERVES 4

I N G R E D I E N T S

Potato Base (see page 228)

Special Tomato Sauce (see page 14)

200 g/7 oz frozen seafood cocktail, defrosted

1 tbsp capers

1 small yellow (bell) pepper, chopped

1 tbsp chopped fresh marjoram

½ tsp dried oregano

60 g/2 oz Mozzarella, grated

15 g/½ oz Parmesan, grated

12 black olives

olive oil, for drizzling

salt and pepper

sprig of fresh marjoram or oregano, to garnish

1 Roll out or press out the potato dough, using a rolling pin or your hands, into a 25 cm/10 inch circle on a lightly floured work surface.

2 Place the dough on a large greased baking tray (cookie sheet) or pizza pan and push up the edge a little with your fingers to form a rim.

3 Spread the tomato sauce evenly over the base almost to the edge.

4 Arrange the seafood cocktail, capers and yellow (bell) pepper on top of the tomato sauce.

5 Sprinkle over the herbs and cheeses. Arrange the olives on top. Drizzle over a little olive oil and season with salt and pepper to taste.

6 Bake in a preheated oven, at 200°C/ 400°F/Gas Mark 6, for 18–20 minutes or until the edge of the pizza is crisp and golden brown.

7 Transfer to a warmed serving plate, garnish with a sprig of marjoram or oregano and serve immediately.

Salmon Pizza

You can use either red or pink salmon for this tasty pizza. Red salmon will give a better colour and flavour but it can be expensive.

NUTRITIONAL INFORMATION

Calories 321   Sugars 6g
Protein . . . . .12g   Fat 14g
Carbohydrate . . .39g   Saturates 6g

1¼ HOURS   20 MINS

SERVES 4

I N G R E D I E N T S

1 quantity Scone (Biscuit) Base (see
    page 227)

1 quantity Tomato Sauce (see page 14)

1 courgette (zucchini), grated

1 tomato, sliced thinly

100 g/3½ oz can red or pink salmon

60 g/2 oz button mushrooms,
    wiped and sliced

1 tbsp chopped fresh dill

½ tsp dried oregano

45 g/1½ oz Mozzarella cheese, grated

olive oil, for drizzling

salt and pepper

sprig of fresh dill, to garnish

1 Roll out or press the dough, using a rolling pin or your hands, into a 25 cm/10 inch circle on a lightly floured work surface (counter). Place on a large greased baking tray (cookie sheet) or pizza pan and push up the edge a little with your fingers to form a rim.

2 Spread the tomato sauce over the pizza base, almost to the edge.

3 Top the tomato sauce with the grated courgette (zucchini), then lay the tomato slices on top.

4 Drain the can of salmon. Remove any bones and skin and flake the fish. Arrange on the pizza with the mushrooms. Sprinkle over the herbs and cheese. Drizzle with a little olive oil and season with salt and pepper.

5 Bake in a preheated oven, at 200°C/400°F/Gas Mark 6, for 18–20 minutes or until the edge is golden and crisp.

6 Transfer to a warmed serving plate and serve immediately, garnished with a sprig of dill.

COOK'S TIP

If salmon is too pricy, use either canned tuna or sardines to make a delicious everyday fish pizza. Choose canned fish in brine for a healthier topping. If fresh dill is unavailable, you can use parsley instead.

Pissaladière

This is a variation of the classic Italian pizza but is made with ready-made puff pastry (pie dough). It is perfect for outdoor eating.

NUTRITIONAL INFORMATION

Calories 612   Sugars 13g
Protein . . . . .12g   Fat 43g
Carbohydrate . . .47g   Saturates 11g

20 MINS   55 MINS

SERVES 8

INGREDIENTS

4 tbsp olive oil

700 g/1 lb 9 oz red onions, sliced thinly

2 garlic cloves, crushed

2 tsp caster (superfine) sugar

2 tbsp red wine vinegar

350 g/12 oz fresh ready-made puff pastry
   (pie dough)

salt and pepper

TOPPING

2 x 50 g/1¾ oz cans anchovy fillets

12 green stoned (pitted) olives

1 tsp dried marjoram

1 Lightly grease a swiss roll tin (pan). Heat the olive oil in a large saucepan. Add the red onions and garlic and cook over a low heat for about 30 minutes, stirring occasionally.

2 Add the sugar and red wine vinegar to the pan and season with plenty of salt and pepper.

3 On a lightly floured surface, roll out the pastry (pie dough) to a rectangle, about 33 x 23 cm/13 x 9 inches. Place the pastry (pie dough) rectangle on to the prepared tin (pan), pushing the pastry (pie dough) into the corners of the tin (pan).

4 Spread the onion mixture over the pastry (pie dough).

5 Arrange the anchovy fillets and green olives on top, then sprinkle with the marjoram.

6 Bake in a preheated oven, at 220°C/425°F/Gas Mark 7, for 20-25 minutes or until the pissaladière is lightly golden. Serve the pissaladière piping hot, straight from the oven.

VARIATION

Cut the pissaladière into squares or triangles for easy finger food at a party or barbecue (grill).

Vegetable Calzone

These pizza base parcels are great for making in advance and freezing – they can be defrosted when required for a quick snack.

NUTRITIONAL INFORMATION

Calories 499	Sugars 7g	
Protein 16g	Fat 9g	
Carbohydrate ...95g	Saturates 2g	

1½ HOURS 40 MINS

SERVES 4

INGREDIENTS

DOUGH

450 g/1 lb/3½ cups strong white flour

2 tsp easy-blend dried yeast

1 tsp caster (superfine) sugar

150 ml/¼ pint/¾ cup vegetable stock

150 ml/¼ pint/¾ cup passata (sieved tomatoes)

beaten egg

FILLING

1 tbsp vegetable oil

1 onion, chopped

1 garlic clove, crushed

2 tbsp chopped sun-dried tomatoes

100 g/3½ oz spinach, chopped

3 tbsp canned and drained sweetcorn

25 g/1 oz/¼ cup French (green) beans, cut into 3

1 tbsp tomato purée (paste)

1 tbsp chopped oregano

50 g/1¾ oz Mozzarella cheese, sliced

salt and pepper

1 Sieve the flour into a bowl. Add the yeast and sugar and beat in the stock and passata (sieved tomatoes) to make a smooth dough.

2 Knead the dough on a lightly floured surface for 10 minutes, then place in a clean, lightly oiled bowl and leave to rise in a warm place for 1 hour.

3 Heat the oil in a frying pan (skillet) and sauté the onion for 2–3 minutes.

4 Stir in the garlic, tomatoes, spinach, corn and beans and cook for 3–4 minutes. Add the tomato purée (paste) and oregano and season with salt and pepper to taste.

5 Divide the risen dough into 4 equal portions and roll each on to a floured surface to form an 18 cm/7 inch circle.

6 Spoon a quarter of the filling on to one half of each circle and top with cheese. Fold the dough over to encase the filling, sealing the edge with a fork. Glaze with beaten egg. Put the calzone on a lightly greased baking tray (cookie sheet) and cook in a preheated oven, at 220°C/425°F/Gas Mark 7, for 25–30 minutes until risen and golden. Serve warm.

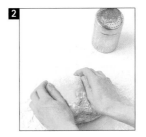

Potato & Tomato Calzone

These pizza dough Italian pasties are best served hot with a salad as a delicious lunch or supper dish.

NUTRITIONAL INFORMATION

Calories	508	Sugars	........8g
Protein	........14g	Fat	...........7g
Carbohydrate	..104g	Saturates	.......2g

1½ HOURS   35 MINS

SERVES 4

INGREDIENTS

DOUGH

450 g/1 lb/4 cups white bread flour

1 tsp easy blend dried yeast

300 ml/½ pint/1¼ cups vegetable stock

1 tbsp clear honey

1 tsp caraway seeds

milk, for glazing

FILLING

225 g/8 oz waxy potatoes, diced

1 tbsp vegetable oil

1 onion, halved and sliced

2 garlic cloves, crushed

40 g/1½ oz sun-dried tomatoes

2 tbsp chopped fresh basil

2 tbsp tomato purée (paste)

2 celery sticks, sliced

50 g/1¾ oz Mozzarella cheese, grated

1 To make the dough, sift the flour into a large bowl and stir in the yeast. Make a well in the centre of the mixture.

2 Stir in the vegetable stock, honey and caraway seeds and bring the mixture together to form a dough.

3 Turn the dough out on to a lightly floured surface and knead for 8 minutes until smooth. Place the dough in a lightly oiled mixing bowl, cover and leave to rise in a warm place for 1 hour or until it has doubled in size.

4 Meanwhile, make the filling. Heat the oil in a frying pan (skillet) and add all of the remaining ingredients except for the cheese. Cook for 5 minutes, stirring.

5 Divide the risen dough into 4 pieces. On a lightly floured surface, roll them out to form four 18 cm/7 inch circles. Spoon equal amounts of the filling on to one half of each circle.

6 Sprinkle the cheese over the filling. Brush the edge of the dough with milk and fold the dough over to form 4 semi-circles, pressing to seal the edges.

7 Place on a non-stick baking (cookie) tray and brush with milk. Cook in a preheated oven, at 220°C/425°F/Gas Mark 7, for 30 minutes until golden and risen. Serve hot.

Index